THE COMPLETE BOOK OF
CACTI
&
SUCCULENTS

THE COMPLETE BOOK OF
CACTI
& SUCCULENTS

TERRY HEWITT

DK PUBLISHING, INC.
www.dk.com

LONDON, NEW YORK, MUNICH,
MELBOURNE, AND DELHI

Project editor
Annelise Evans

Art editor
Jo Grey

Editor
Blanche Sibbald

Senior editor
Rosie Pearson

Senior art editor
Tracy Timson

Senior managing editor
Daphne Razazan

Managing art editor
Carole Ash

Senior production controller
Rosalind Priestley

Main photographer
Peter Anderson

US editor
Jill Hamilton

First American edition, 1993
14 16 18 20 19 17 15

Published in the United States by
Dorling Kindersley, Inc., 375 Hudson Street
New York, New York 10014

Library of Congress Cataloging-in-Publication Data

Hewitt, Terry.
   The complete book of cacti and succulents / by Terry Hewitt.
1st American ed.
      p.   cm.
   Includes index.
   ISBN-13: 978-0-7894-1657-5
   ISBN-10: 0-7894-1657-3
   1. Cactus. 2. Succulent plants. 3. Cactus–Pictorial works.
4. Succulent plants–Pictorial works.   I. Title.
SB438.H44   1993   93–22107
635.9'3347–dc20   CIP

Reproduced by Colourscan, Singapore
Printed and bound by L.Rex Printing Co.,Ltd.China

CONTENTS

INTRODUCTION

ANATOMY AND DISCOVERY

STYLE GUIDE

PLANT CATALOG

A photographic guide with details of size, shape, flowers, and cultivation needs

CARE AND CULTIVATION

INTRODUCTION

TO MOST PEOPLE, cacti and succulents are their great aunt's jade plant (which survived all these years despite her) or the cowboy cactus seen in films. At my nursery, Holly Gate, it is a pleasure to see the dumbfounded look on the face of the uninitiated when presented with an array of such a varied group of plants as that of cacti and succulents. Should the plants actually be in flower, the visitor is inevitably amazed by their beauty and is often converted into a lifelong aficionado on the spot.

Some plants have a tiny diameter and yet produce large flowers that can completely obscure the plant itself; others may be towering columns or large spiny globes or have long, leaflike stems. Gnarled old trunks, "living stones," colorful rosettes, or cacti with dazzling flowers all bewilder the newcomer. The range is so diverse that anyone with a love of plants will find at least one group of interest.

Many cacti and succulents are quite tough and therefore much easier to grow than people suspect. They are ideal plants for the beginner and grow well as pot plants indoors, in a conservatory, or in a greenhouse. In warmer climates, they make a splendid contribution to the planting in a garden.

I am fortunate in having had the opportunity to make my hobby my work (and it remains my hobby). Through this book, I hope to impart some of my interest in these unique plants. The information and advice, given in the text and illustrated in the many color photographs, most of which were taken at Holly Gate, should prove useful to both beginners and enthusiasts. Over the years, I have met many cactus collectors from all over the world and most are interested, friendly, and generous. While some can be dogmatic, most are eager to discuss the plants and share their knowledge. Their fervor is contagious and I have made many good friends among them.

In my opinion, the only self-styled "experts" who know all about cacti and succulents are those people who possess approximately 20 plants. As soon as you have acquired a few more species, you begin to realize that you do not know as much as you thought. As the collection expands, you discover that in fact there is more and more to learn about the subject. When you have amassed a large collection, you recognize that plants, like people, do not always obey the rules that have been laid down for them.

Plants in the wild are not conveniently labeled, so a universal system of botanical names was devised for them. However, cacti and succulents are notoriously difficult to classify into neat groups. They are very adaptable plants that often hybridize easily and, in the wild, vary hugely in form according to local conditions. Plants from different groups that grow in the same habitat can evolve, or converge, to look very similar. On the other hand, plants of the same species that live in different regions may diverge in appearance until they look as if they belong to completely different groups.

Individual botanists also emphasize different plant characteristics when they are classifying cacti and succulents, which often leads to clashes of opinion and confusion about the identity of a particular plant. Until very recently the classification of the cactus family had been based on an old system, which was constantly updated, with plant species being lumped together under the same name and then being separated out again by various botanists.

Common names are just as confusing because they are based on local cultures and are often applied incorrectly or to more than one species. For example, many succulents in the *Agave* genus are called aloes although they are botanically distinct from the *Aloe* genus, and both *Crassula arborescens* and *Dudleya brittonii* are known as the silver dollar plant.

Precision in nomenclature is not important to the beginner, but the enthusiast must be able to distinguish between plants that appear to differ, or those that look the same, in order to choose plants.

To make matters easier, for all plant names in this book I have followed two major authorities. The Convention on International Trade in Endangered Species of Wild Fauna and Flora (CITES) recently sponsored the CITES *Cactaceae Checklist* (compiled by David Hunt, Royal Botanic Gardens, Kew, 1992), which reduces the number of cactus species from over 6,000 to just over 3,500 species. For succulents, I have adhered to the classification system used in

Hermann Jacobsen's *Lexicon of Succulent Plants* (Blandford Press, 1974), which is still widely used. I have also included in the index any old plant names, or synonyms, which may still be in use. These are cross-referenced to the current names used in the book's Plant Catalog, so that relevant information is not missed for want of a name.

The important thing is to have fun growing cacti and succulents. Once you have accumulated a few plants, much satisfaction can be achieved by sowing a few seeds and watching them grow and flower for the first time. Batches of seedlings often show a marked variability and it can be hard to decide which of them to part with when thinning them out.

To ensure their continued survival, collection of many wild species is now banned. Many of those species that are threatened by extinction are more likely to be at risk from climatic changes, urbanization, pollution, or agricultural expansion than collecting, but there is no need to endanger wild populations still further by taking specimens from their habitats. The more that cacti and succulents are propagated and grown in cultivation, the better they are understood, and by entrusting specimens to enthusiastic amateurs, the chances of survival for rarer species is increased.

Lastly, a warning: once bitten by the cactus collecting bug there is no known cure!

ANATOMY
&
DISCOVERY

This exploration of the world of cacti and succulents begins with an explanation of their extraordinary anatomy, which enables them to colonize diverse natural habitats. It continues with the story of the plants' introduction into cultivation, as well as a description of their many properties and uses.

WHAT ARE CACTI AND SUCCULENTS?

SUCCULENT PLANTS, INCLUDING the cactus family, have a highly specialized anatomy to enable them to survive prolonged drought. All are able to store moisture in fleshy tissue in their stems, roots, or leaves, and most have developed distinctive features to help reduce water loss and withstand their hostile habitats. They can also cease active growth and become dormant in severe conditions. Their bizarre appearance reflects a unique evolution, in which plant form, function, and survival are inextricably linked. Cacti are discernable from other succulents by their areoles, or padlike buds (see below).

STEM SUCCULENTS

These plants retain large volumes of watery mucus in their swollen stems, which are most often round, columnar, or barrel-shaped. Nearly all cacti are stem succulents and do not have any leaves, thereby reducing moisture loss though evaporation. The stems contain the green pigment chlorophyll used in photosynthesis, or food production.

Some jungle cacti are epiphytes, which anchor themselves by their roots to other plants or in crevices where there is decaying vegetation. They do not need to conserve moisture in the humid shade of the jungle. Instead, they mostly have flattened stems with a large surface area to absorb as much light as possible.

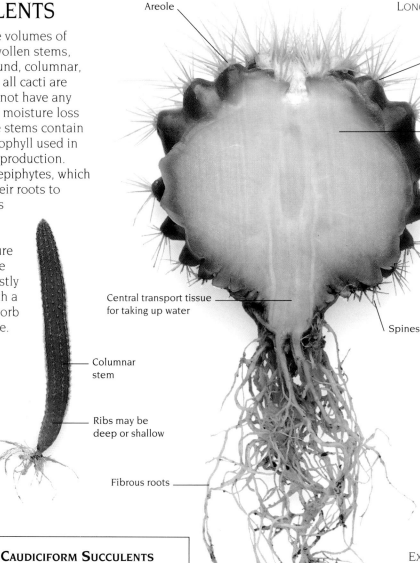

Areole

LONGITUDINAL SECTION

Tubercles, or notched ribs, allow ribs to expand or contract vertically

Water storage tissue

Central transport tissue for taking up water

Spines

Fibrous roots

RIBBED STEM
Stem succulents are often ribbed like a concertina, allowing them to expand or contract sideways as their water stocks are restored or depleted.

Columnar stem

Ribs may be deep or shallow

AREOLE
Only cacti have modified padlike buds from which spines, shoots, and flowers grow. Areoles are not always easily visible.

EXTERNAL VIEW

CAUDICIFORM SUCCULENTS
Some succulents that grow in very harsh habitats with thin soil have a caudex, or swollen base, formed from both root and stem. This provides the plant with greater capacity to store moisture. Such plants are known as caudiciform, but the term is used more broadly for any succulent with a swollen stem or root above ground.

GLOBULAR STEM SUCCULENT
A sphere is the optimum shape for a stem succulent as it has the smallest possible surface area in proportion to volume, keeping water loss to a minimum.

ROOT SUCCULENTS

A number of succulents survive prolonged dry conditions by storing water underground in their tuberous, or swollen, roots. Since the roots are below the soil, moisture loss occurs relatively slowly and there is less risk of damage to the plant from grazing animals or bush fires. The leaves or stems of many root succulents are deciduous; other species' top-growth is shed during long droughts and then regenerates from the roots. The stems or leaves can be thick and fleshy, providing the plant with additional water-storing capacity, as in *Senecio coccineiflorus*, shown below. In cultivation, root succulents with large tubers such as *Brachystelma* are grown with the tuber exposed to prevent rot.

WATER-SEEKING ROOTS
Most cacti and succulents live in deserts and must be able to collect moisture from dewfalls or sporadic rains quickly, before the precious water evaporates. Many have very shallow, but extensive, fibrous root systems that spread out just beneath the soil surface, enabling the plant to take up water from a wide area. If the ground becomes damp, the plants immediately form new root hairs to collect water. Epiphytes produce aerial roots from the stems to seek out moisture in dry conditions.

EXTERNAL VIEW

Fleshy leaves

LONGITUDINAL SECTION

ROOT SUCCULENT
This succulent's main water-storing tissue lies in the tuberous roots. It also has a fleshy stem and leaves.

Succulent stem

Swollen, potato-like storage roots

Fibrous roots

Simple leaves have few pores to reduce evaporation

LEAF SUCCULENTS

This large group includes the cactus *Pereskia* and many succulents, which vary greatly in form, from *Senecio rowleyanus* with pendant leaves to the daggerlike foliage of many *Haworthia*. These plants store water in their thick fleshy leaves, which shrivel in drought and swell up again when water is available. In very long droughts, the leaves are shed.

Some leaf succulents, such as *Lithops*, that live in very arid habitats are made up of little more than a pair of united leaves. Most of the time, they are buried in the soil with just the leaf tips exposed to the sun. Their stonelike appearance camouflages them from grazing animals.

Window

Leaf pair

New leaf bud

PROTECTIVE "WINDOWS"
Calcium oxalate in the translucent sacs at the leaf tips diffuses the hot sun before it reaches the plant body.

Fleshy leaves store water

LEAF SUCCULENT
Many leaf succulents have virtually no stems, forming low rosettes of overlapping leaves, which help to reduce evaporation from both the plant and the soil beneath.

SURFACES

Cacti and succulents have developed a wide range of surface textures. These often striking features are the result of adaptation to different habitats, but they have similar protective functions. For example, some species from high altitudes or areas with fogs have a felted or hairy surface that helps to trap moisture from the air. In hotter regions, lightly-colored foliage reduces heat absorption. Succulent leaves and cacti stems have few stomata, or surface pores, to minimize water loss. In cacti and many succulents, these pores are closed by day. When the temperature drops at night, the pores open to absorb carbon dioxide, which is used the next day for photosynthesis.

Leaf with powdery bloom

Waxy leaf

Downy leaf

Glossy stem

LEAF AND STEM TEXTURES

Some leaves have a leathery or glossy surface, others a waxy coating. Leaves with a very thick waxy layer appear to have a powdery bloom. All these surfaces reduce evaporation and help to deflect the sun's rays. Fine hairs act as insulation against extreme heat or cold. Other species have more conventional barklike stems.

Barklike stem

SPINES AND THORNS

Nearly all cacti and some succulents have spines, which are modified leaves. Cacti spines grow from areoles (see p. 10) and detach easily, but succulent spines grow directly from the stem tissue. Spines vary widely in shape, texture, and length: some are short and bristly; others are softly curved but viciously barbed. They range in color from white, red, or yellow to black. Although spines provide a defense against predators, their main function is to condense moisture so that it drips onto the ground above the plant roots. Spines that are woolly and hairlike also help to shield plants from cold or fierce sun. Some succulents have thorns, which are either modified flowers, leaf stalks, or leaf buds.

PSEUDOCEPHALIUM

This mass of woolly spines grows on one side of the stem. Only Melocactus *(see inset) and* Discocactus *have a true cephalium on the crown.*

NEEDLELIKE SPINES

Many cacti, especially globular species such as Parodia, *have fine, straight, sharp spines, which are often strikingly colored.*

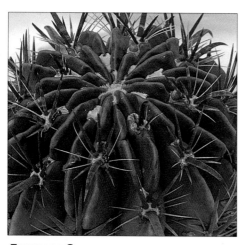

FISHHOOK SPINES

Broad curved spines with a sharp point are colored red or yellow on many barrel cacti.

TEETH AND SPINES

The sawteeth and terminal spines on succulent rosettes are outgrowths of the leaf margins.

THORNS

Some succulents, such as Huernia, *develop thorns that grow directly from the stem tissue.*

FLOWERS

In very arid regions, where long dry spells enforce a dormant state for most of the year, many cacti and succulents have developed a very short growing season. Once rain falls, they burst into growth, forming leaves, flowers, and seeds in less than a month. Cactus flowers have evolved in several ways to attract pollinators. Most desert cacti are day-flowering and produce brightly colored, unscented blooms that attract flying insects. Many jungle cacti have large blooms that open at dusk; these are pale and richly perfumed so that pollinating moths can easily locate them. By contrast, some night-flowering species have foul-smelling, fleshy flowers that are attractive to bats. Others have tubular flowers to accommodate the long beaks of hummingbirds. Succulents have a wide variety of flowers: some are similar to cactus blooms, others are more conventional, and some are tiny and surrounded by petal-like leaf bracts.

FRUITS AND SEEDS

Once the flower has been pollinated, it withers and the ovary develops into a fruit containing seed. Many cacti have fleshy fruits or berries. Succulent seeds and fruits are very diverse, and are distributed by water, wind, insects, birds, or rodents. *Mesembryanthemum* seeds are sealed in woody pods, which open when dampened by rain so that some of the seeds are washed out to germinate while water is available. If the pods dry out, they close until more rain arrives.

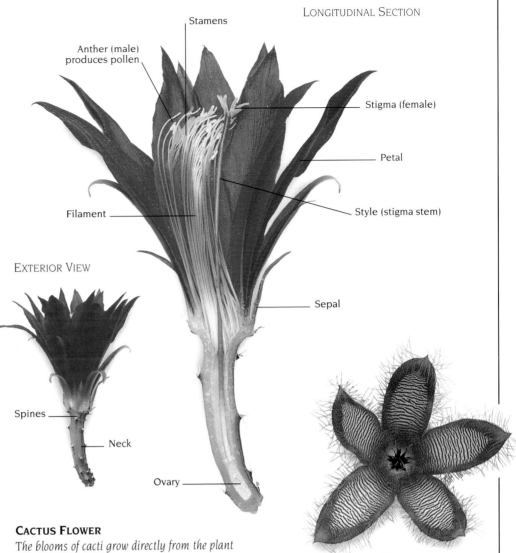

LONGITUDINAL SECTION

Stamens

Anther (male) produces pollen

Stigma (female)

Petal

Filament

Style (stigma stem)

Sepal

EXTERIOR VIEW

Spines

Neck

Ovary

CACTUS FLOWER
The blooms of cacti grow directly from the plant stem and are often funnel-shaped. Some have long necks, which can be spiny or scaly. The flower neck can also be covered in numerous sepals of the same color as the petals; sepals and petals that are similar in appearance (see above) are known collectively as tepals.

SUCCULENT FLOWER
This large Stapelia *flower is very fleshy so that it lasts several days, increasing the chance of pollination.*

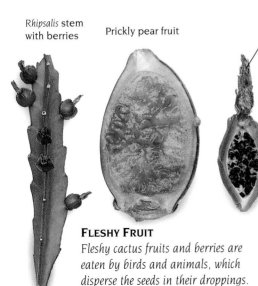

Rhipsalis stem with berries

Prickly pear fruit

Faded flower

Echinopsis fruit

FLESHY FRUIT
Fleshy cactus fruits and berries are eaten by birds and animals, which disperse the seeds in their droppings.

DRY SEEDPODS
Some dry pods split open and expel their seed, while others are composed of fluffy "parachutes," which gently drift away in the wind to distribute the seed.

Aloe
Split capsule

Jatropha
Woody pod

Cotyledon
Dustlike seed

Senecio
Parachuted seed

Withered flower

Seed

Echinocactus
Woolly seedpod

NATURAL HABITATS

CONTRARY TO POPULAR BELIEF, succulents and cacti do not inhabit only conventional deserts. They have a rich range of habitats, from snow-clad Alpine slopes and arid Colorado plains to humid jungles in the Amazon basin. They grow in conditions that often seem inimical to survival; indeed their success partly depends on lack of competition from other, less robust plant life. Looking at their habitats reveals much about their evolution and cultural needs.

DESERT PLAINS

In harsh dry habitats, cacti and succulents reign unchallenged, enduring great temperature extremes of scorching days and freezing nights. Although a few can survive without water for years at a stretch and live in true deserts, which have less than 10 in (25 cm) of rainfall a year, most grow in semideserts, which receive sporadic rainfalls between droughts. Semideserts have very poor soil with sparse vegetation and rocky outcrops, rather than pure sand. The low rainfall is sometimes augmented by heavy dews or coastal mists.

Cacti and succulents may grow in small pockets, as on Argentine savannahs, or in large colonies (see right). On dry plains and plateaus, known as chaparrals in Mexico or veldt in South Africa, small plants like *Haworthia* thrive in the shade of grasses and scrub, and even survive occasional bush fires.

Desert cacti and succulents have the capacity to conserve moisture and withstand drought, by becoming dormant, and to produce new growth in favorable conditions. This growth pattern can be copied by keeping the plants dry in their dormant period and watering them in the growing season.

DESERT IN BLOOM, above
A rare rainfall can stimulate a dramatic spurt of growth, with every succulent plant rapidly flowering and setting seed before returning to a semidormant state.

ARID LANDSCAPE, right
In the parched desert of Baja California in Mexico colonies of Pachycereus cacti tower over low succulents and scrub. The thick, columnar cacti stems can store enough moisture to enable them to survive long droughts.

SNOW SURVIVAL, below
An occasional desert snowfall insulates the cacti against the night cold and, when the snow melts, provides their roots with water.

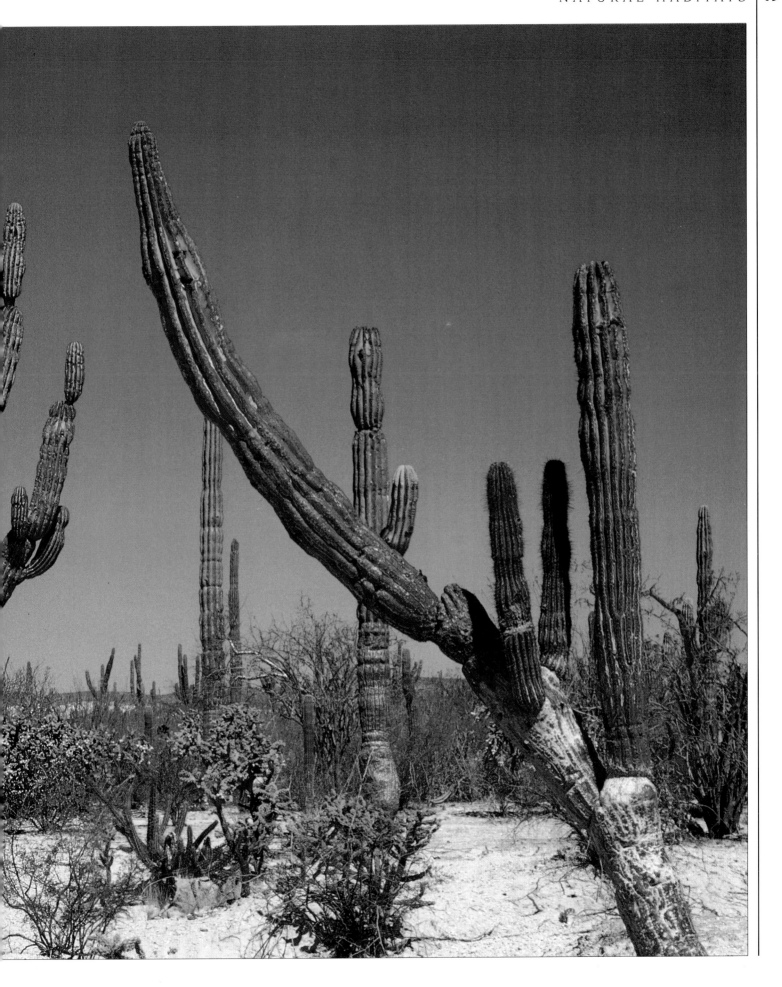

MOUNTAINOUS DESERTS

In mountainous terrain, including high plateaus, screes, and rocky slopes, the soil is often very thin, does not retain much water, and has a high mineral content that can be toxic to nonsucculent plants. In a mountain desert like the Andes, conditions vary dramatically with the altitude and so, too, do the native cacti and succulents. On high peaks, plants are exposed to intense sunlight, nighttime temperatures as low as -4°F (-20°C), fierce winds, and snow. Above the cloud layer, there is often no rain but the plants gain moisture from melting snow. Only small globular or creeping cacti and succulents can survive such conditions, but lower down, where the slope affords some shelter, larger succulents and columnar cacti can grow. Here, the cloud belt diffuses the harsh sunlight and provides some moisture. On dry, overcast foothills below the clouds, small cushion cacti predominate.

As a shield from the harsh cold and brilliant sun, many cacti in mountain regions have a dense coat of woolly spines, and succulents develop thick, waxy skins. Low-growing succulents also grow in many rocky habitats in temperate regions. *Sempervivum* species colonize the alpine parts of Europe, and many *Sedum* thrive in much of the Northern Hemisphere. Even the soilless wastes of lava rock in the Galapagos Islands provide a home for cacti such as *Brachycereus nesioticus*.

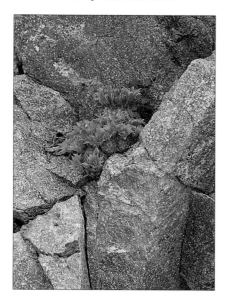

ROCKY FOOTHOLD

In mountain regions, cacti like these Mammillaria *and succulents often lodge themselves in rocky crevices where enough water collects for them to survive. The rocks also provide shelter from winds and retain the heat from the sun. Cultivated plants can be grown in this way, tucked into wall crevices or even between roof tiles.*

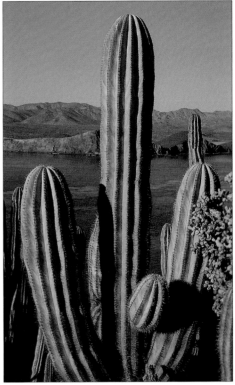

CACTI BY THE SEA
Although rarely thought of as coastal plants, cacti such as these Pachycereus *grow on rugged mountain foothills overlooking the sea. In this type of terrain, they can obtain vital moisture from the sea mists that roll in over the shore.*

HIGH-ALTITUDE HABITAT
Few plants can grow in the hostile conditions found on high rocky slopes like these in Mexico. Columnar cacti that branch at the base and robust barrel cacti are able to withstand the strong winds that sweep across exposed hillsides.

JUNGLES

Although most cacti and succulents grow in arid deserts and mountain areas, many species inhabit subtropical and tropical rainforests such as those in Central and South America, Africa, Sri Lanka, and the West Indies. Here, the climate is constantly hot and humid and sunlight is filtered through a thick tree canopy. Cacti and succulents are amply provided with moisture from the atmosphere and regular rainfalls, so they have adapted to survive a lack of light rather than water, although they can survive periods of drought. Similarly, in cultivation, these plants are best grown in humid, light shade.

Many jungle cacti such as flamboyantly flowered *Epiphyllum*, and some succulents like *Hoya*, which grow in northeastern Australia, are epiphytes. They anchor themselves to the stems of other plants or grow in pockets of decaying leaves. Often they inhabit the upper branches of trees where there is more light. Other species have a climbing or scrambling habit, which enables them to grow over or through other plants toward the light.

A few succulents inhabit the gloom of the forest floor and some small cacti such as *Gymnocalycium* grow in the broken shade of rainforest margins.

AERIAL CACTI, above
In Venezuelan and other tropical rainforests or jungles, epiphytic cacti such as Aporocactus swathe the branches of trees with their long trailing stems.

JUNGLE GIANTS, right
Treelike succulents that grow on the jungle floor, such as Espeletia schultzii, often have a mass of broad leaves to maximize absorption of the limited light that is filtered through the thick canopy of foliage above them.

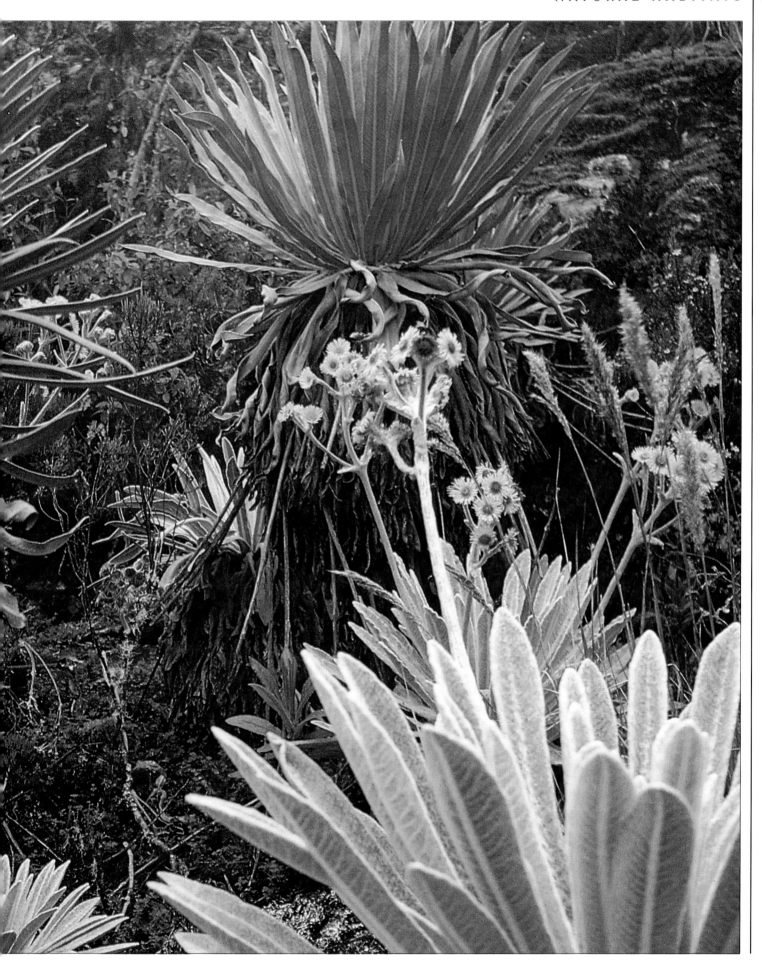

DISCOVERY AND DISTRIBUTION

ORIGINALLY CACTI GREW ONLY on the American continents. Succulents were native to many regions from northern Europe to the Far East, although most were concentrated in southern and eastern Africa. As the map shows, exploration and trading over the last four centuries, and natural distribution, enabled cacti and succulents to establish in new habitats across the world.

MAJOR EXPEDITIONS

In the late 15th century, the race to find fresh sea routes to India and its riches gave rise to a surge in European exploration and thereby to the discovery of new plants. Christopher Columbus is reputed to be the first to have taken cacti to Europe; he found weird, leafless plants in the West Indies (*Melocactus* and *Opuntia*) and presented them to Queen Isabella of Spain. Meanwhile, the Portuguese discovered a wealth of succulents in Africa and India. Like da Gama (see box), Bartolemeu Dias landed at several bays in southwestern Africa and found *Aloe* and *Gasteria* species, among many others. Spanish missionaries colonized Central and parts of northern South America in the next two centuries and sent cacti to Europe on their trading ships. In the 17th century, the Dutch East India Company, which was formed to exploit trade routes to the Cape of Africa, shipped many succulents to Holland and then to the Royal Botanic Gardens at Kew.

As the interest in cacti and succulents increased, botanical expeditions became more frequent. In 1777–87, King Charles III of Spain sponsored several major expeditions to America. Captain Arthur Phillip, founder of Sydney, introduced *Opuntia* cacti into Australia in 1788 to establish a cochineal dye industry (see p. 25). But the zenith of explorers such as Thomas Bridges (see box) and botanists who specialized in cacti and succulents came in the 19th century. Thomas Nuttall traveled widely, from North Dakota to San Diego, New Orleans and the southern US, while he was based in Philadelphia. He discovered many new species, including some *Coryphantha*.

More recently, Dr. Joseph Nelson Rose collected cacti in almost every South American country, as well as the West Indies, Baja California, and the southern US. He donated many new species to the Ministry of Agriculture and the Carnegie Institute in Washington. Even today, new species are constantly being introduced into cultivation.

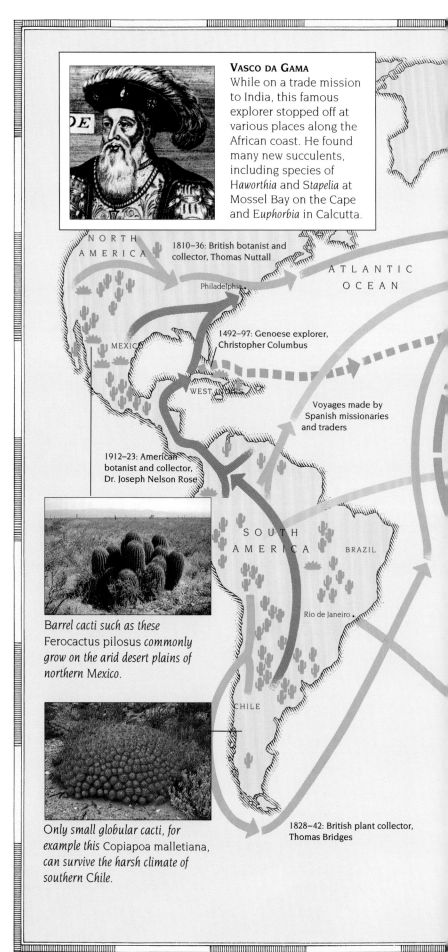

VASCO DA GAMA
While on a trade mission to India, this famous explorer stopped off at various places along the African coast. He found many new succulents, including species of *Haworthia* and *Stapelia* at Mossel Bay on the Cape and *Euphorbia* in Calcutta.

1810–36: British botanist and collector, Thomas Nuttall

Philadelphia

1492–97: Genoese explorer, Christopher Columbus

Voyages made by Spanish missionaries and traders

1912–23: American botanist and collector, Dr. Joseph Nelson Rose

Barrel cacti such as these *Ferocactus pilosus* commonly grow on the arid desert plains of northern Mexico.

Only small globular cacti, for example this *Copiapoa malletiana*, can survive the harsh climate of southern Chile.

1828–42: British plant collector, Thomas Bridges

NORTH AMERICA · MEXICO · WEST INDIES · ATLANTIC OCEAN · SOUTH AMERICA · BRAZIL · Rio de Janeiro · CHILE

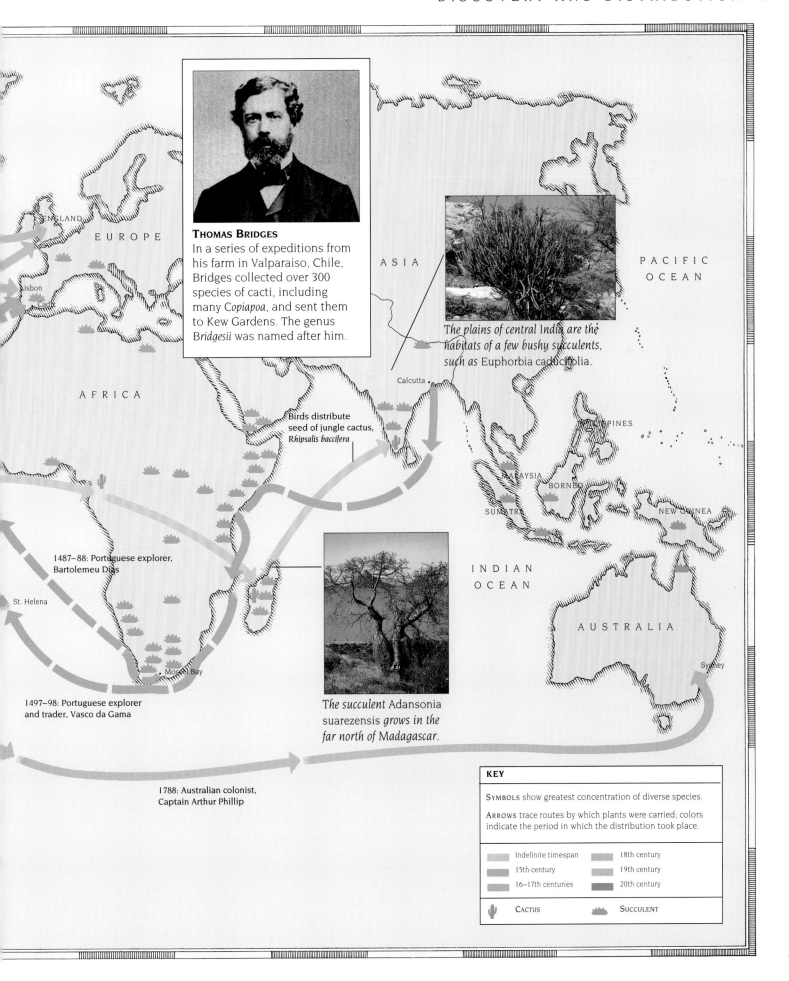

THOMAS BRIDGES
In a series of expeditions from his farm in Valparaiso, Chile, Bridges collected over 300 species of cacti, including many *Copiapoa*, and sent them to Kew Gardens. The genus *Bridgesii* was named after him.

EUROPE

Lisbon

Cad

AFRICA

ASIA

PACIFIC OCEAN

The plains of central India are the habitats of a few bushy succulents, such as Euphorbia caducifolia.

Calcutta

Birds distribute seed of jungle cactus, *Rhipsalis baccifera*

PHILIPPINES

MALAYSIA

BORNEO

SUMATRA

NEW GUINEA

1487–88: Portuguese explorer, Bartolemeu Dias

St. Helena

INDIAN OCEAN

AUSTRALIA

Mossel Bay

Sydney

1497–98: Portuguese explorer and trader, Vasco da Gama

The succulent Adansonia suarezensis grows in the far north of Madagascar.

1788: Australian colonist, Captain Arthur Phillip

KEY

SYMBOLS show greatest concentration of diverse species.

ARROWS trace routes by which plants were carried; colors indicate the period in which the distribution took place.

Indefinite timespan	18th century
15th century	19th century
16–17th centuries	20th century

CACTUS   SUCCULENT

BOTANISTS AND COLLECTORS

BEFORE EARLY EXPLORERS such as Columbus stumbled upon these strange plants in their native habitats, all cacti and many succulents were known only to the local native populations. A few plants were first introduced into Europe in the 15th and 16th centuries as curiosities, but after more species were described and classified by botanists in the 17th century, interest in the plants increased. Wealthy collectors sponsored botanists to search out new species with which to build up public and private gardens. Cacti and succulents are still collected today, but attention is focused on conservation.

ANCIENT CIVILIZATIONS

Cacti were well known to the Inca civilization in Peru, the Aztecs of Mexico, and the North American Indians a long time before European explorers and collectors discovered them. The plants were familiar elements of their everyday environments and were frequently incorporated into their cultures, having religious significance as well as many practical uses. The Indians were well acquainted with the intoxicating effect of the sap of some cacti and the ancient cult which uses the cactus *Lophophora* in its ceremonies still exists today.

In Africa, the Bantu, Bushmen, and Kaffir tribes have exploited the many indigenous succulent species for centuries, finding many different uses for them (see pp. 24–5). No African religious rites involving succulents, however, have been recorded.

FOUNDING OF A CITY
According to legend, an Aztec priest dreamed that Huitzilopochtli, the God of the Sun, told the Aztecs to build a capital city where they saw an eagle perched on a tall cactus. They did so, in 1325, as recorded in an Aztec manuscript of 1541 (right) that shows the site of Tenochtitlán, the new capital, and the ten Aztec tribes that built it. The town became Mexico City and the symbol of an eagle and a cactus is still used on its flag.

CLASSIFICATION

Many of the earliest recorded cacti and succulents appear in English herbals of the late 16th century. The most famous of these is John Gerard's *The Herball or Generall Historie of Plants*, published in 1597. In his book, Gerard described four cactus species: the "Hedgehogge Thistle," which was in fact a *Melocactus*; the "Torch or Thorne Euphorbium," a *Cereus*; the "Thorne Reede of Peru," another *Cereus*; and the "Indian Fig Tree," now known to be an *Opuntia*.

Many of the succulent plants gathered by early travelers were classified by the Swedish botanist Linnaeus in his *Species Plantarum* in 1753. Other botanists of the time who mentioned cacti included Philip Miller, whose *Gardener's Dictionary* of 1731 classified cacti into four genera, and Richard Bradley, who saw many new species of succulent that were sent to Amsterdam by explorers and traders. In 1718 he published a *History of Succulent Plants*. Like Gerard, Bradley described *Cereus* as a torch thistle, but he also lists the "star-pointed ficoid or fig marigold," known today as *Trichodiadema stellatum*.

Cacti and succulents were shipped to Europe in increasing numbers as trade routes opened up because the plants could survive long sea voyages without soil on their roots. The Royal Botanic Gardens at Kew first sent a collector, Francis Masson, to South Africa in 1772. He sailed with Captain Cook on the ship *Endeavour*, and in three years gathered over 100 succulents for classification, including some *Euphorbia*, *Stapelia*, and many *Mesembryanthemum* species. The period 1845–83 was a fruitful time for discovery and the recording of cacti and succulents and many new species were named after collectors and botanists of the time, such as Humboldt, Engelmann, Bridges (see p. 21), and Wislizenus. This also led to much confusion of names.

A major work of classification, *The Cactaceae*, published in four volumes in 1919–23 by Britton and Rose (see p. 20) and Curt Backeberg's six-volume *Die Cactaceae* in 1958–62 did much to rationalize cacti names. On succulents, Jacobsen's *Lexicon of Succulent Plants* (1974) remains an invaluable reference.

HOW THE CACTUS GOT ITS NAME
Carolus Linnaeus (1707–78) created a universal system of botanical plant names, based on Latin and Greek, that is still in use today. Linnaeus first chose the Greek word kaktos, *meaning thistle, to name the cactus family.*

GREAT COLLECTORS

The first private collections of cacti and succulents were created in the 17th century, when plants and seed became available. Only the wealthy owners of heated orangeries could provide the necessary conditions of light and warmth. The Hortus Medicus garden in Amsterdam was set up at this time, mainly to grow medicinal plants for doctors. As early as 1820, greenhouse gardens were all the rage. Most collectors were noblemen, such as the English Dukes of Devonshire and Bedford, who could afford to build large greenhouses and heat them with steam.

By 1835, the German Prince Salm-Dyck had one of the best collections of cacti and succulents in Europe. He studied his plants carefully and painted fine portraits of them. The Russian Prince Kotschoubey of St. Petersburg funded many collectors. In 1830 one of them named an *Ariocarpus* cactus after the Prince, then sold another *Ariocarpus* for 1,000 francs, which far exceeded the value of the plant's weight in gold.

In 1850, the craze was at its height; the general public flocked to admire the strange plants at gardens such as Kew and huge sums were paid for cactus plants. But by the century's end, the increasing cost of funding expeditions and a new enthusiasm for orchids led to declining interest in cacti and many fine old collections were broken up.

GARDENERS OF PRIVILEGE
Until the 20th century, most gardens and major collections of cacti and succulents were owned by the wealthy, who became patrons of botanists in return for new species for their gardens.

GARDENS AND CONSERVATION

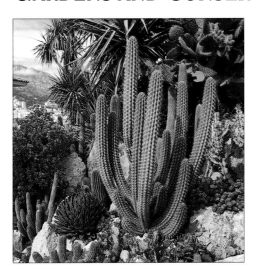

EXOTIC COLLECTION
One of the most famous botanical gardens with a collection of cacti and succulents is the steeply terraced Jardin Exotique in Monaco.

Today, interest in cacti and succulents as both garden and indoor plants is as strong as it ever was and there are national cactus and succulent societies in many countries. Botanists continue to discover new species in the wild and their research uses modern technology, such as electron microscopes and computers, to provide an increasing store of knowledge about the strange anatomy of these plants.

Impressive collections of cacti and succulents have been established in various parts of the world, in both private gardens and botanical institutions. Among the best known are the Huntington Botanical Garden, California, the collection in Zürich, Switzerland, the Palmengarten in Frankfurt, Germany, and the oldest surviving collection at the Royal Botanic Gardens, Kew. A collection in Brisbane, Australia, has also been established.

As with many other groups of plants, the conservation of cacti and succulents has gained increasing importance in this century. Greater control is required to protect endangered species in the wild, not only from unscrupulous collectors and smugglers, but also from ever-expanding numbers of grazing herds and from land development, climatic changes, pollution, and the depletion of natural pollinators.

The collection of some species of cacti and succulents from the wild is now illegal in many countries. Bodies such as the International Union for the Conservation of Nature, or I.U.C.N, encourage growers to raise rare species from seed, rather than buy plants that may have been taken from the wild.

PROPERTIES AND USES

THE APPEAL OF CACTI AND SUCCULENTS lies in their intriguing and unusual appearance, but many of these astonishing species also have a hidden value. From ancient times, they have been used as a source of food, drink, and medicine, and even for making tools and constructing buildings. Their use in the future promises to be even more diverse. The cactus *Cereus hildmannianus* may have the potential to absorb harmful radiation from CRT screens. The stems of certain *Opuntia* can be processed to produce an alcohol fuel, which could be used instead of gasoline; unlike fossil fuels, cacti are a renewable resource.

FOOD AND DRINK

Few plants look less edible than cacti and succulents, so it is surprising to learn that many species are cooked and eaten as vegetables, while others produce mouth-watering fruits. The best known fruits are from *Opuntia ficus-indica* (prickly pear); the yellow, white, or red fruits are commonly sold in Mexican markets and are also available in Australia and many Mediterranean countries. The claret cup hedgehog cactus, *Echinocereus triglochidiatus*, has fruits that become pink when ripe and are made into a delicious jam.

On the high plains of Bolivia, the cactus *Neowerdermannia vorwerkii* is cooked and eaten in the same way as potatoes. In Mexico, the flat joints of young stems of *Opuntia subulata* are peeled, cut up, and boiled to make *nopalitos*. The tubers of *Ceropegia* and *Brachystelma* form part of the diet, in the southern African bush, of the Bantu and Bushmen tribes. Some cacti and succulents can even be made into sweets: pieces of the aromatic, sweet-and-sour flesh of *Ferocactus wislizeni* are candied in a sugar solution.

Perhaps the most internationally well known product is tequila, the fiery distilled liquor from Mexico that is made from the boiled and fermented hearts of *Agave* plants. *Agave* species are the source of another local alcoholic drink called *pulque*, which is made from the heart's sap.

PRICKLY PEAR
The ripe fruits are eaten raw or made into jam; the yellow fruit (above) is the sweetest.

TASTE OF TEQUILA
Tequila is traditionally drunk straight, with a pinch of salt and a squeeze of lime.

COSMETICS AND MEDICINES

Succulents and cacti, like many other plants, have been used since ancient times as a source of cosmetics and medicines. The healing properties of *Aloe* species were known to the Greeks and Romans who used them to treat a variety of ailments, from serious wounds to minor skin complaints. These same properties are recognized today and the mucilaginous sap from freshly split leaves can be applied directly to the skin to soothe minor cuts and burns.

The *Aloe* is also a popular natural ingredient in cosmetics; its sap is added to a wide range of beauty products. *Aloe barbadensis* (syn. A. *vera*) is the most commonly used species in the cosmetics industry, and is cultivated extensively in Florida, Texas, and the West Indies. Queen of the night, the night-flowering *Selenicereus grandiflorus*, also has therapeutic properties.

Its freshly cut blooms are used in the preparation of medicines for improving blood circulation and the cactus is cultivated widely in South America for this purpose.

In the early 20th century, the fleshy tuber of *Testudinaria elephantipes* was used as a source of cortisone, an anti-inflammatory agent. Many *Testudinaria* species are still used today in the manufacture of the contraceptive pill.

A small species of cactus, *Lophophora williamsii*, known as *peyote*, was valued in the past for its medicinal use as a treatment for disorders such as rheumatism and asthma. The Aztecs believed that this "sacred mushroom" had mystical powers because it has hallucinogenic properties. Although it is still used today by some North American Indians in their religious ceremonies, possession of this cactus is now illegal in many countries.

NATURAL BEAUTY
Clear sticky Aloe *sap is used in moisturizers, aftershave lotions, and shampoos.*

PRODUCTS AND MATERIALS

Cacti and succulents have other unexpected uses, most of which have been developed throughout the Americas and in Africa where the plants have always grown wild. For example, the cactus *Oreocereus celsianus*, a native of Argentina and Bolivia, has fine, soft, hairy spines that are gathered and used like down to stuff pillows and bedding.

Commercially, the most important succulent is *Agave sisalana*, which is used to make rope, as well as twine, bags, and rough mats. It is grown widely in Kenya and also in Madagascar, where forests have been cleared to make way for large *Agave* plantations.

In the past, succulents provided the Indians from northern Mexico with a way to catch fish: the stems of *Stenocereus gummosus* were crushed and thrown into the water to release their toxic sap, stupefying the fish, which could then be scooped up easily by hand. In southern Africa, the poisonous sap of *Euphorbia cereiformis*, *E. heptagona* and *E. virosa* was boiled into a syrup and then applied to arrow tips for hunting.

Perhaps the oldest tradition of cultivating cacti for specific uses dates back to the Aztec civilization, which

ROPE PLANT
Agave sisalana *is grown on Madagascan plantations to make sisal hemp. The leaves are harvested (below) and then shredded to extract their long fibers. These fibers, or the hemp, are hung over racks to dry (left), before being woven into rope and other products.*

flourished in Mexico from the 14th to the 16th century. *Opuntia coccenillifera* was grown by the Aztecs as a host plant for the cochineal scale, a type of mealybug. Large quantities of the female insects were crushed to produce a rich purple dye, which was used for coloring royal and ceremonial robes. Male scales yielded a brilliant scarlet dye. When the Spanish arrived in Mexico in the 16th century, they set up their own cactus plantations and sent the dye back to Spain. Today, cochineal dye is produced extensively in South America for use as an organic food coloring and in lipsticks.

DYE FROM THE PAST
In this 16th-century illustration, Spanish overseers supervise the collection of cochineal scales for dye.

A LIVING FENCE
Some columnar cacti, such as Pachycereus, *are planted in rows to form a barrier.*

IMPLEMENTS AND CONSTRUCTION

Almost every part of both cacti and succulents can be exploited for practical purposes. In South America, some cactus spines are used as toothpicks and to make combs, while the long sharp spines of the columnar cactus *Cereus hildmannianus* are used as sewing needles. In Mexico, the curved spines of *Mammillaria bocasana* were employed for many centuries as fishhooks.

The Mexican succulent *Calibanus hookeri* has grasslike leaves that contain a substance similar to soap. This substance, combined with the roughly serrated leaf edges, makes the leaves extremely effective when used to scour pans. *Calibanus hookeri* also yields a plentiful supply of tough leaves, which are ideal for thatching roofs.

In Namibia, the flammable resinous coating of *Sarcocaulon burmannii*, a small shrubby succulent, has earned it the

nickname of "bushman's candle" because the whole plant can be set alight and used as a torch.

Some cacti are surprisingly strong and have woody stem tissue that makes a good construction material in regions where wood is difficult to obtain. In the treeless area along the Bolivian border with Argentina, *Trichocereus pasacana* is used to build houses and also for firewood; in Venezuela, *Pilosocereus* species serve the same purpose.

The columnar habit and fierce spines of some cacti and succulents make them valuable for hedging. *Euphorbia milii*, known as crown of thorns, is commonly used in this way and is often seen planted as an impenetrable barrier along the center of wide roads in Madagascar, while in Mexico, the large columnar cactus *Pachycereus marginatus* is grown as a formidable fence.

STYLE GUIDE

*A dazzling sample of the beautiful shapes and
flower colors of cacti and succulents leads into
a section on how to exploit the decorative qualities
of these plants both indoors and out. Practical
projects show step-by-step how to create imaginative
arrangements in different types of containers.*

CACTI SHAPES

THE DECORATIVE APPEAL OF CACTI lies predominantly in their strange forms. They bear little resemblance to conventional "leafy" plants, ranging in shape from tiny globes, creeping, candlelike stems, and squat barrels to huge, branching candelabra. Their stark profiles give them a sculptural, almost abstract quality, making them striking as feature plants and ideal subjects for the visual drama of a formal composition. The shape of a cactus may be disguised by spines and the plant body may be fluted with deeply indented ribs or studded by chunky, divided ribs known as tubercles.

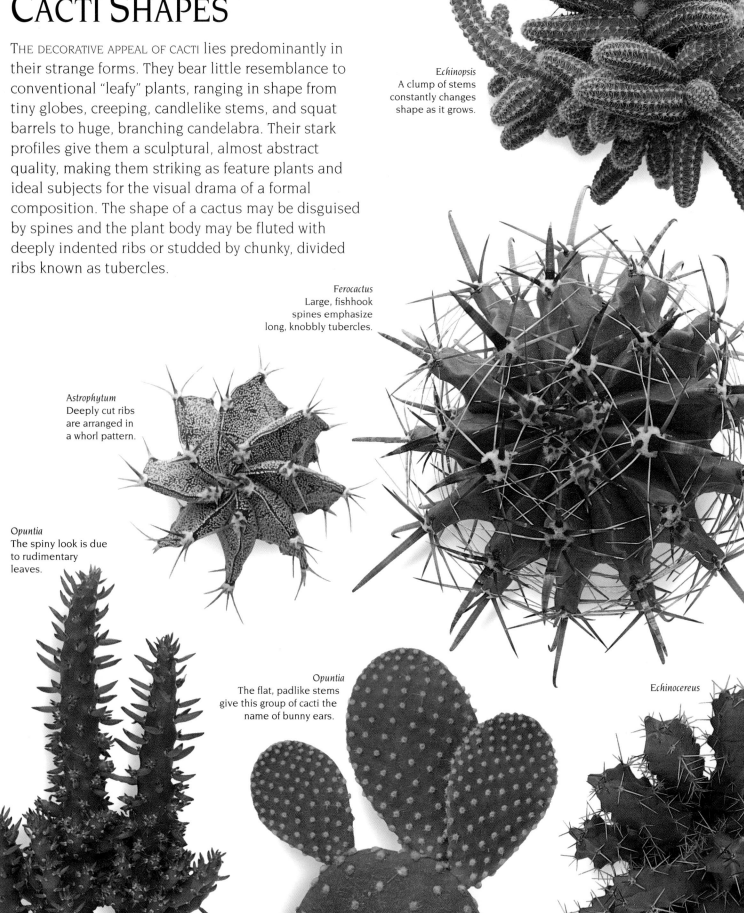

Echinopsis
A clump of stems constantly changes shape as it grows.

Ferocactus
Large, fishhook spines emphasize long, knobbly tubercles.

Astrophytum
Deeply cut ribs are arranged in a whorl pattern.

Opuntia
The spiny look is due to rudimentary leaves.

Opuntia
The flat, padlike stems give this group of cacti the name of bunny ears.

Echinocereus

Oreocereus
The shape of this cactus is softened by its thick, woolly coat of spines.

Echinopsis
The strong ribs reinforce the linear shape of this cactus.

Echinocactus
Spine cushions, body shape, and tubercles all create a bold, symmetrical pattern.

Cleistocactus

Cleistocactus
The elegant simplicity of a column is perhaps the most familiar of cacti shapes.

Opuntia
Short, jointed stems branch freely to form an irregular shape.

SUCCULENT SHAPES

SUCCULENTS DISPLAY A GREAT DIVERSITY of exotic forms, from simple, cactuslike plants to more complex shrublike or treelike species that have beautifully shaped leaves and stems as well as attractive outlines. Some plants show the perfect symmetry of the rosette, which may be starkly elegant or softly pretty; others have a more fluid and graceful profile of arching or trailing stems and foliage. There are also some bizarre bulbous or tubular forms. Shapes of succulents lend themselves to many differing styles of display and provide a perfect contrast for other types of plants in mixed arrangements.

Stem

Testudinaria
The squat, bulbous stem contrasts with the delicate, heart-shaped leaves.

Lithops
These are known as living stones because of their smooth, rounded shape.

Agave
Long leaves with terminal spines form a spiky rosette.

Echeveria
The symmetrical rosette is a classic succulent shape.

Sedum
Creeping rosettes form leafy mats of foliage.

Echeveria
New offsets echo the shape
of the larger parent plant.

Faucaria
The arrangement of teeth
on the leaves gives the
plant the common name of
tiger's jaws.

Crassula
Although bushy in form,
this plant has slender,
lance-shaped leaves.

Kalanchoe
Tiny plantlets adorn the
ends of the tubular leaves.

Cotyledon
The large, spoonlike
leaves are softened
by slightly frilled tips.

STEM AND LEAF SHAPES

SOME CACTUS STEMS look like leaves, some succulent leaves look like stems – and both can vary in form even within a single plant genus. The majority of leaves and stems have strong, fleshy shapes and their visual impact is as powerful as the outline of the plant. Stems and leaves may be deeply serrated, twisted and angular, long and slender, round and fat, scalelike, or delicate and heart-shaped; such a wide array of shapes provides scope for effective groups of contrasting and complementary forms.

Crassula
The corrugated appearance of these pendant succulent stems is due to tightly furled leaves.

Senecio
Succulent stem

Senecio
Small, pealike leaves form a string of beads along this succulent's stem.

Crassula
Opposite pairs of fat little leaves appear to be threaded onto this succulent stem.

Epiphyllum
Because of its deeply serrated form, this type of cactus stem is often described as rickrack.

Haworthia
Succulent leaves

Aloe
Sawlike teeth give these succulent leaf margins a fierce look.

Leaves

Senecio
Succulent stem

Echinopsis
Cactus stem

Senecio
Succulent leaf

Aeonium
Succulent leaf

Heliocereus
This elongated,
three-sided cactus stem
looks more like a leaf.

Epiphyllum
Cactus stem

Testudinaria
Succulent leaf

Crassula
A fleshy, oval leaf
is common to
many succulents.

Crassula
Succulent leaf

Epiphyllum
Scalloped edges add a
touch of grace to the broad,
straplike cactus stem.

Kalanchoe
The elegant line of this
arrow-shaped succulent leaf
is highlighted by the soft,
velvety texture.

FLOWER COLORS

WHEN IN BLOOM, both cacti and succulents provide a glorious show: their petals range from pure whites, silvery grays, and subtle greens to vibrant reds, hot pinks, and dazzling yellows, in a single, vivid wash of color or blended in strange and exquisite patterns. Commercial hybridizing has added many spectacular shades to this palette; only blue still eludes the breeder's skill. The massed petals and sepals of cactus blooms are indistinguishable in hue but succulent flowers usually have green sepals.

Echinopsis

Glottiphyllum
Mustard-colored stamens surrounded by butter-yellow petals draw the eye.

Matucana

Aloe
These tubular buds, when fully open, have a tiny fringe of pale petals at the mouth.

Matucana

Rebutia
Bright colors, such as this intense orange, make the flower easily visible to pollinators.

Matucana

Epiphyllum
These blooms open at night and are large and pale so that they are visible to their pollinators in the dusk.

Epiphyllum
Cool white petals contrast in tone with pale green, elongated sepals.

Sempervivum
Subtle hues of maroon, green, and silver highlight the daintiness of the flowers.

Epiphyllum
The long crimson sepals fade to apricot as they age.

Echinocereus

Matucana

Rebutia

Stenocactus

Brachystelma
Curved-over petals reveal striking, pale green undersides.

Gymnocalycium

Gymnocalycium
This group of cacti often has unusually colored flowers.

Harrisia
Purplish green sepals fringe a deep flowercup of pure white petals.

Stapelia
The strange mottling can be deep yellow, purple, or brown.

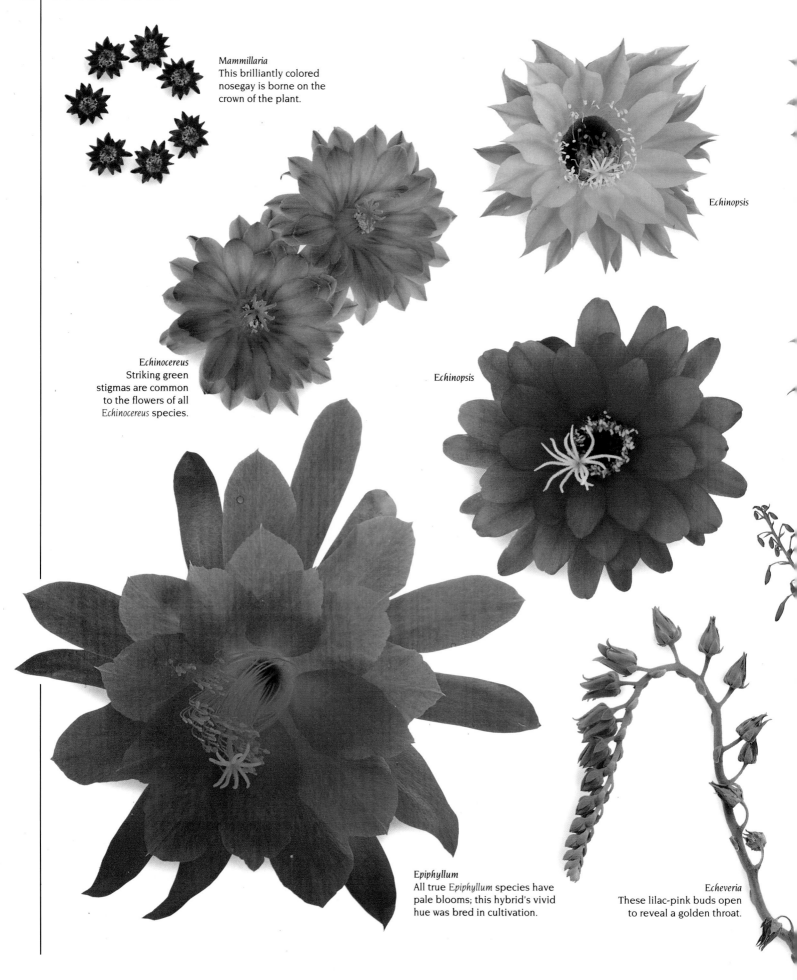

Mammillaria
This brilliantly colored nosegay is borne on the crown of the plant.

Echinopsis

Echinocereus
Striking green stigmas are common to the flowers of all *Echinocereus* species.

Echinopsis

Epiphyllum
All true *Epiphyllum* species have pale blooms; this hybrid's vivid hue was bred in cultivation.

Echeveria
These lilac-pink buds open to reveal a golden throat.

Echinopsis

Echinopsis
Striped pink petals frame the rich green of the flower's pollen tube.

Euphorbia
The true flowers are the tiny, central cups; the colorful "petals" are leaf bracts.

Senecio
Many small, tubular flowers form a ball of bright color.

Echinopsis

Hoya
This "wax flower" shows a dramatic contrast of pale and deep pink.

Aloe
Stem and flowers are the same coral hue.

Matucana

Pachycormis
Clusters of tiny pink flowers form a haze of color.

Lewisia
Fine veins accentuate the delicacy of pale pink petals.

Echinocereus

CHOOSING CONTAINERS

From rustic wooden tubs to traditional terracotta troughs or ornate stone urns, there are containers to suit every style and setting, whether indoors or out. Cacti and succulents usually thrive in containers and, because most are slow growing, they do not outgrow their pots quickly. Unless they are very heavy, pots can be moved, like a portable garden, to create new schemes. It is also easy to bring plants indoors for winter, if necessary. A container should complement rather than compete with the planting and its setting, and be in proportion to both. Shape also has an impact: for a unified effect, use similarly shaped containers or, to create a striking contrast, choose pots with markedly different forms. Most indoor and all outdoor containers must have drainage holes.

Crassula ovata
Jade plant

Senecio scaposus

Mammillaria pringlei

WOVEN BASKETS
Baskets are available in a variety of textures and shapes, and go well with both spiny and smooth-skinned plants. Place a protective plastic lining or a dish in the bottom of the basket before filling it with potting mix.

Sedum burrito
Donkey's tail

PLANT STANDS
Create an attractive display by using stands with tall pedestals to bring plants nearer eye level. Like hanging containers, they suit trailing and epiphytic plants. Cuttings may be planted through the sides to create a fuller effect.

Agave filifera

Euphorbia trigona
'Red Form'

TIMELESS TERRACOTTA
Available in a wide array of shapes and sizes, terracotta containers suit classic and contemporary settings, both indoors and out. Because of its weight, terracotta is ideal for tall plants that might otherwise be top-heavy. Upright pots echo the forms of erect cacti and succulents, while a wide, flared dish flatters low spreading plants. If using deep pots, fill the bottom with broken crocks; most cacti and succulents do not need a great depth of potting mix.

Agave victoria-reginae
Queen Victoria century plant

Agave toumeyana

Sphagnum moss lining

Pachypodium lamerei
Madagascar palm

Weberbauerocereus johnsonii

Crassula ovata
Jade plant

Stetsonia coryne

Opuntia vestita
'Cristate'

Mammillaria
pringlei

Mammillaria
spinosissima 'Cristate'

Euphorbia
triangularis

Cereus validus

AN UNUSUAL ALTERNATIVE

Metal containers have an unconventional appeal and, while striking in a modern room or on a patio, some can be equally at home in a rustic setting. Choose containers made from a metal that will not corrode, such as aluminum or stainless steel. Plants with white spines or a milky bloom will subtly echo the gleam of silver-gray metal.

PATTERNED EARTHENWARE

When using very striking containers, such as this ethnic earthenware, keep the planting bold but simple, so that it is neither dominated by the pots nor detracts from their impact. Use large, heavy pots only for permanent displays.

Agave victoria-reginae
Queen Victoria
century plant

Echinopsis
scopulicola

Mammillaria
microhelia

PAINTED POTS

Bright colorful pots contrast well with plants that have strong silhouettes. Terracotta pots or wooden planters are easy to paint with primary colors and simple patterns. If placing the pots outside, use a weatherproof paint or finish them with a protective varnish.

DISPLAY IDEAS

FROM THE MATTE, PEBBLELIKE leaves of some species to the jointed, trailing stems or ribbed spiny bodies of others, cacti and succulents show great diversity of form, size, texture, and color. The bold architectural outlines of some can be used to create a striking display of arresting shapes; others have waxy or hairy leaves and silky or hooked spines that can be combined for subtle contrasts. The potential for developing imaginative schemes is limitless; the only restriction is to choose plants that need similar conditions if you want to grow them together.

INDOORS

Cacti and succulents make a refreshing change from conventional house plants. Before deciding where to put them, bear in mind their practical needs of light, temperature, and humidity (see pp. 150–51). Take the time to assess how plants look in different parts of a room and place them where they will have the most visual impact. Many small succulents, particularly those with rosettes of leaves such as *Aloe* and *Haworthia*, look striking when viewed from above, forming mosaics of color and texture. By contrast, species with pendant stems look best in hanging containers. Spiny species should be set well away from areas where people might brush against them.

Consider, too, whether an individual plant or a group of plants will be more appropriate. A large single specimen is most impressive sited against a plain wall. Smaller plants can be placed in formal pairs to frame a window or at either end of a table. Grow groups of plants in a single container, or in individual pots to allow greater flexibility for changing the display throughout the year.

It is important to match planting arrangements to the decorative style of a room. In a modern setting, for example, with spare clean lines and unfussy decor, a columnar cactus makes a bold yet congruous addition. In a more traditional room with antique furniture, a collection of leafy *Crassula*, *Echeveria*, or *Kalanchoe* in an ornamental china bowl is more appropriate.

Light can also be used to enhance the plants: cacti with interesting spines or hairs are eye-catching if placed on a sunny windowsill or artificially lit from behind. A strong outline or particularly fine shape can be emphasized by backlighting to reveal its dramatic shadow.

LIVING ART, above
The distinctive form of a single specimen like this Cereus hildmannianus v. monstrose *creates a living sculpture that echoes its modern setting.*

FRAMED DISPLAY, left
Small plants placed on glass shelves in front of a window create an ornamental screen, which draws individual plants together into a cohesive design.

A CONTRAST OF MOOD, right
The simple shapes of cacti and succulents in terracotta pots provide a calm counterpoint to the background of brilliant colors and busy patterns.

PATIOS AND TERRACES

The warm, sheltered conditions typically provided by patios and terraces make them an ideal place for growing cacti and succulents, either in raised beds or containers. The strong geometrical shapes of the plants provide a good link between the hard lines and materials of the house and patio and the softer shapes and textures of the garden plants. It is important to choose plants that are in proportion to the style and space available. In a large formal setting, for example, a single specimen plant with a dominant stature and shape can make an unusual focal point, or two plants placed sentry-like on either side of a flight of steps can be an unconventional alternative to traditional topiary.

Planting in containers allows greater flexibility for exploiting the plants' display potential, using them as movable design elements. For a strongly patterned design, plant up several containers with the same species and set the pots in a row on top of a low wall, or at one edge of the patio.

In an informal garden, many succulents, especially small *Sedum*, look effective planted into the crevices of a drystone wall. If space allows, create a succulent bed at one edge or corner of the patio for a luxuriant effect. If space is limited, remove just one or two paving stones and plant one species in the resulting gap; surround the clump with complementary ground cover. If the patio is made of loose gravel, use the same material to top-dress the bed. Alternatively, use a different material – rounded pebbles if the patio is made of stone slabs, for example – for an interesting contrast of textures. Opt for materials in muted colors, because these enhance the plants without competing with them.

TRADITIONAL DISPLAY, above
For a formal effect, plant a single decorative urn or handsome terracotta pot with a spiky rosette-shaped succulent such as Agave americana 'Medio-picta alba' *and raise the urn on a plinth or pedestal.*

COORDINATED ELEGANCE, left
Make sure the style of the container and its planting blends well with the surrounding plants, as well as the background and setting. A classical trough planted with several plants of Agave attenuata *makes an elegant display on an ornate table. The warm tone of the terracotta container also harmonizes with the color of the painted wall behind it.*

CONTEMPORARY STYLE, right
In a stark modern setting, keep the planting strong but simple. Use large plants of arresting architectural form such as this Carnegiea gigantea *in undecorated containers.*

GARDEN SETTINGS

There is scope to give your imagination free rein in an open garden, especially if there is space to prepare a well-drained bed. Even in cooler climates, a wide variety of plants may be grown outdoors (see pp. 163–6) and tender plants can be sunk into the bed in pots during the summer to give seasonal interest to the display.

When grouping plants, consider scale, shape, texture, and color. If plants are large, shape and form are likely to be most important and have the strongest impact, whereas if smaller plants are featured – perhaps grown in a raised bed to be viewed at close hand – differences in texture and color are more noticeable.

Combine plants that flower one after the other for succession of color; if flowering times overlap, ensure that the colors of the blooms complement each other. Also include species with unusual forms and textures to provide year-round interest: for example, the globular form, glossy skin, and sparse spines of *Gymnocalycium horstii* can be contrasted with the candlelike stems of *Mammillaria elongata* encased in golden, comblike spines.

Top-dressing the bed with a suitable material and adding a few large, well-shaped stones gives the planting a sense of substance and permanence. Cacti and succulents may also be grown with other plants, provided that all thrive in the same conditions. For example, the rich burgundy foliage of *Euphorbia amygdaloides* 'Purpurea' creates a stunning contrast to the platelike rosettes of *Aeonium tabuliforme*, or a spreading carpet of evergreen *Juniperus squamata* 'Blue Star' can offset the smooth waxy rosettes of *Sempervivum*.

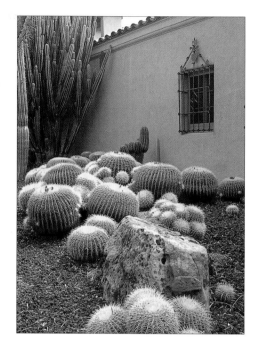

FORM AND CONTRAST, above
The rounded cushions of golden barrel cacti, Echinocactus grusonii, *form a well-sculpted group that resembles living boulders. A bold contrast is provided by the vertical lines of the majestic columnar cactus.*

SCULPTURAL CENTERPIECE, below
The tentacle-like, undulating leaves of Agave americana 'Marginata' *create a focal point in this border, while a soft cascade of bougainvillea provides a colorful backdrop.*

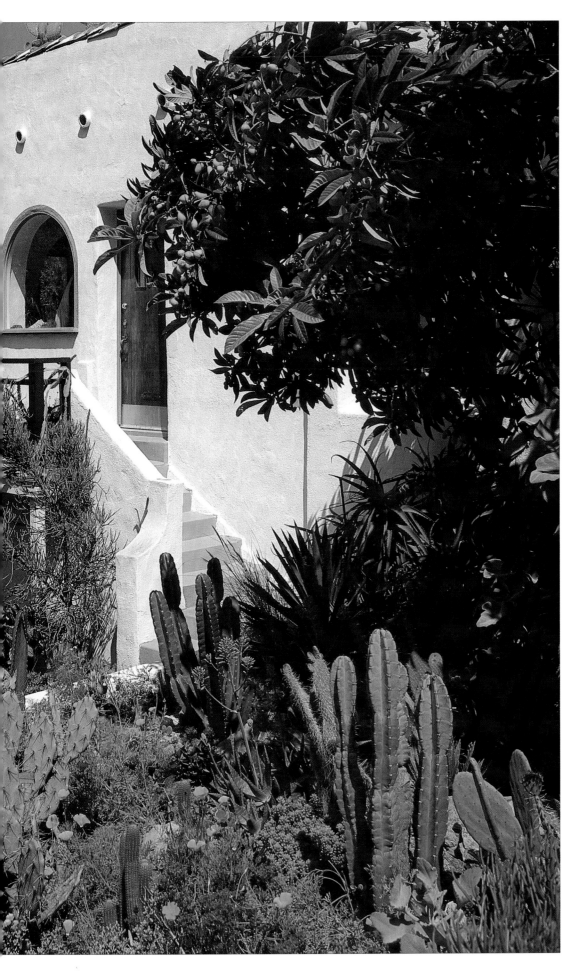

INFORMAL GROUPING
Plant cacti and succulents in informal groups or drifts for a natural effect. Here, deeply ribbed columnar plants add a strongly vertical dimension, echoed by the dark spire of a cypress behind, while low succulents and other plants weave a contrasting tapestry of color and texture beneath them.

CREATING A DESERT LOOK

MAINLY FROM DRY HABITATS, cacti and succulents offer enormous scope for creating desert-style displays with their diverse range of shapes, colors, and textures. Try a few small or slow-growing plants in a miniature desert garden for a long-lasting arrangement that should be placed in a brightly lit position indoors. Most species need very little water (so they will not suffer if you travel often) and are dormant during the winter; make sure to choose plants that are compatible in these respects (see pp. 56–143). Take care to avoid overwatering the plants if the container has no drainage holes.

Peat

Pebbles

Small washed grit

Thick brown paper

Fine brush

Spoon

9 in (23 cm) diameter terracotta bowl

Trowel

Opuntia species
Prickly pear

Aeonium haworthii
Pinwheel

Mammillaria magnimamma

Echeveria fimbriata

Echeveria elegans

PLANTS, TOOLS, AND MATERIALS

Because cacti and succulents have shallow roots, the bowl need be only 3 in (8 cm) deep. It does not matter if the bowl has drainage holes since the planting mix is composed of peat and grit. A layer of coarse grit on top gives desertlike appeal.

PLANTING THE ARRANGEMENT

1 A free-draining planting mix is essential for healthy plants; to make this up, mix two parts peat with one part small washed grit. Add more grit if needed to ensure good drainage. Cover the bottom of the bowl with a thick layer of the fresh mix.

2 With the plants still in their pots, try different arrangements, keeping in mind whether the display will be viewed from all sides. Note the arrangement you like best, then remove the plants and loosely fill the bowl with more planting mix.

BOLD SCHEME
To appreciate the plants' sculptural shapes and contrasting textures, do not overcrowd the container.

3 Starting with the tallest, remove each plant from its pot. Wrap a strip of folded brown paper around the stem of each cactus to form a handle and gently lift the plant from its pot. Fluff out the roots of each plant a little. Scoop out a hole in the planting mix for each plant as you go.

4 Lower the plant into its hole. Make sure it is sitting at the same depth in the hole as it was in its pot, spread out its roots, and fill in around them with more mix. Once all the plants are in place, lightly firm the surface of the planting mix.

5 Gently remove any planting mix that has lodged between the plants' spines or leaves with a fine, soft brush.

6 Position a few decorative pebbles on top of the planting mix and spoon on a layer of grit. Brush the surface and spray it with water to wash the stones clean. Leave it for three to four days, then water lightly.

The treelike *Aeonium haworthii* gives focus to the planting

Pebbles provide the finishing touch

Dainty rosettes of *Echeveria* contrast in shape with the globular, spiny *Mammillaria magnimamma*

DESERT DISPLAY
Once planted, a desert garden will survive happily for two to three years. After this time, renew the planting mix and replace any of the plants that have outgrown the container.

PLANTING A HANGING BASKET

SOME CACTI AND SUCCULENTS look spectacular in a hanging basket. Try the jungle cacti with slender, arching stems and showy, pendant flowers or any of the vast array of trailing succulents. One large plant looks elegantly impressive, while a mixed planting can create dramatic contrasts. Check that the plants all have the same cultural needs (see pp. 150–51) and growing periods (see the relevant entries in the Plant Catalog, pp. 56–143). Most species or hybrids that thrive in hanging baskets need some shade from the hot summer sun; hang them from tree branches in the garden or in bright indirect light indoors.

10 in (25 cm) diameter wire-mesh basket with chain

Small saucer

Terracotta pot

Sphagnum moss

Small washed grit

Standard soilless potting mix

Trowel

Schlumbergera 'Frida'

PLANTS, TOOLS, AND MATERIALS

A wire-mesh hanging basket is both lightweight and free-draining. Choose a green one so that the mesh blends in with the sphagnum moss lining for a natural look. A saucer is useful for an indoor basket because it prevents water from dripping onto the floor. Use several plants of the same type for a luxuriant planting.

HOW TO PLANT UP THE BASKET

1 Sit the basket in the top of a large pot to steady it while planting it up; make sure that the chains are untangled. Line the basket with sphagnum moss, pressing it down firmly so that it forms a layer at least 2 in (5 cm) thick.

2 Combine 1 part grit to 2 parts of the soilless potting mix. Add more grit if needed for good drainage. Put the saucer in the bottom of the basket and loosely fill two-thirds of the basket with the planting mix.

3 Ease each plant out of its pot by supporting the base of the stems and the root ball in one hand and turning the pot upside down with the other.

4 Hold the top of the root ball firmly in one hand and gently tease out some of the roots with your fingers, allowing any old loose planting mix to fall away. Take care not to damage the roots.

5 Position each plant in the basket so that the top of its root ball will be level with the surface of the potting mix. Space the plants evenly to allow room for future growth: three plants in a triangular formation work well. Once all the plants have been positioned, fill in around them with more planting mix.

A TERRACOTTA BOWL
As an alternative to a wire-mesh basket, try planting a hanging container made of terracotta. It makes an attractive contrast to the foliage and is convenient indoors because it has no drainage holes so there is no dripping. Take care not to overwater the planting mix.

Sturdy chain to support the weight of the planted basket

Masses of flowers create a show of brilliant color

6 Firm the surface of the planting mix gently, leaving about 1/2 in (1 cm) below the rim of the basket to allow for watering. Do not water the basket for 2–3 days so that any damaged roots have time to heal; otherwise, they may rot.

HANGING GARDEN
Hang the basket in a cool place until the cacti produce flower buds. Then move it to its final position to enjoy the show of blooms. Planted baskets are heavy, especially just after watering, so use a high-quality support; pulleys are very useful for lowering the basket to within easy reach.

WINDOW BOX DISPLAY

THE STRONG, ARCHITECTURAL FORMS and complementary colors of cacti and succulents make them ideally suited for either a semipermanent or a permanent arrangement in a window box or trough. Choose plants in a variety of contrasting shades, shapes, textures, and sizes for a striking display. Remember to check that all the plants prefer similar conditions (see pp. 56–143). In areas that suffer frost, move the trough under cover or indoors for the winter.

Washed gravel

Small washed grit

Potting mix

Clay pellets

Fine brush

Spoon

Cleistocactus strausii
Silver torch cactus

Echinopsis spachiana

Crassula ovata
Jade plant

Aeonium arboreum 'Atropurpureum'
Purple rose tree

Ferocactus herrerae

Ferocactus latispinus
Crow's claw

Mammillaria bombycina

Echeveria elegans

Protective gloves

Broken crocks

Brown paper

Trowel

6 in (15 cm) deep terracotta trough

CONTAINERS AND MATERIALS

The trough must have a minimum depth of 4 in (10 cm), and drainage holes to prevent it from becoming waterlogged. Extra drainage is provided by a layer of clay pellets and the grit, which is added to the potting mix. Washed gravel makes a natural-looking top-dressing.

PLANTING THE ARRANGEMENT

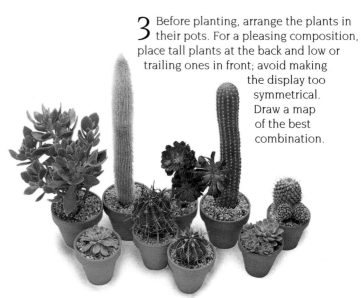

1 Combine equal parts of grit and potting mix; add extra grit if needed for good drainage. Cover each drainage hole with broken crocks. Add a thin layer of clay pellets; cover with a double layer of brown paper.

2 Half fill the container with planting mix. The paper stops loose potting mix from clogging up the drainage layer and, after the mixture has settled down, will eventually disintegrate.

3 Before planting, arrange the plants in their pots. For a pleasing composition, place tall plants at the back and low or trailing ones in front; avoid making the display too symmetrical. Draw a map of the best combination.

4 Gently ease each plant out of its pot by supporting the plant in one hand and turning the pot upside down. Wear gloves when handling spiny plants. Prepare each root ball by breaking it up slightly; this helps the roots to grow out into the new planting mix.

5 Make a depression in the planting mix and lower each plant into it so that its root ball is at the same depth as it was in the pot. Insert the largest plants first, spacing them so that they have room to grow. Fill in with planting mix around the roots and between the plants. Gently firm the planting mix surface.

6 Carefully brush off any stray particles of planting mix from the plants' leaves or from between the spines. Spoon a layer of washed gravel over the surface of the mix, taking care not to let any fall on the plants. The top-dressing keeps the surface from drying out and prevents any growth of unsightly algae. Leave the trough for a few days and then lightly water it; this ensures that the newly planted roots will not rot.

THE FINAL ARRANGEMENT
This window box planting will require only very occasional care to keep it healthy and attractive. After 3–5 years, refresh the display by changing all the mix and replanting. Replace any plants that are overgrown or damaged with new ones.

Cleistocactus strausii, a columnar cactus, gives height to the display

Purplish leaf bracts of *Aeonium arboreum* 'Atropurpureum' strike a colorful high note

Eventually, rosettes of *Echeveria elegans* will tumble over the sides of the trough

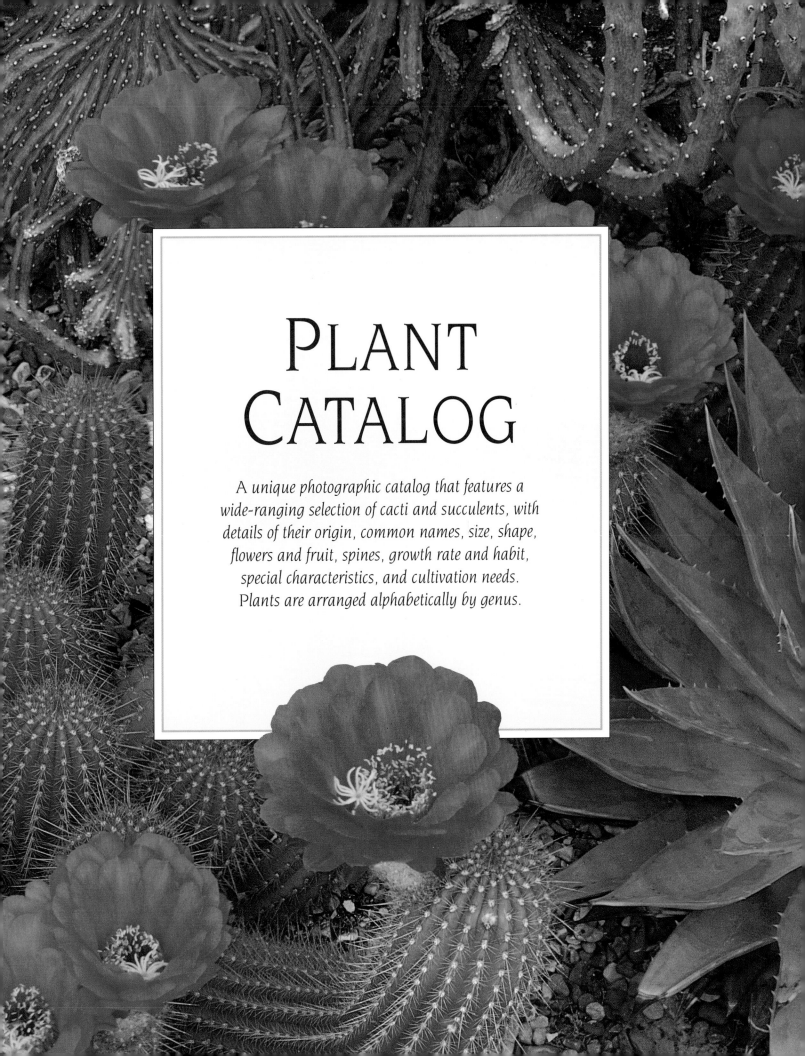

PLANT CATALOG

A unique photographic catalog that features a
wide-ranging selection of cacti and succulents, with
details of their origin, common names, size, shape,
flowers and fruit, spines, growth rate and habit,
special characteristics, and cultivation needs.
Plants are arranged alphabetically by genus.

How to Use this Section

The Plant Catalog has been divided into two parts, the first devoted to cacti and the second to other succulents. Within each part, the genera, or plant groups, are arranged in alphabetical order by their scientific, or botanical, names. The significance of the parts of a plant name is explained below (see box). Each genus entry features a representative selection of species or forms. Many species of cacti and succulents vary greatly in appearance from plant to plant, whereas other species are fairly uniform. Where the species is variable, the plant shown is usually a common form of the species.

Information in the Catalog

The cacti and succulents in the Plant Catalog, unless otherwise stated, are easy to grow, dormant in winter, may be grown outdoors or indoors in suitable conditions, and need watering only when in growth. They have unscented flowers and are evergreen perennials.

In comparison to many garden plants, most cacti and succulents grow slowly. The terms "fast-growing" or "slow-growing" and "small" or "large" in genus introductions are used in reference to other succulents or cacti. Many factors, including local conditions, affect how these plants grow; details given here are a general indication. Special propagation tips are also given.

GENUS NAME Scientific, or botanical, name of the plant group.

GENUS INTRODUCTION Gives the place of origin and number of species in the genus, as well as the main features and common characteristics of the group, such as body shape and size, spines, flowering, fruits, growth habit, and light needs. If applicable, common names, recent name changes, or special cultural needs are noted.

HEIGHT AND SPREAD PROFILES A profile for each plant indicates its growth habit, shape, and size after five years indoors in a pot (*top*) or ten years in a bed (*bottom*). Five-year profiles show growth achievable by a beginner growing plants in a greenhouse or on a windowsill, although individual plants vary. Experienced collectors may obtain better results. Most plants grow faster in a bed than in a pot. Ten-year profiles show likely growth with low maintenance. The largest scales are deepest green.

SCIENTIFIC PLANT NAME For succulents, the *Lexicon of Succulent Plants'* classification system has been followed. The authority for cacti is the CITES *Cactaceae Checklist*. Names for forms or varieties are not yet recorded in this work so there are many visually different plants in one species. If featured, such plants are here provisionally given the status of a form (e.g. *Rebutia heliosa* f. *perplexa*).

COMMON PLANT NAME If applicable, vernacular names in common use are given.

CAPTION Details may include form, growth habit, flower type if not shown, flowering season, unusual features, and special cultivation advice. The terms "fast-growing" or "slow-growing" and "small" or "large" highlight growth rates and sizes that are atypical of the genus. Some species vary in appearance; important variations of habit, size, spination, or flower color are noted.

SIZE AND TEMPERATURE Indicates the plant's maximum height (H), or length of trailing or creeping stems (L), and its maximum spread (S). Read with the profiles for an idea of how fast or slowly the plant reaches mature size. Some plants take 100 years, others are full-sized in a few years. Also given is the minimum temperature at which the plant can be cultivated. Latitudes less than 45° North or South often have a lower night temperature which rises significantly by mid-morning. Cacti and succulents can survive such temperatures, but not frosts, for short periods.

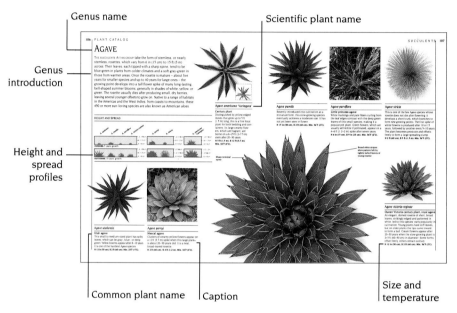

Genus name

Scientific plant name

Genus introduction

Height and spread profiles

Common plant name

Caption

Size and temperature

Plant Names

Genus (first scientific word): group of plants, often of diverse appearance, with common characteristics in the structure of their flowers or seedpods.

Intergeneric hybrid (denoted by x before the genus name): natural or cultivated cross between two genera.

Species (second scientific word): naturally occurring plant type in genus with several distinct botanical features.

Variety (denoted by v. before third scientific word): plant with varying botanical structure from a species, often with a distinct variance in look.

Form (denoted by f. before third scientific word): plant differing slightly from the species, as in flower color.

Hybrid or cultivar (denoted by second or third word in single quote marks): a hybrid is a cross between two species of one genus; a cultivar is a hybrid or form selected or bred in cultivation.

CACTI

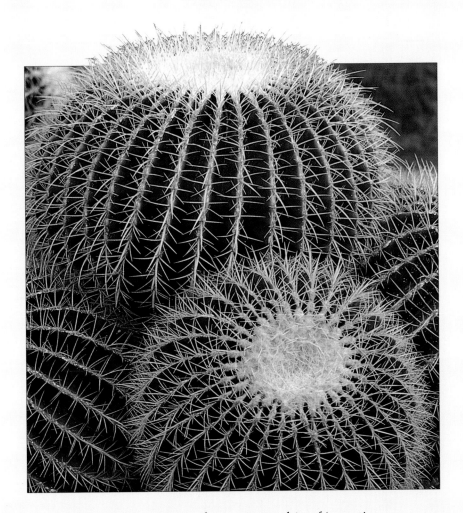

The wide variety of cacti covered in this section
includes small and globular, or tall and columnar
desert species, as well as trailing or climbing
jungle species.

APOROCACTUS

IN THE WILD IN MEXICO, these epiphytic rat's-tail cacti (see pp. 10–11) grow on trees and in rocky crevices. They make good plants for hanging baskets. There are now only two true species: both have slender stems that are studded with short tufts of bristly spines and can creep or trail for a considerable length. Among the first cacti to flower in early spring, they bear a profusion of vividly hued, long-necked blooms on the previous year's growth. Very easy to grow, these plants need a fairly rich planting mix and a bright situation shaded from hot sun. Water lightly now and then in winter to avoid dieback of the stem tips, and cut out old or discolored stems at the base to encourage new growth.

LENGTH AND SPREAD

Aporocactus species and forms	Aporocactus species and forms
4 ft/1.2 m	8 ft/2.4 m
2 ft/60 cm	4 ft/1.2 m
0 in/0 cm	0 in/0 cm
INDOORS: 5 years' growth	**OUTDOORS:** 10 years' growth

Petals and sepals of each flower are arranged in layers

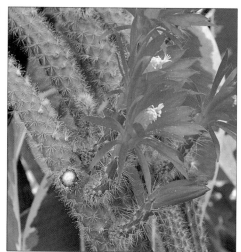

Aporocactus martianus f. conzatianum

Although the flowers of this form are less abundant than those of A. *flagelliformis*, they are larger. The stems, which are most often densely covered with short, golden brown spines, are also thicker. This cactus rarely produces any berries.

L and S unlimited. Min. 43°F (6°C).

Aporocactus flagelliformis f. flagriformis

A different form of the species A. *flagelliformis*, this cactus has slimmer stems and fewer spines. Variable in growth habit, its flowers are a deep shade of carmine-pink and the berries are red. It is not as common in cultivation and less tolerant of overwatering.

L and S unlimited. Min. 43°F (6°C).

Aporocactus flagelliformis

This cactus bears an abundance of beautiful, double cerise flowers, 2–3 in (5–8 cm) across, which sometimes produce small red berries. Its pencil-thin stems are densely clothed in short golden spines and, as in other *Aporocactus*, grow up to 12 in (30 cm) a year. Easier than A. *martianus* to grow, this species is also more tolerant of cold.

L and S unlimited. Min. 41°F (5°C).

X APOROPHYLLUM

THIS GROUP IS NOT a true genus but a collection of intergeneric hybrids developed by crossing the *Aporocactus* species with other epiphytic cactus groups, predominantly *Epiphyllum* hybrids. Most of the characteristics of *Aporophyllum* hybrids have been inherited from the *Aporocactus* genus, but the hybrids are distinguished by their larger, open-faced flowers in brilliant shades of orange, cerise, scarlet, and purple as well as white. The stems grow over 6 ft (2 m) long and root into the soil to form large mats. The plants need shade and temperatures no lower than 43°F (6°C), and flower best if fed well each spring and summer. Water them lightly from time to time in winter. Propagate from 6 in (15 cm) cuttings to obtain plants that are similar to the parent.

LENGTH AND SPREAD

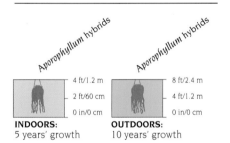

Aporophyllum hybrids

4 ft/1.2 m	
2 ft/60 cm	
0 in/0 cm	

INDOORS:
5 years' growth

Aporophyllum hybrids

8 ft/2.4 m	
4 ft/1.2 m	
0 in/0 cm	

OUTDOORS:
10 years' growth

x *Aporophyllum* 'Sussex Pink'

x *Aporophyllum* 'Dawn'

x *Aporophyllum* 'Vivide'

x *Aporophyllum* 'Edna Bellamy'

ARIOCARPUS

THESE SIX SPECIES OF living rock, or fossil, cacti from southern Texas and Mexico are endangered in the wild. The small, cone-shaped plants grow very slowly, largely underground, and have gray or brown, almost spineless tubercles. They grow in short bursts in late spring and in autumn, when their white, yellow, pink, or red, open-faced flowers and pale fleshy berries appear. Especially challenging to grow in cooler areas, these sun-loving cacti need careful watering during their growth period; water once in spring, occasionally in summer, and thoroughly a few times in early autumn. Some ground limestone in the potting mix benefits the roots. Mature plants are seldom legally available but seed germinates easily.

Smooth, pointed tubercles

HEIGHT AND SPREAD

A. trigonus
A. fissuratus

12 in/30 cm
6 in/15 cm
0 in/0 cm
INDOORS: 5 years' growth

12 in/30 cm
6 in/15 cm
0 in/0 cm
OUTDOORS: 10 years' growth

Triangular tubercles with a wrinkled surface

Ariocarpus trigonus

Only the rosette of long, curving, leaflike tubercles is visible on this plant; the flat, tuberous body is below the soil. Yellow flowers and small white berries appear in a ring on the crown. A plant only 10 in (25 cm) in diameter may be 100 years old.
H 4 in (10 cm), S 8 in (20 cm). Min. 45°F (7°C).

Ariocarpus fissuratus

Sought by collectors, this rare and curious species has fleshy tubercles tightly packed on its crown into flat or slightly domed rosettes. Woolly tufts of spines grow in the center. Its open-faced pink flowers last for three or four days. This cactus can take 50 years to reach a diameter of 6 in (15 cm). It is very prone to rot if overwatered.
H 2 in (5 cm), S 6 in (15 cm). Min. 41°F (5°C).

ASTROPHYTUM

THERE ARE ONLY FOUR species in this sun-loving genus from Mexico, but many hybrids. Mostly small, rotund cacti that are often flecked with white scales, they are quite variable, especially in the type of spine and number of ribs. Many large, bright yellow, daisylike flowers appear at the plant crown in spring to late summer. Each bloom opens fully in bright light and is long lasting. The fleshy green seedpods split open to reveal large, helmet-shaped seeds. The slow-growing body becomes columnar after many years. Add some ground limestone to the planting mix to improve the plant's roots and vigor.

HEIGHT AND SPREAD

A. ornatum
A. asterias
A. capricorne
A. myriostigma

12 in/30 cm
6 in/15 cm
0 in/0 cm
INDOORS: 5 years' growth

12 in/30 cm
6 in/15 cm
0 in/0 cm
OUTDOORS: 10 years' growth

Woolly brown areoles, or spine cushions, line the ridges of the ribs

Astrophytum ornatum

The fastest-growing and largest Astrophytum, this variable species bears many large flowers after 5–6 years. The ribs, usually flecked with silver and with mostly pale, curving spines, spiral toward the crown.
H 4 ft (1.2 m), S 8 in (20 cm). Min. 45°F (7°C).

Astrophytum asterias

Sea urchin, silver dollar cactus

This small, spineless cactus has a gray-green to white-green body. It is a sensitive plant and rots if overwatered, so it is best grown grafted. Flowers with deep red throats appear after about five years. In winter, when dry and dormant, the globular or saucerlike body shrinks to a flat disc.
H 2 in (5 cm), S 5 in (13 cm). Min. 50°F (10°C).

Astrophytum capricorne

Goat's horn cactus

The wiry, gray to brown spines that twist around this small cactus are easily broken off if handled. The body, which is usually dark, is sometimes flecked with white. Its flowers often have a wine-red throat.
H 4 ft (1.2 m), S 4 in (10 cm). Min. 41°F (5°C).

Astrophytum myriostigma

Bishop's cap, bishop's miter, monk's hood

This species is prized for a look that is distinctly uncommon among cacti. Initially squat, it is the size of a small melon when about ten years old. Its bare body may be green, blue, or purple, with 4–8 ribs, and eventually becomes slightly columnar. The speckled look is due to innumerable white scales, which are in fact rudimentary spines. Large plants readily bear blooms that are 2½ in (6 cm) across and last 2–3 days.
H 6 in (15 cm), S 8 in (20 cm). Min. 41°F (5°C).

CARNEGIEA GIGANTEA

THIS IS KNOWN AS A MONOTYPIC GENUS because it contains only one species: the giant saguaro cactus. In the wild, in the southwestern US and northwest Mexico, this cactus often forms large colonies. It takes about 150 years to reach its full impressive stature of some 40 ft (12 m) and sometimes develops a few branches once it is 10–15 ft (3–5 m) tall. Huge, funnel-shaped, creamy white blooms, followed by red, plum-shaped, edible fruits, first appear on the stem tip in late spring when the plant is about 40 years old or more. Mature plants in the wild can produce up to ten million seeds a year but usually only one seedling in 50 million is successful, so a mature cactus may reproduce only once in every five years. Collecting plants from the wild is now illegal. Fortunately, the seed germinates very readily in cultivation. This sun-loving species is moderately easy to grow at a minimum temperature of 41°F (5°C).

HEIGHT AND SPREAD

INDOORS:	OUTDOORS:
5 years' growth	10 years' growth

12 in/30 cm · 6 in/15 cm · 0 in/0 cm

CEPHALOCEREUS

FROM TROPICAL AND SUBTROPICAL Mexican habitats ranging from seashores to mountains, the five sun-loving species in this genus are blue-green, slow-growing, columnar plants. In the wild, they reach about 50 ft (15.2 m) in 200 years; in cultivation, they are usually no taller than 3 ft (90 cm). The spines vary but are sometimes long and silky on the upper stem, forming a pseudocephalium, or "beard." Trumpet-shaped, white, pink, or yellow summer flowers briefly appear at night on plants that are at least 20 years old. The round seedpods split open when ripe.

Spines can
vary in length

HEIGHT AND SPREAD

C. senilis · *C. senilis*

12 in/30 cm · 6 in/15 cm · 0 in/0 cm

INDOORS:	OUTDOORS:
5 years' growth	10 years' growth

Cephalocereus senilis

Old man cactus
The long downy spines are thickest at the stem tip, especially on very old plants (see inset), which eventually bear cream to pink nocturnal flowers and rosy seedpods. If the down becomes dirty, wash and comb it gently. The columnar stem seldom branches. Add extra calcium to the potting mix or soil for healthy growth.
H 50 ft (15.2 m), S 12 in (30 cm). Min. 41°F (5°C).

CEREUS

DIVERSE HABITATS in eastern South America and the West Indies are home to the 60 or so species of mostly large, robust, columnar cacti in this genus. Their stems, often blue-green and spiny, grow up to 4 ft (1.2 m) a year and branch freely. Funnel-shaped, pink, white, or green flowers appear near the plant's crown, opening mostly at night to fade at dawn in spring or summer. The round or oval edible fruits are green, red, or purple. These sun-loving cacti make good focal or hedge plants.

HEIGHT AND SPREAD

C. aethiops C. h. v. monstrose C. validus

4 ft/1.2 m
2 ft/60 cm
0 in/0 cm
INDOORS: 5 years' growth

8 ft/2.4 m
4 ft/1.2 m
0 in/0 cm
OUTDOORS: 10 years' growth

Cereus aethiops

Mature plants form stately clumps of tall, slender blue-green stems studded with distinctive black spines. Once the stem is 3–4 ft (90 cm–1.2 m) tall, it blooms several times at night in summer. Plum-shaped purple-brown fruits follow.
H 10 ft (3 m), S 4 ft (1.2 m). Min. 45°F (7°C).

Buds open into white or pale pink flowers

Cereus hildmannianus v. monstrose

Curiosity plant
The contorted stem of this variable, white-flowering cactus is caused by deformed growing points. In a small pot, the stem is often more squat than the plant shown here. It has brown fruits.
H 15 ft (5 m), S 10 ft (3 m). Min. 41°F (5°C).

Short spines range from gold to red

Cereus validus

An attractive focal plant, this variable cactus flowers freely at intervals in summer. Its long thick spines are glossy black on new growth. The fruits are greenish purple. The stem offsets in time to form a clump.
H 25 ft (7.5 m),
S 10 ft (3 m).
Min. 45°F (7°C).

Flowers are predominantly white with salmon or pink tints

Cactus flowers once the stem is 4 ft (1.2 m) tall

CLEISTOCACTUS

DENSE, NEEDLELIKE SPINES in hues of white, beige, or gold often clothe these branching columnar cacti. The 49 species are widespread in most South American countries, from Ecuador and Argentina to Uruguay. Some have tubular flowers. Others, formerly classified as *Borzicactus*, have more open, lopsided flowers, tend to have slimmer stems, and form arching mounds. Between spring and autumn, most of these sun-loving, fast-growing plants produce masses of small scarlet, orange, green, or golden blooms, usually from the upper part of the stem. The round berries are green, yellow, or red.

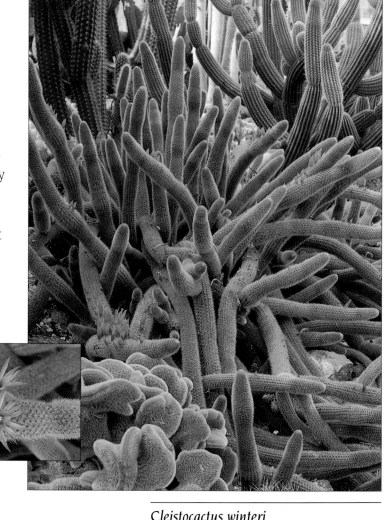

HEIGHT AND SPREAD

	C. winteri	C. brookeae		C. strausii
				4 ft/1.2 m
				2 ft/60 cm
				0 in/0 cm

INDOORS: 5 years' growth

OUTDOORS: 10 years' growth

Cleistocactus winteri

Large, tangled mounds of long, slender, arching stems covered in short golden spines make this a distinctive bedding plant. The stems may also be cristate, or wavy, in form (see foreground). Mature plants flower almost constantly in spring and summer. The fruits are green. Small plants are ideal for hanging baskets.
H 3 ft (90 cm), S unlimited. Min. 45°F (7°C).

Cleistocactus brookeae

The slender, semierect stem of this species, which often becomes prostrate with age, usually has straight, pale gold spines, although in one form the spines are white. In summer, slightly S-shaped flowers appear along the upper part of the stem. Small purple-red berries follow. The cactus slowly spreads into a clump.
H 5 ft (1.5 m), S unlimited. Min. 41°F (5°C).

Cleistocactus strausii

Silver torch cactus
This variable, fast-growing cactus has eye-catching silvery spines. Solitary when young, the spring-flowering stem branches and clumps as it matures. Its fruits are green. Allow the roots plenty of room.
H 10 ft (3 m), S 6 ft (2 m). Min. 41°F (5°C).

Tubular flowers grow directly from stem

COPIAPOA

THIS GROUP OF SUN-LOVING Chilean cacti includes about 26 species. Some are globular, with small brown bodies and tiny spines, or larger, blue-green bodies and short spines; others are slightly columnar, freely offsetting species with fierce spines. After some years, most develop a powdery or waxy sheen. All have small, open-faced yellow summer flowers that grow from the woolly plant crown. Small green seedpods develop inside the crown and emerge when ripe. These tuberous-rooted plants slowly offset into large clumps. They need a dry winter and moderate summer watering.

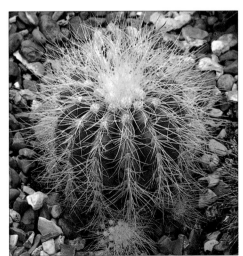

Light, waxy sheen develops after 5–10 years

HEIGHT AND SPREAD

C. cinerea *C. hypogaea* *C. coquimbana* *C. krainziana*

12 in/30 cm
6 in/15 cm
0 in/0 cm

INDOORS: 5 years' growth

12 in/30 cm
6 in/15 cm
0 in/0 cm

OUTDOORS: 10 years' growth

Copiapoa cinerea

This striking cactus is challenging to grow. It varies in shape, type of spine, and number of ribs. The large, slow-growing, globular body is solitary at first. Only with great age, does it become slightly columnar and begin to produce a few offsets. Pale gold, open-faced flowers appear after about 20 years.
H and S 4 ft (1.2 m). Min. 45°F (7°C).

Copiapoa hypogaea

This small, globular, gray-brown cactus flowers freely as soon as it is 2 in (5 cm) in diameter. It has large, felty areoles and is very variable in shape and in the color and density of its spines. Protect it from winter cold to avoid bad scarring.

H 6 in (15 cm), S 15 in (38 cm). Min. 45°F (7°C).

Copiapoa coquimbana

One of the larger-growing *Copiapoa* species, this free-flowering plant is globular at first, then slightly columnar in shape. It readily produces offsets to form a clump. The straight spines vary in color and density but are usually dark and quite long.

H 18 in (46 cm), S 3 ft (90 cm). Min. 45°F (7°C).

Copiapoa krainziana

This small, usually gray to green cactus is distinguished by long whiskery spines that vary in color. White-spined forms need to be large before flowering; darker-spined plants grow faster. The globular body freely offsets into a mound.

H 8 in (20 cm), S 12 in (30 cm). Min. 41°F (5°C).

CORYPHANTHA

CHUNKY TUBERCLES GIVE THESE CACTI the common name of beehive cacti. The 60 or so small sun-loving species from the US and Mexico generally have dense spines. A few are columnar but most are globular and slow-growing with a tuberous root. They usually do not flower for several years, then produce large, daisylike flowers from the plant crown in spring and summer; these are often glossy yellow but some species have pink or red blooms. Green seedpods, which contain large brown seeds, follow.

HEIGHT AND SPREAD

INDOORS: 5 years' growth

OUTDOORS: 10 years' growth

Tubercles vary in size from plant to plant

Coryphantha guerkeana

Pale starry spines and short, curved, often black-tipped central spines encase the body of this species. It is globular or slightly flattened in shape. The plant offsets slowly to form clumps and when it is about five years old, pale yellow flowers appear.
H 4 in (10 cm), S 8 in (20 cm). Min. 41°F (5°C).

Areoles, or spine cushions, are very woolly at the crown

Coryphantha pseudoechinus

The chief attraction of this cactus is its spines, which range from pale or red-brown to black. After five years, small, violet-pink flowers appear. The gray-green body is globular at first, becoming columnar; it is usually solitary but may offset with age.
H 7 in (18 cm), S 12 in (30 cm). Min. 41°F (5°C).

Coryphantha bumamma

Very large glossy green tubercles make this flattened globular species distinctive. Its stout spines are yellow and after about five years, golden flowers are produced. This slow-growing cactus is moderately easy to care for and offsets freely. Detach the offsets for use in propagation.
H 5 in (13 cm), S 15 in (38 cm). Min. 41°F (5°C).

Coryphantha clava

This stubbly cactus has yellow to brown spines that fade to off-white. Clumping with age, it bears golden flowers only when mature. The areoles exude a nectarlike secretion on which mold grows; regular spraying with water in summer and autumn and good ventilation help to avoid this.
H 15 in (38 cm), S 2 ft (60 cm). Min. 41°F (5°C).

ECHINOCACTUS

AT ONE TIME, MOST CACTI were called *Echinocactus* but now this genus consists of only six slow-growing species from the US and Mexico. When in flower, they produce a ring of open-faced flowers ranging from golden yellow to purple-red on the plant crown. The smaller species are globular and the larger ones are barrel-shaped, resembling the *Ferocactus* (see pp. 74–5). The easiest to grow and best known is E. *grusonii*; other species are best left to the enthusiast because they need constant care.

HEIGHT AND SPREAD

E. grusonii

12 in/30 cm
6 in/15 cm
0 in/0 cm
INDOORS: 5 years' growth

12 in/30 cm
6 in/15 cm
0 in/0 cm
OUTDOORS: 10 years' growth

Echinocactus grusonii

Golden barrel, mother-in-law's seat
Bright golden spines that emphasize its distinctive barrel shape make this beautiful species ideal as a specimen plant. Potgrown plants take 30–40 years to reach a flowering size of about 15 in (38 cm) in diameter. Small, funnel-shaped, summer blooms are followed by papery seedpods. Keep the plant warm and dry in winter.
H 4 ft (1.2 m), S 10 ft (3 m). Min. 50°F (10°C).

ECHINOCEREUS

THESE PRETTY, SPINY hedgehog cacti come from the southern US and Mexico. There are about 50 species, which vary widely in shape and flower color. Densely spined species flower profusely at an earlier age than those with fewer spines. The flower buds form inside the stems, then burst through the skin near the stem tips in late spring and early summer. The large, mostly funnel-shaped flowers with green stigmas open fully only in sun and are long lasting. The soft, spiny berries range from green to purple. These plants need full sun and summer feeding. Most are hardy – many even tolerate light frost – but they flower best if kept at 50°F (10°C) in winter. Densely spined species may rot if they are watered too early in spring.

Echinocereus chloranthus

Cylinder bells
Strangely colored flowers are a feature of this small variable species: they are a brownish green and appear freely in spring near the plant crown. The spines range in color from red or brown to cream, and the small berries are green. This plant slowly forms a clump. It needs a dry, winter rest.
H 5 in (13 cm), S 12 in (30 cm). Min. 41°F (5°C).

HEIGHT AND SPREAD

E. chloranthus *E. stramineus* *E. knippelianus* *E. scheeri* *E. triglochidiatus* *E. rigidissimus* v. *rubrispinus* *E. cinerascens* *E. subinermis*

12 in/30 cm
6 in/15 cm
0 in/0 cm

INDOORS: 5 years' growth

12 in/30 cm
6 in/15 cm
0 in/0 cm

OUTDOORS: 10 years' growth

White areoles, or spine cushions

Needlelike spines

Echinocereus stramineus

Porcupine hedgehog
When young, this robust cactus is short and columnar. Its flowers – the largest in the genus – open in spring and keep growing to reach 6 in (15 cm) across. The spines vary in color and the berries are wine-red.
H and S unlimited. Min. 41°F (5°C).

Echinocereus knippelianus

Bold coloring and strength of form make this a striking cactus. Pink spring flowers and green berries are borne near the stem tip. In the wild, the tuberous root pulls the plant below ground to avoid the hot sun.
H 5 in (13 cm), S 15 in (38 cm). Min. 41°F (5°C).

Mature clump of small, slow-growing stems

Echinocereus scheeri

This very variable species has abundant spring flowers that open at dusk and partly close during the day. They appear all along the young, fingerlike stems and change color, usually from pink to vermilion or orange, as they age. Green fruits follow.
H and S unlimited. Min. 41°F (5°C).

Bright green stigmas contrast with scarlet petals

Echinocereus triglochidiatus

Claret cup hedgehog
Corrugated ribs and vividly hued blooms distinguish this species. It bears small pink berries in summer. The length and number of spines vary from plant to plant.
H 8 in (20 cm), S 2 ft (60 cm). Min. 36°F (2°C).

Small, slowly offsetting body may be short and columnar or globular in shape

Echinocereus rigidissimus v. *rubrispinus*

Rainbow cactus
The short spines often occur in red and white bands. Its erect stem slowly forms a clump, but the plant flowers readily when quite small. A ring of pink to magenta spring flowers with pale throats, followed by green berries, appear on the crown of each stem. It needs a long, dry, winter rest.
H 9 in (23 cm), S 2 ft (60 cm). Min. 41°F (5°C).

Echinocereus cinerascens

The shape, spines and flower color of this species vary enormously. It does not flower well until it is about 8–12 in (20–30 cm) in diameter. Its large blooms appear in spring near the stem tips and are followed by green berries that soften when ripe. This cactus forms large spreading mounds of thick prostrate stems.
H and S unlimited. Min. 41°F (5°C).

Echinocereus subinermis

One of the few Echinocereus to have yellow flowers, this small cactus is almost hidden by its clusters of large summer blooms. These are followed by gray-green berries. The small body has few ribs and short, pale, needlelike spines. Plants grow and form offsets slowly and are moderately easy to care for.
H 6 in (15 cm), S 15 in (38 cm). Min. 45°F (7°C).

ECHINOPSIS

THE ROBUST SPECIES in this large genus range in shape from small and globular to tall and columnar, with flowers and spines that differ greatly in size and hue. This diversity is due to the recent amalgamation into one genus of the former genera Echinopsis, Lobivia, Pseudolobivia, Soehrensia, and Trichocereus, which originated in countries such as Chile, Argentina, Ecuador, and Peru. The 150 species include night-flowering plants that have several flushes of summer blooms and others that flower more erratically in daytime from spring to summer with displays lasting one or two days. The round berries are often green. Most of these cacti can withstand neglect and near-freezing winter temperatures.

Long neck

Blooms may be deep red to purple

Echinopsis mamillosa f. *kermesina*

When it is only 3 in (8 cm) in diameter, this small cactus produces flowers that open on summer nights and last about 24 hours. Protect the plant from cold to avoid unsightly scarring and grow it in full sun.
H 12 in (30 cm), S 9 in (23 cm). Min. 45°F (7°C).

HEIGHT AND SPREAD

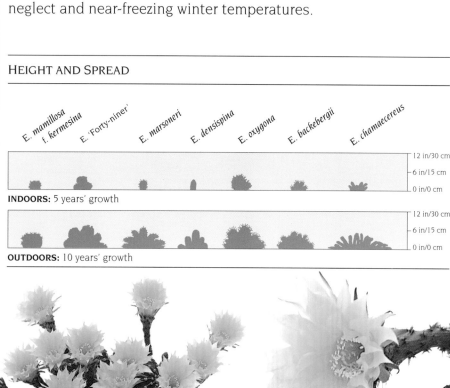

E. mamillosa f. kermesina · E. 'Forty-niner' · E. marsoneri · E. densispina · E. oxygona · E. backebergii · E. chamaecereus

12 in/30 cm
6 in/15 cm
0 in/0 cm
INDOORS: 5 years' growth

12 in/30 cm
6 in/15 cm
0 in/0 cm
OUTDOORS: 10 years' growth

Pale areoles, or spine cushions

Echinopsis 'Forty-niner'

Like all Echinopsis hybrids, this pretty cactus was developed to create a more handsome and larger body than that of the species, as well as more vividly colored flowers. The dazzling golden blooms open at dusk, at intervals throughout spring and summer, and fade after 24 hours; their necks can be up to 10 in (25 cm) long. This sun-loving, globular plant is very robust.
H 12 in (30 cm), S 4 ft (1.2 m). Min. 36°F (2°C).

Echinopsis marsoneri

Cob cactus

The shape and spines of this small cactus vary. Open, short-necked flowers, which are gold with a red throat, appear on the sides of the stem in summer. This plant grows well in sun or shade, slowly becoming prostrate.
H and S 15 in (38 cm). Min. 41°F (5°C).

Echinopsis densispina

Often labeled with its old name of *Lobivia famatimensis*, this cactus flowers when 1–2 in (2.5–5 cm) tall. In spring or summer, it bears a profusion of fairly large, funnel-shaped flowers with the daisylike petals that are typical of *Lobivia*. They range from white, yellow, and orange, to pink, purple, or red. The pale spines are bristly. This species prefers light shade or, when in bloom, sun.
H and S 2 ft (60 cm). Min. 41°F (5°C).

Echinopsis oxygona

Widely grown for a century because it is robust and easily propagated, this cactus is a fine flowering plant. The long-necked blooms, some scented, are white to lavender in hue. They are about 5 in (13 cm) across. They appear intermittently in spring and summer, and open at night for up to 24 hours. The globular body is usually dark green and the spines range from black to white in color.
H 12 in (30 cm), S 4 ft (1.2 m). Min. 41°F (5°C).

Spiny neck

Flowers open to 5 in (13 cm) across

Echinopsis backebergii

The spines, flower and body color of this small globular species differ greatly from plant to plant. Its flat-faced summer blooms are often red or purple with a pale throat and are borne freely around the upper stem. The spines may be red, brown, yellow, purple, or grayish. This is a good beginner's plant because it flowers and forms offsets readily. It will grow in either sun or light shade.
H 9 in (23 cm), S 3 ft (90 cm). Min. 41°F (5°C).

Echinopsis chamaecereus

Peanut cactus

This small slender plant has very short white spines, and branches rapidly, forming a cluster of creeping candlelike stems. It flowers prolifically, producing funnel-shaped blooms, which open fully only in sun, all along the stem in late spring or early summer. The small berries are spiny. This cactus tolerates neglect and prefers slight shade. It is easily grown from offsets.
H 6 in (15 cm), S unlimited. Min. 32°F (0°C).

ECHINOPSIS

HEIGHT AND SPREAD

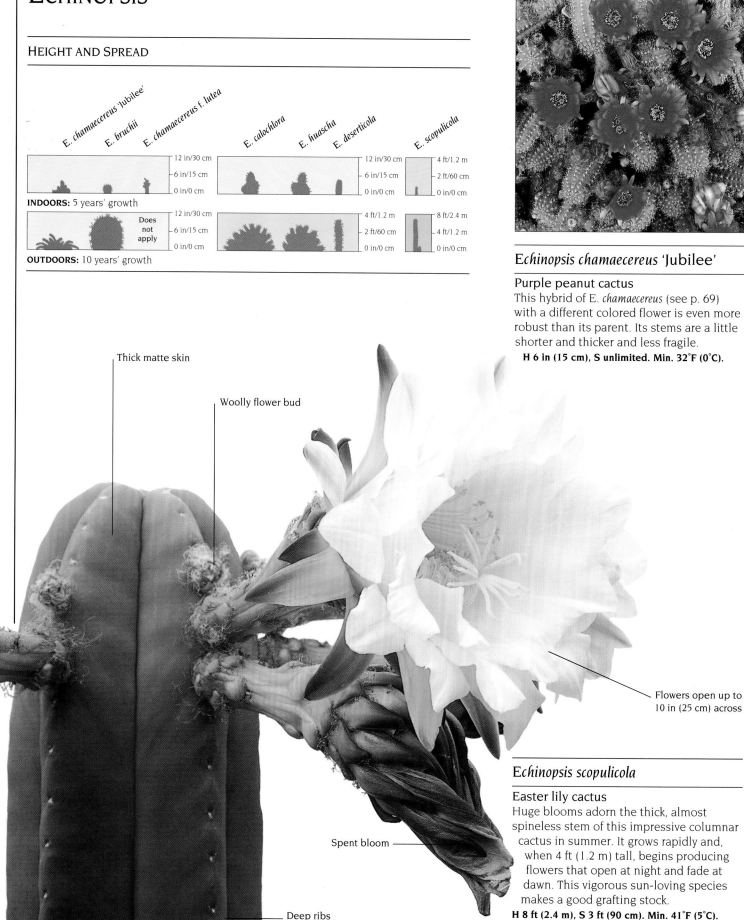

	E. chamaecereus 'Jubilee'	E. bruchii	E. chamaecereus f. lutea	E. calochlora	E. huascha	E. deserticola	E. scopulicola

INDOORS: 5 years' growth — 12 in/30 cm, 6 in/15 cm, 0 in/0 cm | 12 in/30 cm, 6 in/15 cm, 0 in/0 cm | 4 ft/1.2 m, 2 ft/60 cm, 0 in/0 cm

OUTDOORS: 10 years' growth — 12 in/30 cm, 6 in/15 cm, 0 in/0 cm, Does not apply | 4 ft/1.2 m, 2 ft/60 cm, 0 in/0 cm | 8 ft/2.4 m, 4 ft/1.2 m, 0 in/0 cm

Echinopsis chamaecereus 'Jubilee'

Purple peanut cactus
This hybrid of E. *chamaecereus* (see p. 69) with a different colored flower is even more robust than its parent. Its stems are a little shorter and thicker and less fragile.
H 6 in (15 cm), S unlimited. Min. 32°F (0°C).

Thick matte skin

Woolly flower bud

Flowers open up to 10 in (25 cm) across

Spent bloom

Deep ribs

Echinopsis scopulicola

Easter lily cactus
Huge blooms adorn the thick, almost spineless stem of this impressive columnar cactus in summer. It grows rapidly and, when 4 ft (1.2 m) tall, begins producing flowers that open at night and fade at dawn. This vigorous sun-loving species makes a good grafting stock.
H 8 ft (2.4 m), S 3 ft (90 cm). Min. 41°F (5°C).

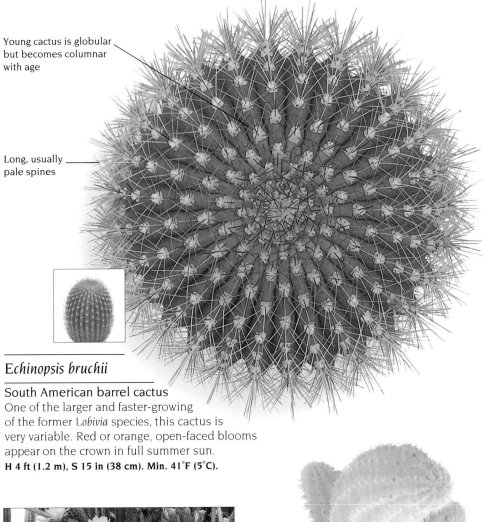

Young cactus is globular but becomes columnar with age

Long, usually pale spines

Echinopsis bruchii

South American barrel cactus
One of the larger and faster-growing of the former *Lobivia* species, this cactus is very variable. Red or orange, open-faced blooms appear on the crown in full summer sun.
H 4 ft (1.2 m), S 15 in (38 cm). Min. 41°F (5°C).

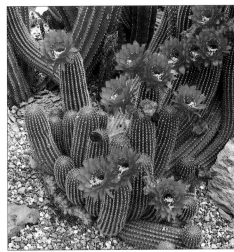

Echinopsis calochlora

The abundant, funnel-shaped blooms of this striking species, which may be various shades of red, open at night in summer and last about two days. Its short spines are yellow or brown. When young, the thick cylindrical body is erect, but it rapidly forms large dense clumps of creeping stems. This is a very robust plant if given full sun.
H 3 ft (90 cm), S unlimited. Min. 41°F (5°C).

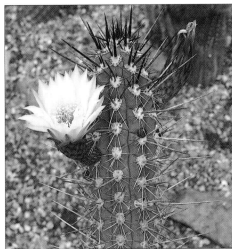

Echinopsis huascha

When mature, this fast-growing species often forms a dense, writhing mound of long, thick, round stems. There are many different forms, some compact, others more prostrate. The spines vary in length and range in hue from red or brown to golden yellow. Once the cactus reaches 12–15 in (30–38 cm), it produces a profusion of red or gold, funnel-shaped flowers in summer. This cactus grows well in sun.
H 3 ft (90 cm), S unlimited. Min. 41°F (5°C).

Echinopsis chamaecereus f. lutea

Yellow peanut cactus
A cactus curiosity, this is grown for its banana-like stems because its red flowers rarely appear. It has no chlorophyll, so it must be grafted onto a green cactus that can supply it with food. The slim elongated stem slowly forms a small clump. Grown only as a pot plant, it needs some care; shade its tender body from summer sun to avoid scorch marks. The grafting stock determines the minimum temperature.
H 5 in (13 cm), S 10 in (25 cm). Av. min. 50°F (10°C).

Echinopsis deserticola

Even when small, this fierce-looking cactus often has dark spines up to 4 in (10 cm) long. Its columnar stem is fast-growing and produces erect branches as it matures into a handsome specimen. The body size, the number of ribs, and the spines can differ greatly among individual plants. This sun-loving plant eventually forms a clump. Pale pink to white flowers appear in summer.
H 6 ft (2 m), S 4 in (1.2 m). Min. 45°F (7°C).

EPIPHYLLUM

THESE ARE KNOWN AS ORCHID CACTI for their large spectacular flowers, strap cacti after their broad, leaflike stems, or phyllocacti because their flowers grow from the stem edges. The 20 species of medium-sized to large, almost spineless epiphytes (see pp. 10–11) grow in the tree canopies of tropical jungles from Mexico to northern South America. The flowers, which are often scented, open at night and last a few hours in warmth but up to a few days in cooler conditions. The plumlike fruits are red or green. *Epiphyllum* are hungry plants, so they need regular feeding. They grow best in warm shade.

Asymmetrical indentations on stems

LENGTH AND SPREAD

E. anguliger | E. crenatum v. chichicastenango | E. ackermannii | Epiphyllum hybrids

4 ft/1.2 m
2 ft/60 cm
0 in/0 cm

INDOORS: 5 years' growth

4 ft/1.2 m
2 ft/60 cm
0 in/0 cm

OUTDOORS: 10 years' growth

Epiphyllum anguliger

Rickrack orchid cactus, fishbone cactus
So named because of its deeply serrated, trailing stems, this species has several forms with zigzag stems. The sweetly scented, white or cream flowers are about 3 in (8 cm) in diameter with long curved necks, and are produced in summer and autumn. Tiny green fruits follow.
L and S unlimited. Min. 45°F (7°C).

Epiphyllum crenatum v. *chichicastenango*

If grown in a hanging basket this bushy cactus is fairly compact, but in a pot it becomes tall and spreading. Its curiously asymmetrical, indented, flat stems are erect at first, then form a prostrate trailing clump. Large, sweetly scented flowers and green fruits appear in spring and summer.
L and S unlimited. Min. 45°F (7°C).

Epiphyllum ackermannii

As the only *Epiphyllum* species with vividly colored, rather than white or cream flowers, this Costa Rican plant's right to inclusion in this genus has long been the subject of debate. It is also confused with an early, red-flowered hybrid of the same name. This clambering cactus can quickly grow up a tree or a wall and it can also form a trailing or arching mound. Aerial roots are produced from the stems wherever they find moisture. The trumpet-shaped flowers are produced in spring and summer and are followed by green fruits.
L and S unlimited. Min. 41°F (5°C).

Epiphyllum hybrids

Thousands of hybrids have been created by crossing E*piphyllum* species, often with other mostly epiphytic cacti, to improve the size, longevity, and color range of their blooms. The flowers average 5–8 in (13–20 cm) across but the largest can be 15 in (38 cm); many of them change hue according to local light and temperature. Large-flowered hybrids must be a good size before they produce full-sized blooms. The hybrids' cultivation needs are similar to those of the species but they need warmer temperatures for an extended growing season and a fine display of flowers. Hybrid cuttings 6–8 in (15–20 cm) long, taken in spring, should flower in 1–2 years. Plant several to a pot for a larger plant.

L and S unlimited. Min 45°F (7°C).

E*piphyllum* 'Reward'

E*piphyllum* 'Lynda Ann'

E*piphyllum* 'J. T. Barber'

E*piphyllum* 'Fantasy'

E*piphyllum* 'Fortuna'

E*piphyllum* 'Ignescens'

E*piphyllum* 'Jennifer Ann'

E*piphyllum* 'Hollywood'

ESPOSTOA

THE LARGE COLUMNAR SPECIES in this variable group are from the high Andes of southern Ecuador and northern Peru. Most are swathed in woolly white spines through which longer, needlelike spines protrude. New growth and young stems are the most woolly in appearance. After 10–30 years, a pseudocephalium, or thick "beard" (see p. 12), of woolly spines develops on one side of the upper stem. From this, tubular flowers, which are mostly pale and sometimes foul-smelling, fleetingly emerge on spring and summer nights – although this happens rarely in cultivation. Red, yellow, or green fruits follow. Most of the 16 species are slow-growing, but some achieve treelike proportions after many years. These plants do best in a very well-drained soil or planting mix in full sun; avoid overwatering because the roots are prone to rot.

HEIGHT AND SPREAD

E. lanata   E. melanostele

12 in/30 cm
6 in/15 cm
0 in/0 cm
INDOORS: 5 years' growth

12 in/30 cm
6 in/15 cm
0 in/0 cm
OUTDOORS: 10 years' growth

Espostoa lanata

Peruvian old-man cactus, snowball cactus
This impressive cactus forms a taller and more slender stem than other species in its genus. Fairly broad, tubular white flowers with a rather unpleasant scent may open once the plant is 3 ft (90 cm) tall. These are followed by cherrylike red berries.
H 12 ft (3.7 m), S 3 ft (90 cm). Min. 41°F (5°C).

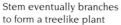

Espostoa melanostele

Often shorter and thicker-stemmed than many Espostoa species, this variable plant branches at its base in time. A mature stem may be totally concealed by very long, woolly spines. Pale flowers and yellow to red berries appear after 15 years. Do not overwater.
H 7 ft (2.1 m), S 3 ft (90 cm). Min. 41°F (5°C).

Yellow spines are shorter, and white wool is sparser, than in other Espostoa species

Stem eventually branches to form a treelike plant

FEROCACTUS

KNOWN AS BARREL CACTI because of their shape, or as fishhook cacti for their spines, these mostly large, sun-loving desert plants come from the southern US and Mexico. There are about 35 species. Large, bell- or funnel-shaped, yellow to violet blooms and small, sticky yellow berries usually appear near the plant crown in summer. The plant body secretes a sugary solution in summer and autumn, thought to attract pollinating ants; wash this off indoor or greenhouse plants to prevent the formation of sooty mold.

HEIGHT AND SPREAD

| F. wislizeni | F. cylindraceus | F. latispinus | F. echidne |

INDOORS: 5 years' growth

OUTDOORS: 10 years' growth

Broad, hooked, central spines up to 4 in (10 cm) long

Ferocactus wislizeni

Candy barrel cactus
Distinctively patterned with white and red or rust-colored spines, this large cactus bears lemon, orange, or red blooms when 12 in (30 cm) in diameter. The plant is tolerant of neglect and eventually becomes columnar in shape.
H 10 ft (3 m), S 3 ft (90 cm). Min. 41°F (5°C).

Fine, needlelike spines, 2 in (5 cm) long

Ferocactus cylindraceus

Fire barrel, compass barrel cactus
The spines, often long, hooked, and flame-red at the crown, become denser as this variable species ages. Columnar in the wild, it remains barrel-shaped in cultivation. Its bell-like flowers are orange or yellow.
H 10 ft (3 m), S 3 ft (90 cm). Min. 41°F (5°C).

Ferocactus latispinus

Crow's claw
With age, the red or straw spines of this slow-growing, ball-shaped or flat-topped, globular plant become broad and hooked and lie flat against the body. Cream to purple flowers appear in spring or autumn.
H 10 in (25 cm), S 15 in (38 cm). Min. 41°F (5°C).

Ferocactus echidne

This globular species, which is one of the smaller *Ferocactus*, usually has deeply indented ribs and relatively few, straight, pale yellow spines. It begins to flower when it is about 5 in (13 cm) in diameter.
H and S 12 in (30 cm). Min 41°F (5°C).

GYMNOCALYCIUM

THESE CHIN OR SPIDER CACTI are small and globular, ranging in hue from blue-green to gray or brown. They often have metallic-colored buds and flower freely when still young. There are 80 species in this extremely variable group. In the wild, in South American countries from Bolivia to Argentina, they grow in the shade of other vegetation, so avoid leaving them in full sun, or they may suffer stunted growth or be scorched. Most species bear funnel-shaped flowers around the crown at intervals from late spring right through summer. These open fully only in bright light. The plum-shaped fruits may be green, blue, or red in color.

Flowers range from pink to orange and open wide in full sun

HEIGHT AND SPREAD

	G. horstii	G. baldianum	G. saglionis	G. quehlianum	G. mihanovichii 'Red Top'	G. bruchii

INDOORS: 5 years' growth

12 in/30 cm
6 in/15 cm
0 in/0 cm

OUTDOORS: 10 years' growth

Does not apply

12 in/30 cm
6 in/15 cm
0 in/0 cm

Gymnocalycium horstii

A small number of ribs and areoles give this species a bold, chunky look. Its fruits are waxy and green. Protect it from winter cold to avoid bad scarring.
H 8 in (20 cm), S 2 ft (60 cm). Min. 45°F (7°C).

Gymnocalycium baldianum

One of the few *Gymnocalycium* species with eye-catching deep red, pink, or purple flowers, it blooms in early summer when it is only 1 in (2.5 cm) across. Green fruits follow. The flattened body has short, curved, pale brown spines. There are many hybrids, with a wide range of flower colors.
H 5 in (13 cm), S 12 in (30 cm). Min. 41°F (5°C).

Gymnocalycium saglionis

This flattened and globular cactus is one of the largest cacti in its group. The solitary, silver- or olive-green body contrasts very attractively with black, white, or red-brown spines. Pale red, round fruits follow the pink summer flowers. This plant likes sun.
H 10 in (25 cm), S 15 in (38 cm). Min. 48°F (9°C).

Gymnocalycium quehlianum

This species has been cultivated for many years. It has a small gray-green body and steel-colored buds, which open in summer into long-necked white flowers with red throats. The straight spines are gray-brown and the berries green. In sun to light shade, this variable plant slowly forms a clump.
H 5 in (13 cm), S 12 in (30 cm). Min. 41°F (5°C).

Petal shape and size may vary

Gymnocalycium mihanovichii 'Red Top'

Ruby ball, hibotan

This novel cultivar is called a neon cactus. To obtain the colored body it has been bred without any chlorophyll and grafted onto a green stock that makes its food. Its pink flowers rarely appear, and then only in summer. Other cultivars differ in body color. Do not leave the plant in sun; its tender body may be scorched and its color may fade.

H and S 6 in (15 cm). Min. 50–61°F (10–16°C).

Gymnocalycium bruchii

Attractive, bell- or funnel-shaped, spring flowers are readily produced by this small flattened cactus, even when it is only 1 in (2.5 cm) across. Its body is very variable in shape and is most often green with straight or curved, white, bristly spines; the fruits are green. Although slow-growing, it eventually forms a densely packed carpet of stems. This plant enjoys sun or light shade.

H 5 in (13 cm), S 18 in (46 cm). Min. 41°F (5°C).

LEUCHTENBERGIA PRINCIPIS

THERE IS ONLY ONE SPECIES in this genus: a very slow-growing, tuberous-rooted species from Mexico that is closely related to the *Ferocactus* (see p. 75). It has very long, slender tubercles, which look like a rosette of leaves and are tipped with fragile, papery spines, giving it the name of agave cactus. After eight years or so, funnel-shaped yellow flowers and smooth green fruits appear at the tubercle tips. The base of the plant becomes increasingly woody with age. This is a demanding plant to grow, but given full sun and a minimum temperature of 41°F (5°C), it forms offsets eventually. Mature plants reach a height of 8 in (20 cm) and a spread of 2 ft (60 cm).

HEIGHT AND SPREAD

12 in/30 cm	12 in/30 cm
6 in/15 cm	6 in/15 cm
0 in/0 cm	0 in/0 cm

INDOORS: 5 years' growth

OUTDOORS: 10 years' growth

MAMMILLARIA

MOST OF THESE PINCUSHION CACTI flower prolifically, making them good subjects for a collection. Some have fingerlike stems, but most *Mammillaria* are small, globular, and thickly covered with spines. Even when very young, the majority bear rings of beautiful flowers around the crown in spring or early summer with a second and sometimes a third flush of blooms later on. The seedpods are red. These 250 or so sun-loving cacti come from Mexico, Colombia, Guatemala, Honduras, the southern US, Venezuela, and the West Indies.

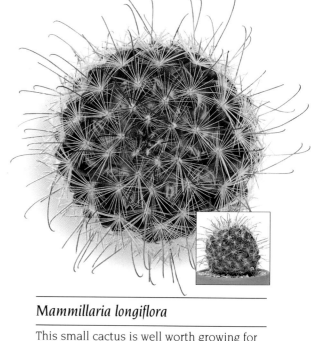

Mammillaria longiflora

This small cactus is well worth growing for its showy, sometimes striped, pink flowers, which are over 1 in (2.5 cm) across and usually the first cactus flowers of spring. The long hooked spines are reddish brown or yellow. The plant needs to be dry when dormant in winter; it rots if overwatered.
H 6 in (15 cm), S 12 in (30 cm). Min. 41˚F (5˚C).

HEIGHT AND SPREAD

M. longiflora   *M. longimamma*   *M. sempervivi*   *M. pringlei*   *M. zeilmanniana*   *M. magnimamma*   *M. bombycina*

12 in/30 cm
6 in/15 cm
0 in/0 cm

INDOORS: 5 years' growth

12 in/30 cm
6 in/15 cm
0 in/0 cm

OUTDOORS: 10 years' growth

White wool is denser at top of stem

Elongated stems

Mammillaria longimamma

Finger mound
In late spring, this small cactus bears large butter-yellow flowers with relatively broad petals near the plant crown. Its green unripe fruits look very similar to its long fat tubercles. Like a number of *Mammillaria* species, this plant has a large tuberous root which is likely to rot if overwatered.
H 6 in (15 cm), S 2 ft (60 cm). Min. 41˚F (5˚C).

Mammillaria sempervivi

This cactus can vary in shape and color. Its spring flowers are usually cerise, but may be yellow or white, and the very short black spines turn white with time. The flattened, globular, stem is often solitary until it is 20–30 years old, when it forms offsets. Older plants can become so woolly that they look like white powder puffs.
H and S 8 in (20 cm). Min. 41˚F (5˚C).

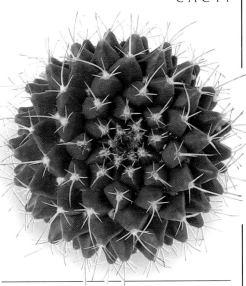

Mammillaria pringlei

Curved golden spines usually densely cover this species. It bears rings of abundant cerise flowers in spring and often again in autumn. After many years, it forms slightly columnar stems that become prostrate; mature plants often branch at the stem tips.
H 12 in (30 cm), S 4 ft (1.2 m). Min. 41°F (5°C).

Mammillaria zeilmanniana

Rose pincushion
Abundant carmine-pink, spring flowers appear when this species is only about ¼ in (6 mm) in diameter. The purplish black body grows rapidly to form a multiheaded mound. It will not tolerate winter dampness.
H 6 in (15 cm), S 2 ft (60 cm). Min. 41°F (5°C).

Mammillaria magnimamma

This sun-loving cactus, one of the easiest *Mammillaria* species to grow, has spines of variable length, shape, and color, and pronounced, sometimes angular tubercles. A ring of pale pink to purple flowers appears in spring. The plant offsets freely to form large clumps. It is often seen under different names because of its variability.
H 12 in (30 cm), S 3 ft (90 cm). Min. 41°F (5°C).

Rings of spring flowers

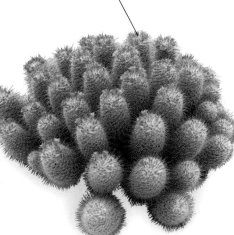

Mammillaria bombycina

Dainty cerise flowers and red, brown, or yellow hooked spines that protrude through a soft white down make this a fine plant. The cactus generally will not flower until it is at least 3 in (8 cm) in diameter. Most often globular in shape, this species offsets easily into a large, showy clump.
H 12 in (30 cm), S unlimited. Min. 41°F (5°C).

MAMMILLARIA

HEIGHT AND SPREAD

M. matudae   M. candida   M. parkinsonii   M. hahniana   M. wiesingeri   M. bocasana v. rubriflora   M. saboae f. haudeana

12 in/30 cm
6 in/15 cm
0 in/0 cm

INDOORS: 5 years' growth

12 in/30 cm
6 in/15 cm
0 in/0 cm

OUTDOORS: 10 years' growth

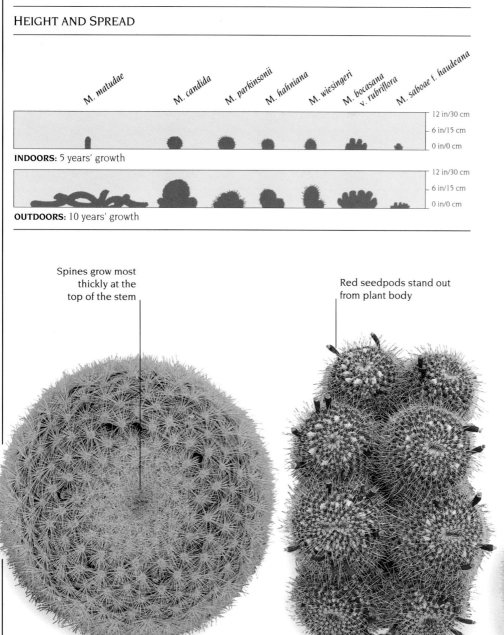

Spines grow most thickly at the top of the stem

Red seedpods stand out from plant body

Mammillaria candida

Snowball pincushion
The body of this plant is cloaked in dense white spines, which are often pink-tipped. It produces rings of spring flowers, usually in succession. These blooms are cream at first, turning pink and then brown as they age. The solitary stem offsets slowly to form a clump. The plant needs extra calcium to flourish: add a teaspoonful of ground limestone to the planting mix.
H 10 in (25 cm), S 2 ft (60 cm). Min. 41°F (5°C).

Mammillaria parkinsonii

Owl's eyes
This species takes many forms but generally has black-tipped white spines. Its usually globular body slowly develops into a large mound by branching into two at each stem tip. The dark-tipped spines on the two new heads look like owl's eyes, giving the cactus its common name. Pink or cream flowers appear around the growing point in spring.
H 6 in (15 cm), S unlimited. Min. 41°F (5°C).

Mammillaria hahniana

Old lady cactus, birthday cake cactus
Cerise flowers are followed in spring by sturdy red pods that stand in a ring on the crown of this cactus, like candles on a cake. The spines are sometimes long, curly, hairlike, and white. Solitary at first, the body eventually offsets or branches at the tip.
H 8 in (20 cm), S 2 ft (60 cm). Min. 41°F (5°C).

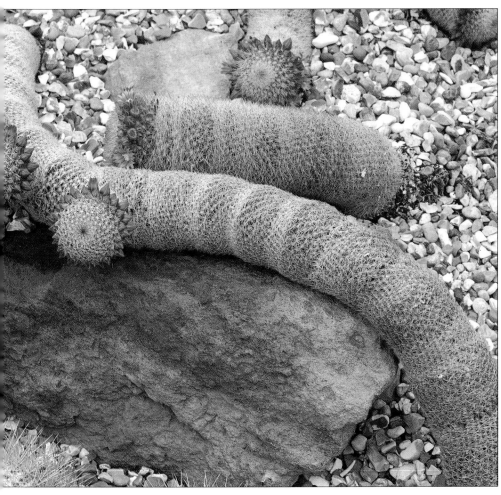

Mammillaria matudae

Mature specimens often develop into a prostrate mound of long, snaking stems that look very effective when planted out in a bed. The stems may also be short and thick. When young, the plant body of this variable species takes the form of a solitary column. Its spines vary in length and density but are usually brown in color. A plant that is only about four years old and 3–4 in (8–10 cm) tall will flower prolifically in the spring.

H 6 in (15 cm), S 7 ft (2.1 m). Min. 41°F (5°C).

Mammillaria saboae f. haudeana

Fairly new to cultivation, this tiny species produces large, dark pink to purple summer flowers, which are up to 1½ in (4 cm) across. The fruits develop inside the plant body and appear when the old tubercles wither at the base. This slow-growing cactus forms a low dense clump in time. It thrives when grown as a grafted plant (see inset) but may rot in winter dampness.

H 2 in (5 cm), S 12 in (30 cm). Min. 41°F (5°C).

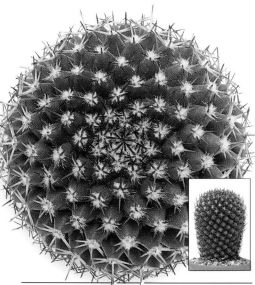

Mammillaria wiesingeri

Wine-red or cerise, starry flowers with a yellow throat often appear in two flushes, in spring and again in autumn. They are produced in rings around the upper part of the short, columnar stem. The straight spines are brown. Eventually, this solitary cactus offsets to form a clump.

H 8 in (20 cm), S 12 in (30 cm). Min. 41°F (5°C).

Mammillaria bocasana v. rubriflora

Powder puff cactus, snowball cactus
Less common than the cream-flowered species, this form bears pink or red flowers repeatedly from spring to autumn. Red or straw-colored spines protrude from long tubercles covered in wispy white spines. The body may rot if cold and damp.

H 8 in (20 cm), S 2 ft (60 cm). Min. 41°F (5°C).

MATUCANA

THIS GROUP OF PERUVIAN CACTI includes globular or short, columnar plants, with spines that can vary in length, color, and density. Globular *Matucana* species flower when still quite small and only 3–5 years old, but the larger cacti must be at least 6 in (15 cm) tall. They flower in spring or summer and sometimes throughout both seasons. The long-necked flowers are often lopsided and range from yellow to scarlet in color. Their small, round green seedpods burst open when ripe to shed their seed. Most of the 20 or so species prefer sun. Keep them at a minimum temperature of 50°F (10°C) to avoid unsightly cold damage and any risk of rot. The former genus *Submatucana* and some *Borzicactus* species are now included in this group.

HEIGHT AND SPREAD

M. intertexta *M. aureiflora* *M. madisoniorum* *M. intertexta f. celendinensis* *M. ritteri*

12 in/30 cm
6 in/15 cm
0 in/0 cm
INDOORS: 5 years' growth

12 in/30 cm
6 in/15 cm
0 in/0 cm
OUTDOORS: 10 years' growth

Matucana intertexta

This small variable cactus has pale brown, needlelike spines and red or orange flowers that sometimes appear singly on the plant crown in spring and summer. The plant may develop into a clump when it is mature.
H 4 in (10 cm), S 8 in (20 cm). Min. 50°F (10°).

Fragile black spines are easily shed

Curved golden spines vary in length

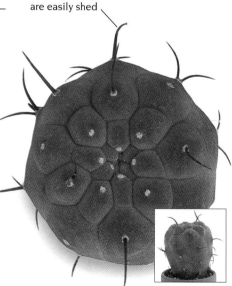

Matucana aureiflora

Rudimentary leaves grow at the tubercle tips on the crown of this small plant. Clusters of golden yellow flowers appear at intervals throughout spring and summer, even when the plant is young.
H 4 in (10 cm), S 8 in (20 cm). Min. 50°F (10°C).

Matucana madisoniorum

Younger specimens of this smooth and almost spineless, globular blue-green cactus are the most striking. The few spines are curved or needlelike. Bright red flowers appear on the crown in summer.
H 6 in (15 cm), S 8 in (20 cm). Min. 50°F (10°C).

Matucana intertexta f. celendinensis

Formerly *Borzicactus celendinensis*, this is a variety of M. *intertexta* and is very similar in appearance. The primary difference between the two is in the flower color.
H 4 in (10 cm), S 8 in (20 cm). Min. 50°F (10°C).

Matucana ritteri

Vivid vermilion flowers appear in summer when this cactus is about five years old. It has needlelike, light brown spines that vary in length. The species is closely related to M. *intertexta* and has a small globular body that offsets slowly to form a clump.
H 4 in (10 cm), S 8 in (20 cm). Min. 50°F (10°C).

MELOCACTUS

A CEPHALIUM, or densely spined crown, grows on these bizarre Turk's cap cacti when each globular body is of mature flowering size. The main plant body then stops growing. Small, mostly red to violet, summer flowers are borne freely but briefly on the cephalium's center. Its spines vary greatly in shape and color. The 40 or so variable, challenging species are slow-growing in pots. They come from the West Indies, Mexico, and northern South America and are now endangered in the wild.

Dense rust-red spines on unusual double cephalium

HEIGHT AND SPREAD

M. matanzanus
M. salvadorensis

12 in/30 cm
6 in/15 cm
0 in/0 cm
INDOORS: 5 years' growth

12 in/30 cm
6 in/15 cm
0 in/0 cm
OUTDOORS: 10 years' growth

Red spines fade with age

Melocactus matanzanus

A visually arresting species, this has dark pink to scarlet flowers and large, pink seedpods in summer. It thrives in sun or shade and grows on Cuban seashores after torrential rains wash the soil clean of salt.
H and S 5 in (13 cm). Min. 61°F (16°C).

Melocactus salvadorensis

This small species produces its cephalium when it is about seven years old. It is very variable but usually has a green hemispherical body with reddish, comblike spines. Pink to cerise flowers appear in summer, followed by large red seedpods. The cactus grows well in sun or shade.
H 5 in (13 cm), S 7 in (18 cm). Min. 61°F (16°C).

NEOPORTERIA

HAVING CONFUSED COLLECTORS for years, this large group of very variable cacti from western South America was recently reclassified into about 30 species. The cacti are mostly small, gray to brown in color, and differ widely in shape. The flowers appear freely in spring, summer, or autumn. They are large, open-faced, and usually bicolored in shades of rose and yellow. The barrel-shaped seedpods are red or green. If possible, keep these sun-loving plants above 50°F (10°C) and water them occasionally in winter to prevent unsightly scarring and withered roots.

Neoporteria subgibbosa f. *litoralis*

This large cactus has white, brown, or straw-colored spines and red seedpods. It flowers when quite small, in autumn and sometimes spring. The globular body becomes columnar and semiprostrate.
H 3 ft (90 cm), S 5 in (13 cm). Min. 45°F (7°C).

HEIGHT AND SPREAD

N. subgibbosa f. litoralis
N. curvispina
N. clavata

12 in/30 cm
6 in/15 cm
0 in/0 cm
INDOORS: 5 years' growth

12 in/30 cm
6 in/15 cm
0 in/0 cm
OUTDOORS: 10 years' growth

Red buds open into pink and yellow flowers

Cactus flowers freely once it is 2–3 in (5–8 cm) in diameter

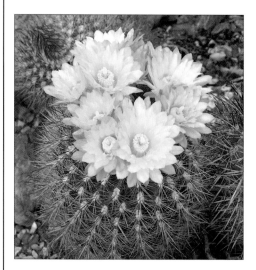

Neoporteria curvispina

One of the largest in its genus, this cactus is globular at first but becomes columnar and creeping in habit. Its spines are red to yellow. Once it is 3–4 in (8–10 cm) tall, it bears flowers and dry red berries in spring and summer. The body scars easily if cold.
H 3 ft (90 cm), S 5 in (13 cm). Min. 45°F (7°C).

Neoporteria clavata

The dark spines of this small cactus provide a dramatic contrast for its pink or purple flowers. These appear in spring and autumn. The seedpods are green or red. With age, the dark body becomes slightly columnar.
H 12 in (30 cm), S 5 in (13 cm). Min. 45°F (7°C).

OPUNTIA

THIS IS THE LARGEST cactus genus, with over 360 sun-loving species from Canada to Chile and Argentina. Known as prickly pear, cholla, Indian fig, or bunny ears, the plants can be several yards or a few inches tall. The genus includes some with fleshy pads or branching stems and mat-forming alpine species. Barbed spines and tufts of bristles protect the body. Most species grow very readily; in parts of Australia, some are pernicious weeds. The vivid flowers appear in spring to autumn, followed by green, red, or purple, often edible, fruit.

HEIGHT AND SPREAD

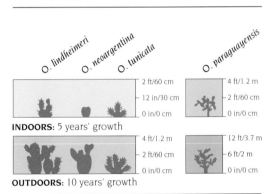

INDOORS: 5 years' growth

OUTDOORS: 10 years' growth

Opuntia lindheimeri

Vivid golden, orange, or deep red flowers are produced from the edges of the pads in summer when this spreading, bushy species is only two or three pads high. The blooms give way to pear-shaped, purple fruits. The pads are studded with dense spine cushions of golden brown bristles, known as glochids.
H 4 ft (1.2 m), S 10 ft (3 m). Min. 41°F (5°C).

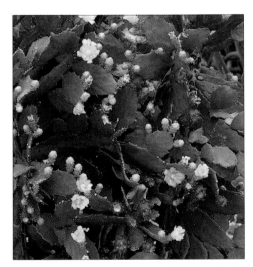

Opuntia neoargentina

Tree opuntia
The pads of this large robust cactus slowly swell in the middle to form a trunk. In dry areas, old pads are deciduous. Cuttings of 6 in (15 cm) readily flower in summer.
H 15 ft (5 m), S 4 ft (1.2 m). Min. 41°F (5°C).

Small, spreading bush

Opuntia tunicata

The barbed spines have a silver sheen in bright sunlight and are encased in papery sheaths. Young plants have few spines. In summer, gold to pink, poppylike flowers and greenish yellow pears adorn the stem tips.
H 3 ft (90 cm), S 6 ft (2 m). Min. 41°F (5°C).

Opuntia paraguayensis

Riverina pear
This fast-growing, treelike species flowers abundantly over a long period in summer; its small fruits are purple. It is banned in Australia but widely grown elsewhere.
H and S 12 ft (3.7 m). Min. 41°F (5°C).

OREOCEREUS

FROM THE HIGH ANDES, these cacti are wrapped in a down of long, white, hairlike spines to protect them from the hot sun and mountain cold. In strong light, this down thickens and conceals the long, needlelike, central spines, which may be white, straw-colored, or red. The 11 mostly columnar, variable species in this genus take many years to become large and bushy. Only then do they bear crimson summer flowers; these are often lopsided and arching with a vertical face and grow near the stem tip. Hollow green berries follow. Keep these sun-loving plants above 50°F (10°C) to avoid scarring or rot.

HEIGHT AND SPREAD

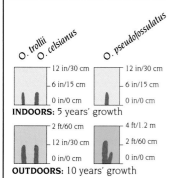

O. trollii O. celsianus   O. pseudofossulatus

12 in/30 cm | 12 in/30 cm
6 in/15 cm | 6 in/15 cm
0 in/0 cm | 0 in/0 cm
INDOORS: 5 years' growth

2 ft/60 cm | 4 ft/1.2 m
12 in/30 cm | 2 ft/60 cm
0 in/0 cm | 0 in/0 cm
OUTDOORS: 10 years' growth

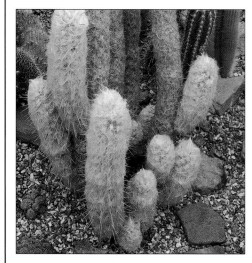

Oreocereus celsianus

Old man of the mountains
The usually stout woolly stems of this large, very variable species only branch with age. It has pink, lopsided flowers and red or straw-colored central spines.
H 10 ft (3 m), S 3 ft (90 cm). Min. 50°F (10°C).

Oreocereus pseudofossulatus

The stems are taller and more slender than most Oreocereus, and they branch more readily, often forming a lax bush. Faster-growing than other large Oreocereus, this cactus flowers sooner, producing lopsided, violet-red flowers after 10–15 years. Its white wool is wispy, and the strong central spines are red or yellow.
H 9 ft (2.7 m), S 3 ft (90 cm). Min. 45°F (7°C).

Oreocereus trollii

Old man of the Andes
Only very old specimens of this curiously woolly species flower. The blooms are lopsided and violet or carmine. The central spines vary greatly in length and can be golden yellow or red in color. The plant needs full sun to thrive.
H 3 ft (90 cm), S 2 ft (60 cm). Min. 45°F (7°C).

Sturdy spines protrude through "cotton batting" of fine white spines

Thick solitary stem very slowly forms a small clump

OROYA

ONLY THREE SPECIES OF small, slow-growing, Peruvian cacti make up this sun-loving genus. They are flattened and globular in shape and have comblike spines that vary widely in density and range from straw or gold to brown in hue. After about five years, summer flowers, which are similar to those of *Neoporteria* (see p. 84), cluster on the plant crown. The small hollow berries are golden red.

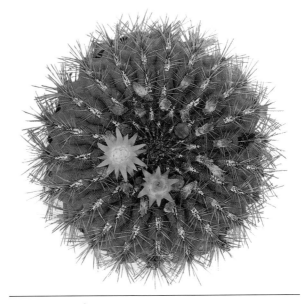

Oroya peruviana

The amalgamation of other former *Oroya* species into this one has created a species with many varied forms. Its spines, once always gold-colored, now range from yellow to brown. Orange or red buds open into small, yellow-tinged, carmine to crimson flowers. Protect the cactus from cold to prevent unsightly scarring.
H 4 in (10 cm), S 8 in (20 cm). Min. 50°F (10°C).

HEIGHT AND SPREAD

O. peruviana
- 12 in/30 cm
- 6 in/15 cm
- 0 in/0 cm
INDOORS:
5 years' growth

O. peruviana
- 12 in/30 cm
- 6 in/15 cm
- 0 in/0 cm
OUTDOORS:
10 years' growth

PACHYCEREUS

THESE HUGE COLUMNAR CACTI make impressive feature plants. Some have solitary stems but many branch readily to form clumps or even trees. Only mature plants that are about 6–15 ft (2–5 m) tall will flower. The nocturnal blooms, which are funnel-shaped and shaded white or pink, are produced on the stem tip in spring to early summer. They are followed by large spiny fruits that are green, yellow, or reddish in color. The 12 sun-loving species are native to parts of the southern US and Mexico. Some forms are sensitive to low temperatures.

Pachycereus schottii v. *monstrose*

Totem pole
This slow-growing form rarely flowers. It is prized for its strange knobbly stem; this mutation may be caused by a virus.
H 20 ft (6 m), S 8 ft (2.4 m). Min. 50°F (10°C).

Scar tissue from cold damage

Pachycereus schottii

Senita cereus, whisker cactus
This multistemmed cactus bears cream to dark pink flowers and small red berries. When the plant is about 6 ft (2 m) tall, its gray spines become long and curly at the stem tip, making the stem look like a brush.
H 20 ft (6 m), S 8 ft (2.4 m). Min. 50°F (10°C).

HEIGHT AND SPREAD

P. schottii v. monstrose
P. schottii
- 12 in/30 cm
- 6 in/15 cm
- 0 in/0 cm
INDOORS:
5 years' growth

P. schottii v. monstrose
P. schottii
- 4 ft/1.2 m
- 2 ft/60 cm
- 0 in/0 cm
OUTDOORS:
10 years' growth

PARODIA

ORIGINALLY FROM ARGENTINA, Bolivia, Brazil, Paraguay, and Uruguay, these neat, mainly globular cacti flower freely from spring through to early fall. Their funnel-shaped blooms range from gold to scarlet and are followed by small, spiny berries or red pods. Included in the current 100 *Parodia* species are those formerly classified as *Eriocactus*, *Malacocarpus*, and *Notocactus*. Most *Parodia* thrive in sun or light shade and need an occasional light misting in winter. They may lose their roots if they dry out, but do not water them if it is cold since they can rot.

Daisylike flowers with long necks

HEIGHT AND SPREAD

P. concinna
P. schwebsiana
P. penicillata v. nivosa
P. graessneri
P. mammulosa
P. magnifica
P. herteri

12 in/30 cm
6 in/15 cm
0 in/0 cm
INDOORS: 5 years' growth

12 in/30 cm
6 in/15 cm
0 in/0 cm
OUTDOORS: 10 years' growth

Parodia concinna

Large golden flowers with maroon stigmas appear on the neat, globular body of this former *Notocactus* species throughout the spring and summer. The spines are soft and curved and can vary from pale yellow to red. The small, very spiny fruits are dry and papery when ripe. This sun-loving plant grows offsets after some years to form a clump.
H 5 in (13 cm), S 6 in (15 cm). Min. 41°F (5°C).

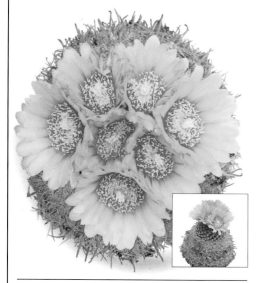

Parodia schwebsiana

Twisted ribs and short, hooked brown spines give this sun-loving cactus a strange appearance. It produces repeated flushes of orange-yellow, funnel-shaped flowers at the plant crown from spring until autumn. This species develops a columnar shape and offsets to form a small clump.
H 12 in (30 cm), S 4 in (10 cm). Min. 45°F (7°C).

Parodia penicillata v. nivosa

The long, slender buds of this pretty species open in sun to flame-red, daisylike flowers in spring and early summer. Given sun and moderate summer watering and feeding, this small, flattened, globular plant grows quite fast and forms a clump with age. The tiny fruits are papery when ripe.
H 7 in (18 cm), S 12 in (30 cm). Min. 45°F (7°C).

Parodia graessneri

Yellowish green blooms that appear very early in the year and fine, dense, golden spines make this an attractive species. Its small green fruits are papery when ripe. Flattened and globular in shape, the plant grows slowly and is usually solitary, although it may produce a few offsets. It needs full sun to thrive and cannot tolerate winter moisture or long, dry periods.
H 6 in (15 cm), S 2 ft (60 cm). Min. 50°F (10°C).

Parodia mammulosa

This robust cactus tolerates some neglect and flowers repeatedly throughout spring and summer. Its large blooms have striking, red to purple stigmas. The species has many forms but is generally flattened and globular, or a solitary column, and is dark green with short, stiff, pale spines. Its hollow, cerise-red berries are papery when ripe. This fast-growing plant enjoys full sun.
H 12 in (30 cm), S 5 in (13 cm). Min. 45°F (7°C).

Parodia herteri

Formerly a *Notocactus*, this cactus is prized for its pink or purple blooms because most flowers of this genus are yellow. The flattened body flowers profusely in summer once it is about the size of a tennis ball. The species has two dominant forms, dark or pale green, which may have white or brown spines. This solitary, sun-loving plant has small, purple-red, papery fruits
H 8 in (20 cm), S 10 in (25 cm). Min. 45°F (7°C).

Parodia magnifica

Both main variants of this handsome, sun-loving species make impressive clumps: the form with fewer ribs (above) has a larger, bluer body with shorter, paler spines and forms offsets far less freely; the other (right) is densely covered with soft golden spines. Open-faced butter-yellow flowers appear on the plant crown in summer. The small fruits are dry and papery when ripe.
H 12 in (30 cm), S 5 ft (1.5 m). Min. 45°F (7°C).

PARODIA

HEIGHT AND SPREAD

P. horstii P. chrysacanthion P. crassigibba P. leninghausii P. otaviana

12 in/30 cm
6 in/15 cm
0 in/0 cm

INDOORS: 5 years' growth

12 in/30 cm
6 in/15 cm
0 in/0 cm

OUTDOORS: 10 years' growth

Crimson stigmas

Funnel-shaped flowers open wide in sun

Parodia horstii

The summer flowers of this variable cactus display shades of tangerine and orange-red that are atypical of the genus. Its spines are most often long, straight, and colored red and white. One of the larger *Parodia* species, it is globular in shape at first but becomes columnar and prostrate with age. The plant rarely forms offsets.

H 2 ft (60 cm), S 12 in (30 cm). Min. 45°F (7°C).

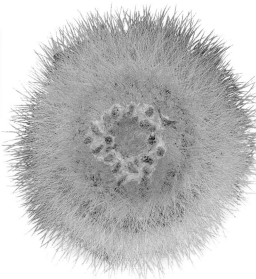

Parodia chrysacanthion

Golden powder puff
A thick mantle of often bristlelike golden spines and dense white wool on the new growth and crown of mature plants gives this cactus its name. Small yellow flowers appear in spring to summer. This slow-growing and solitary plant prefers sun.
H and S 8 in (20 cm). Min. 41°F (5°C).

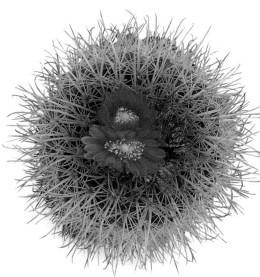

Parodia crassigibba

Clusters of large flowers adorn this small cactus when it is only 2–3 in (5–8 cm) in diameter. They can be lemon-yellow or purple in hue and open only in sunshine in spring and early summer. The spines vary from short and bristly to long and curved and range in color from yellowish gray to rust-brown. This sun-loving plant has a flattened or globular body with relatively few ribs. When ripe, the fruits are dry and papery. This species was formerly a *Notocactus*.
H 5 in (13 cm), S 6 in (15 cm). Min. 45°F (7°C).

Parodia leninghausii

Goldfinger, golden ball cactus
In the wild, the sloping crown of this cactus faces the sun. Its short, thick, columnar stem is slightly curved at the base and is covered in long, soft golden spines. Clusters of large, buttercup-yellow, open-faced flowers are produced on the plant crown in summer. The cactus offsets freely when it is about 5–10 years old.
H and S 3 ft (90 cm). Min. 45°F (7°C).

Parodia otaviana

The long, hooked, golden or rust-brown spines of this small cactus contrast dramatically with its scarlet blooms. These are freely produced in spring and summer once the plant body has reached 2–3 in (5–8 cm) in diameter. Tiny papery fruits follow. The slow-growing, globular green body eventually becomes slightly columnar in shape. This sun-loving plant is one of the easiest *Parodia* species to grow.
H 8 in (20 cm), S 7 in (18 cm). Min. 45°F (7°C).

PERESKIA

SAID TO BE THE most primitive of cacti, these 16 sun-loving Barbados gooseberries, or rose cacti, are mostly huge, fast-growing bushes, trees, or climbers from the West Indies, and Central and northern South America. They have stout, sharp spines, deciduous leaves, and roselike blooms and small berries in summer to autumn.

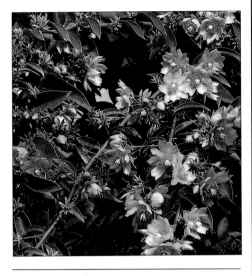

Pereskia aculeata

Barbados gooseberry
Masses of large, sharply scented, autumn flowers in shades of white, cream, or rose cluster on new growth. Edible, small, spiny, yellow berries follow. When young, the plant resembles any other shrub, but as it develops into a climber, its dark thorns become thick and rigid. Prune it in the same way as a grapevine and repot annually.
H 30 ft (9 m), S unlimited. Min. 39°F (4°C).

HEIGHT AND SPREAD

INDOORS: 5 years' growth

OUTDOORS: 10 years' growth

Pereskia aculeata 'Godseffiana'

Grown as a house plant for its pink or bronze young foliage, this cultivar of P. *aculeata* is slightly slower-growing and less free-flowering than the species.
H 30 ft (9 m), S unlimited. Min. 39°F (4°C).

PILOSOCEREUS

WHEN MATURE, THESE LARGE, columnar, mostly blue cacti develop a pseudocephalium (see p. 12) of woolly spines at the crown. Nocturnal, funnel-shaped flowers grow from the "beard" in spring to autumn; they vary in hue, are often foul-smelling, and last 24 hours. The large, fleshy berries are purple to green. The 60 species from the West Indies and Central and northern South America need warmth and sun.

HEIGHT AND SPREAD

INDOORS:
5 years' growth

OUTDOORS:
10 years' growth

Pilosocereus leucocephalus f. palmeri

This impressively large, clumping cactus has gray or beige spines that are yellow on new growth. Its stem, which can be blue-green, develops a pseudocephalium when 4–6 ft (1.2–2 m) tall. Pale pink to white flowers, which are unpleasantly scented, are followed by large, dark, plumlike fruits.
H 20 ft (6 m), S 5 ft (1.5 m). Min. 50°F (10°C).

REBUTIA

USUALLY AMONG THE FIRST CACTI to bloom each spring, this group of small, mostly globular plants comprises about 40 very free-flowering and colorful species, from Argentina to Bolivia. They differ widely in appearance since they include several hundred forms from the previous genera of *Aylostera*, *Digitorebutia*, *Sulcorebutia*, and *Weingartia*. In the wild, many evolve constantly to adapt to the altitude and local conditions. The berries are hardly visible. Most *Rebutia* do well in sun or light shade; some will tolerate near-freezing temperatures if kept dry. Tinier species make striking specimens when they are grafted.

Dense, white, needlelike spines ——————

HEIGHT AND SPREAD

R. muscula R. fiebrigii f. ithyacantha R. canigueralii f. rauschii R. pygmaea R. marsoneri R. pulvinosa f. albiflora R. heliosa

12 in/30 cm
6 in/15 cm
0 in/0 cm
INDOORS: 5 years' growth

12 in/30 cm
6 in/15 cm
0 in/0 cm
OUTDOORS: 10 years' growth

Rebutia muscula

This handsome, sun-loving cactus flowers profusely in spring and occasionally until autumn. Its long-necked blooms need sun to open. The body is usually globular and readily forms pincushion-like clumps.
H 3 in (8 cm), S 12 in (30 cm). Min. 41°F (5°C).

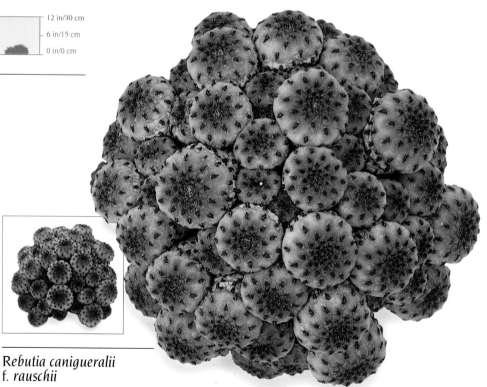

Rebutia fiebrigii f. *ithyacantha*

This pretty species varies hugely in form. It is usually dark green and may become slightly columnar. The plant produces abundant flowers from its lower stem in spring. Keep it in full sun. When mature, it forms a mound.
H 3 in (8 cm), S 12 in (30 cm). Min. 41°F (5°C).

Rebutia canigueralii f. *rauschii*

Many people prize this cactus for its small, buttonlike stems and dramatic royal-purple flowers. Its colors vary from dark green to purple. The funnel-shaped, spring flowers sprout from the lower stems. A sun-lover, the plant is prone to rot and is difficult to grow on its own roots, but thrives when grafted.
H 5 in (13 cm), S 10 in (25 cm). Min. 41°F (5°C).

Short-necked spring flowers

Deep pollen tube

Rebutia pygmaea

Intensely colored scarlet, salmon-pink, or orange flowers are produced in abundance from the lower stem of this variable cactus. Unlike most *Rebutia*, it forms a clump of short, fingerlike stems, which are most often purple-brown and have pale bristly spines. This plant grows best in sun.
H 4 in (10 cm), S 12 in (30 cm). Min. 41°F (5°C).

Rebutia marsoneri

The blooms of this cactus are probably the most brilliant of the yellow-flowered *Rebutia*; their reddish spring buds need bright sun to open fully. The globular, flattened body is solitary or slowly offsetting in habit. It grows best in full sun.
H 3 in (8 cm), S 12 in (30 cm). Min. 41°F (5°C).

Rebutia pulvinosa f. albiflora

One of the few white-flowered species available, this dainty globular plant readily forms a mat of bristly stems. It produces long-necked, pink-tinged flowers from the lower stem, which open fully in the spring sun. This is a tolerant plant, but its central stems tend to die off in mature clumps.
H 3 in (8 cm), S unlimited. Min. 41°F (5°C).

Rebutia heliosa

This species readily develops a mound of tiny heads, which are densely covered in short silver-gray spines. A profusion of funnel-shaped, long-necked, spring blooms that open fully only in sun appears on the lower stem. Grafting produces a healthier, faster-growing and longer-lived plant.
H 3 in (8 cm), S 8 in (20 cm). Min. 41°F (5°C).

REBUTIA

HEIGHT AND SPREAD

R. mentosa f. flavissima	*R. steinbachii v. polymorpha*	*R. steinbachii f. verticillacantha*	*R. wessneriana*	*R. heliosa f. perplexa*	*R. 'Pastel Pink'*	*R. arenacea*	*R. steinbachii f. tiraquensis*			12 in/30 cm

INDOORS: 5 years' growth

OUTDOORS: 10 years' growth

Rebutia mentosa f. flavissima

Eye-catching magenta to carmine flowers with short necks cluster around the lower stem; they need sun to open fully. With age, this solitary cactus slowly offsets into a clump. Its spines are pale yellow to gold.
H 4 in (10 cm), S 5 in (13 cm). Min. 39°F (4°C).

Flower buds grow from the side of plant body

Straight, dark spines may be very long

Globular stems form a compact mound

Rebutia steinbachii v. polymorpha

A profusion of flowers in brilliant, often bicolored hues of daffodil-yellow, orange, scarlet, pink, or purple, are borne on the dark green body in mid- to late spring and again in summer. Very variable in form, the plant often has long spines. It is robust and moderately easy to grow, if given full sun.
H 8 in (20 cm), S 10 in (25 cm). Min. 41°F (5°C).

Rebutia steinbachii f. verticillacantha

Bicolored flowers, which may be violet or vermilion with gold or orange throats, are produced from mid- to late spring and again in summer. These are often larger than the variable body, which offsets to form a dimpled carpet of many dark green stems. The short spines are pale or dark.
H 5 in (13 cm), S 15 in (38 cm). Min. 41°F (5°C).

Rebutia wessneriana

This flat-topped, globular species is prized for its relatively large, orange, red, or deep purple flowers, which grow from the base of the stem in spring. Most plants have dense, soft white spines. Its very short-spined form, R. *w.* f. *krainziana*, is also attractive.
H 3 in (8 cm), S 8 in (20 cm). Min. 41°F (5°C).

Rebutia heliosa f. perplexa

Olive-green, buttonlike stems form a compact mound, which is covered with dainty blooms from mid- to late spring. These flowers, which have long necks and are delicately shaded rose-pink, grow from the lower stem and open fully only in sun. The short spines are ginger-colored. This plant grows best in full sun.
H 3 in (8 cm), S 8 in (20 cm). Min. 39°F (4°C).

Rebutia 'Pastel Pink'

With flowers in various shades of pink, this sun-loving hybrid is a good example of the many fine cacti now available in this genus. The spring blooms appear on the lower stem when the plant is only two years old. The globular, pale to dark green body quickly forms a low mound.
H 4 in (10 cm), S 12 in (30 cm). Min. 39°F (4°C).

Spines may be white or brown

Rebutia arenacea

The areoles, or spine cushions, on the spiraling ribs decrease in size toward the plant crown. Very short, starlike spines encase a brownish green, usually globular body, which offsets slowly into a small clump. In spring, its vivid, relatively large flowers are followed by tiny berries. This cactus, recently introduced from Bolivia, grows best in full sun.
H 4 in (10 cm), S 8 in (20 cm). Min. 45°F (7°C).

Rebutia steinbachii f. tiraquensis

This sun-loving cactus is one of the largest in the genus and is very variable. Its spines may be dark red to brown or white to yellow. From mid- to late spring and again in summer, flowers in one of many shades of pink, cherry-red, or purple appear. Flowers of a deeper hue are produced by the larger, red-spined form. The plant offsets slowly.
H 8 in (20 cm), S 10 in (25 cm). Min. 41°F (5°C).

RHIPSALIS

THE GRACEFUL PENDANT STEMS of these variable mistletoe or wickerwork cacti are tubular or leaflike and are ideal for a hanging basket. Most of these epiphytes (see pp. 10–11) flower in late winter or early spring; small, open-faced blooms, ranging from white to pale pink, are borne along the stems and last for a few days. Bright berries follow, in various colors from white or pink to black. This group of about 40 medium-sized or large, slow- to fast-growing, shade-loving species is widespread in Central and South America.

LENGTH/HEIGHT AND SPREAD

R. pilocarpa   R. crispata   R. cereuscula   R. teres

INDOORS: 5 years' growth

12 in/30 cm
6 in/15 cm
0 in/0 cm

12 in/30 cm
6 in/15 cm
0 in/0 cm

OUTDOORS: 10 years' growth

12 in/30 cm
6 in/15 cm
0 in/0 cm

4 ft/1.2 m
2 ft/60 cm
0 in/0 cm

Rhipsalis pilocarpa

One of the most striking *Rhipsalis* species, this deep green plant is tinged with purple and flecked with silvery spines. Its slender trailing stems branch into whorls when about 6 in (15 cm) long. Rose-white to cream flowers, which are sweetly scented, appear near the stem tips from autumn to spring. The fruits are pale green with yellow bristles.

L 3 ft (90 cm), S unlimited. Min. 50°F (10°C).

Rhipsalis crispata

The edges of the spineless, leaflike stems are often crinkled to differing degrees. The cactus grows slowly, but eventually forms a prostrate or pendant bush. Its small cream flowers are produced from spring to early summer and are followed by greenish white berries. This species is more difficult than most *Rhipsalis* to bring into flower.

H 3 ft (90 cm), S unlimited. Min. 50°F (10°C).

Rhipsalis cereuscula

Coral cactus, rice cactus
When mature, this fernlike species has an abundance of trailing tubular stems, up to 12 in (30 cm) long, which branch at the tip into dense whorls of short shoots. The shoots often produce aerial roots. In winter and spring, small, greenish white flowers appear.

L 4 ft (1.2 m), S unlimited. Min. 45°F (7°C).

Rhipsalis teres

This variable cactus often has slightly thicker, stiffer stems than many other fernlike *Rhipsalis* species. Its dark green tubular stems normally form a pendant bush. Sometimes they have short pale spines. In spring, small, white to greenish white flowers appear, followed by berries of the same color. It is moderate to fast growing.

L 10 ft (3 m), S unlimited. Min. 45°F (7°C).

SCHLUMBERGERA

THIS GENUS FROM BRAZIL consists of only six species, but there are many more hybrids. They are very similar in form, with flat jointed stems arching into a small bush. Plants start into growth in late summer and, after a period of short days with less than 12 hours of light, flower in winter. Too much light, even if it is artificial, can retard flowering. Lopsided, trumpet-shaped, mostly red flowers grow from the truncated tips of new stems, followed by green or reddish, grapelike fruits. These shade-loving plants are known as Christmas cacti in the Northern Hemisphere or winter-flowering cacti in the Southern Hemisphere. They need regular feeding when in active growth in summer and autumn.

HEIGHT AND SPREAD

Species and hybrids

12 in/30 cm
6 in/15 cm
0 in/0 cm
INDOORS: 5 years' growth

12 in/30 cm
6 in/15 cm
0 in/0 cm
OUTDOORS: 10 years' growth

Schlumbergera truncata

Crab cactus, lobster cactus
The truncated stems of this long-cultivated species are much less erect than the newer Schlumbergera hybrids. It changes in form as it grows from a small bush to a clambering, prostrate, or pendant mat. The small, long-necked flowers are produced later than those of the hybrids.
H 12 in (30 cm), S unlimited. Min. 41°F (5°C).

Schlumbergera 'Firecracker' and 'Maria'

Schlumbergera 'Maria'

Schlumbergera hybrids

Most cultivated Schlumbergera are hybrids. They are easier to grow than the species, with larger, more shapely flowers, and make fine pot plants. Their diverse flower colors are affected by local light intensity, temperature, and the season; blooms that open in autumn are paler than winter flowers.
H 12 in (30 cm), S unlimited. Min. 41°F (5°C).

Schlumbergera 'Firecracker'

Schlumbergera 'Joanne'

Schlumbergera 'Lilac Beauty'

Schlumbergera 'Gold Charm'

SELENICEREUS

THESE LARGE, EPIPHYTIC CLIMBERS (see pp. 10–11) are prized for their beautiful pale flowers that open at night. They grow mainly in the forests of Mexico and South America. The 20 or so variable species include some that are similar to *Epiphyllum* (see pp. 72–3) but most have slim tubular stems that cling to a host plant by means of aerial roots. The long-necked summer flowers grow near the stem tips, are often strangely scented, and produce spiny, plumlike fruits. Most of these shade-loving plants do not flower easily until mature, but they grow quite fast. The stems make good grafting stocks for other epiphytes, especially *Schlumbergera* (see p. 97) that are trained as standards.

Selenicereus spinulosus

Large summer blooms up to 8 in (20 cm) across appear on plants that are about five years old. The flowers have white inner petals and green to red-brown outer petals. Even on the same plant, the slender clambering stems vary greatly. They may be angular at first, with deep ribs, but later thicken to become smooth and tubular. The spines are pale and bristly. This species makes a good grafting stock for epiphytes.
H and S unlimited. Min. 41°F (5°C).

HEIGHT AND SPREAD

S. pteranthus *S. spinulosus* *S. grandiflorus*

		8 ft/2.4 m
		4 ft/1.2 m
		0 in/0 cm

INDOORS: 5 years' growth

		15 ft/5 m
		7½ ft/2.2 m
		0 in/0 cm

OUTDOORS: 10 years' growth

Selenicereus pteranthus

This climbing species has slender stems that can be deeply ribbed or smooth and tubular. The spines range in color from pale yellow to brown. White or cream flowers, up to 8 in (20 cm) in diameter, are produced briefly in summer.
H and S unlimited. Min. 41°F (5°C).

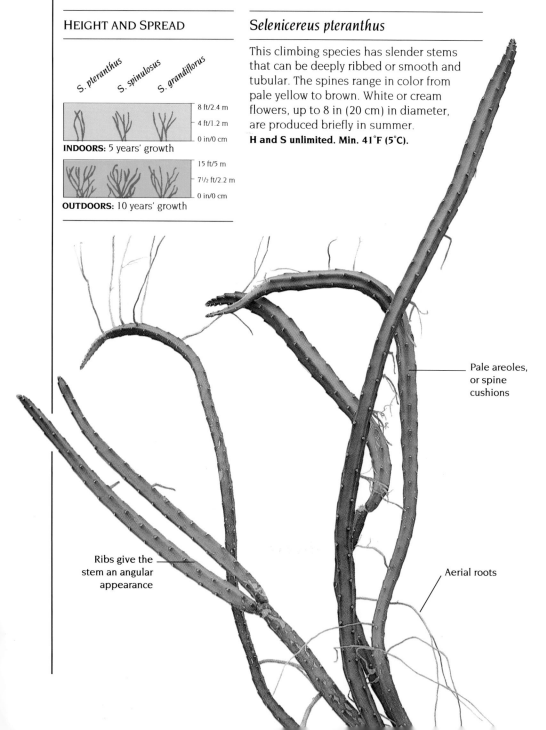

Pale areoles, or spine cushions

Ribs give the stem an angular appearance

Aerial roots

Selenicereus grandiflorus

Queen of the night
Woolly buds open to dramatic, sweetly scented flowers that are up to 12 in (30 cm) across (the largest in the genus). The slim stems are very variable, with deep or shallow ribs and bristly or broad, pale or dark brown spines. In cultivation, the cactus is not very free-flowering.
H and S unlimited. Min. 41°F (5°C).

STENOCACTUS

COMMONLY CALLED WAVE OR BRAIN CACTI because of their crinkly appearance, these can have up to 150 undulating ribs. The 20 or so, mainly solitary, slow-growing species are very variable – no two plants are identical. Many flower in late winter or early spring when only about 2 in (5 cm) across. Funnel-shaped blooms grow from the plant crown between early spring and summer. These are often white, with pink to purple stripes, or yellow. Green seedpods follow. The long spines of these sun-loving Mexican cacti range in color from straw to brown or black.

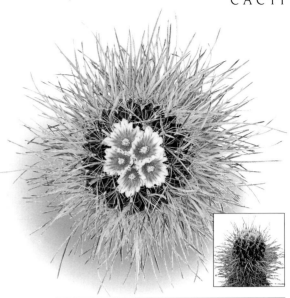

HEIGHT AND SPREAD

S. multicostatus
S. multicostatus v. lloydii
S. coptonogonus

12 in/30 cm
6 in/15 cm
0 in/0 cm
INDOORS: 5 years' growth

12 in/30 cm
6 in/15 cm
0 in/0 cm
OUTDOORS: 10 years' growth

Stenocactus multicostatus

A mature plant can have over 100 thin ribs, each less than $1/32$ in (1 mm) wide, and may possess only a single areole, or spine cushion. The cactus body can be globular to hemispherical. Its pliable spines vary considerably in number and length, with some plants having virtually no spines at all. Their color ranges from pale yellow to copper-brown. Delicately shaded flowers are borne prolifically in spring and periodically in summer.
H and S 5 in (13 cm). Min. 41°F (5°C).

Stenocactus multicostatus v. lloydii

Very similar to S. *multicostatus* in variability of form, spines, and growth habit, this cactus has flowers whose petals are a slightly paler shade of pink.
H and S 5 in (13 cm). Min. 41°F (5°C).

Older spines are longer and paler

Stenocactus coptonogonus

Although it is the type species (used to define the genus characteristics), this cactus is closely related to the *Ferocactus* (see pp. 74–5). It is hemispherical to globular and is the only *Stenocactus* species with so few ribs, which are also straight. Its spines vary in length and hue and the white spring flowers are striped with magenta.
H 5 in (13 cm), S 6 in (15 cm). Min. 41°F (5°C).

THELOCACTUS

THIS GROUP OF MOSTLY SMALL, sun-loving cacti is originally from southern Texas and Mexico. Recently, the 40 species were amalgamated into 13. The plants are various hues of green or metallic gray and can be flat, squat, or conical with dense or sparse spines that are long and curving or straight. An abundance of long-lasting, flat-faced flowers, which range from white or yellow to red or violet, are borne near the crown of mature plants in summer. The small, dry seedpods split at the base to scatter the seed. Most of these cacti grow and produce offsets slowly. Do not overwater them because they are prone to rot.

HEIGHT AND SPREAD

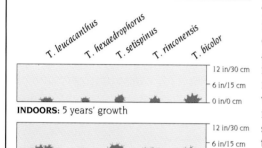

T. leucacanthus   *T. hexaedrophorus*   *T. setispinus*   *T. rinconensis*   *T. bicolor*

12 in/30 cm
6 in/15 cm
0 in/0 cm
INDOORS: 5 years' growth

12 in/30 cm
6 in/15 cm
0 in/0 cm
OUTDOORS: 10 years' growth

Thelocactus leucacanthus

The ability of this variable species to offset freely and form large, spreading clumps of deep green, spiny stems is unusual for this genus. Its long, starry spines vary in color, from straw-yellow to gray, and the flowers range from pale yellow to carmine and violet. The young offsets often develop roots while they are attached to the parent stem, so they are easy to divide up and transplant (see p. 157).
H 6 in (15 cm), S 15 in (38 cm). Min. 41°F (5°C).

Thelocactus hexaedrophorus

Ranging from blue- to gray-green, this cactus has relatively few, sturdy, curved spines, which can be gray or banded red. Some older plants develop pronounced, wartlike tubercles with spines that are often banded red and yellow. The flowers of this flattened globular species can be shaded white, cream, or mauve.
H 5 in (13 cm), S 7 in (18 cm). Min. 41°F (5°C).

Thelocactus setispinus

If grown from seed, this rewarding cactus produces citrus-scented flowers after only three years, when it is 2 in (5 cm) across. The hooked central spines are yellow or red, fading to gray, and are surrounded by long starlike spines. This globular species, formerly classed as *Ferocactus*, offsets slowly.
H 7 in (18 cm), S 10 in (25 cm). Min. 41°F (5°C).

Thelocactus rinconensis

On a young plant, the tubercles of this gray- to blue-green cactus are sometimes very angular. The long, slender spines disintegrate and shred into fibers as the plant matures. White, pale gold, or pink flowers are borne on the upper part of the flattened, globular body.
H 6 in (15 cm), S 12 in (30 cm). Min. 41°F (5°C).

Thelocactus bicolor

Texas pride, glory of Texas
This species, which may be globular or
conical, is spiked with dense, sometimes
flattened, red and yellow spines. Its feathery
blooms appear when it is 2 in (5 cm) across.
H 10 in (25 cm), S 5 in (13 cm). Min. 41°F (5°C).

WEBERBAUEROCEREUS

THE SLENDER, SPINY STEMS of these impressive columnar cacti grow very large
and may be bushy or treelike. Some species have ribs with distinctive
notches and their spines, which range from white to straw-colored or brown,
often turn gray with age. Mature plants flower on summer nights. The blooms,
located near the top of the stem, are tubular or funnel-shaped, often with
long necks, and are sometimes slightly lopsided. They are shaded white,
crimson, or sienna and are followed by red or green, small, scaly berries.
The eight or so species are native to the Peruvian mountains and need
sun to thrive. Like most columnar cacti, they require a good-sized pot.

Indented stem, where
new annual growth
began, may occur in
potgrown plants

HEIGHT AND SPREAD

INDOORS:
5 years' growth

OUTDOORS:
10 years' growth

Weberbauerocereus johnsonii

Golden column
One of the few species in its genus that is densely
covered with golden spines, this makes a handsome
specimen plant, whether it is grown in a large pot or in
an open bed. The spines darken with age. Older stems
branch to form a treelike plant and produce long
tubular flowers, which are white or pale pink. The
berries are green and hairy.
H 20 ft (6 m), S 6 ft (2 m). Min. 45°F (7°C).

SUCCULENTS

A selection of plants ranging in form from tiny living stones and creeping mats to leafy bushes, spiraling rosettes, and palmlike trees.

ADENIUM

THE EXOTIC BLOOMS of these bushy plants are open-faced and white, pink, or crimson; they appear periodically from spring to autumn on young growth. Twin-horned, green seedpods follow. The pithy brown stems are caudiciform, or swollen (see p. 10), with oval leaves. The four species from east Africa or southern Arabia grow slowly, but many more vigorous hybrids with a range of flower colors are available. All of these sun-loving species prefer dry warmth and can rot if damaged.

Flowers up to 5 in (13 cm) wide

Prominently veined, glossy leaves with pale downy undersides

Stem has poisonous milky sap

HEIGHT AND SPREAD

A. obesum

12 in/30 cm
6 in/15 cm
0 in/0 cm

INDOORS:
5 years' growth

A. obesum

2 ft/60 cm
12 in/30 cm
0 in/0 cm

OUTDOORS:
10 years' growth

Adenium obesum

Desert rose, mock azalea, impala lily
The easiest in its genus to grow, this variable plant flowers readily in 3–4 years from seed. Its pink, white, or crimson flowers, which usually have dark outer edges and paler centers, are produced from spring through to autumn.
H 4 ft (1.2 m), S 15 in (38 cm). Min. 61°F (16°C).

ADROMISCHUS

GROWN FOR THEIR DECORATIVE FOLIAGE of varying shapes, colors, and textures, these southern African succulents have dainty, mottled, often fleshy leaves that shed easily. Most of the plants form small lax clumps. Tiny pale flower trumpets appear on long stalks in summer. Although from a range of habitats, in cultivation these frost-tender plants need bright shade or diffuse sun. There are about 50 species, some of which grow slowly, but many newly discovered forms.

Roots

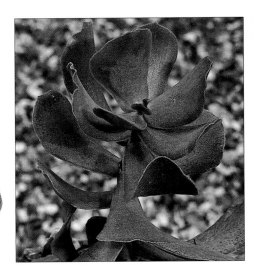

HEIGHT AND SPREAD

A. cooperi   A. maculatus

12 in/30 cm
6 in/15 cm
0 in/0 cm

INDOORS: 5 years' growth

12 in/30 cm
6 in/15 cm
0 in/0 cm

OUTDOORS: 10 years' growth

Adromischus cooperi

The small, purple-blotched, gray-green leaves are most often spoon-shaped with a flattened wavy edge. The centers of the pale green flowers darken to purple. This succulent is very easily propagated from leaf cuttings.
H 4 in (10 cm), S unlimited. Min. 41°F (5°C).

Adromischus maculatus

Calico hearts, clam plant
With age, the caudex, or swollen stem (see p. 10), becomes very bulbous. The leaves are pale to dark gray-green with purple flecks and often heart-shaped with a wavy margin and waxy tips. This usually low carpeting succulent has white or purple flowers.
H 4 in (10 cm), S unlimited. Min. 41°F (5°C).

AEONIUM

THE FAST-GROWING, ROSETTE-SHAPED SUCCULENTS in this diverse group can be stemless or shrublike, small or medium-sized, sun- or shade-loving. The growing point in the center of a mature rosette develops into a stem with clusters of small, long-lasting, starry blooms that are white, yellow, pink, or red. After flowering, the rosette, and in some species the entire plant, dies. The tiny seedpods are papery when ripe. Most of the 30 species of pinwheel plants are dormant in summer and start growing in autumn. Largely from the Canary Islands and the Mediterranean region, they tolerate dry cold, but can rot in cold, damp conditions.

HEIGHT AND SPREAD

A. arboreum 'Atropurpureum'
A. tabuliforme
A. arboreum
A. haworthii
A. arboreum 'Albovariegatum'
A. arboreum 'Schwartzkopf'

Does not apply						4 ft/1.2 m
						2 ft/60 cm
						0 in/0 cm

INDOORS: 5 years' growth

Does not apply						4 ft/1.2 m
						2 ft/60 cm
						0 in/0 cm

OUTDOORS: 10 years' growth

Mature rosette is the size and shape of a dinner plate

After flowering, the terminal rosette dies back

Side rosettes grow on to replace terminal one

Glossy rosettes can be bright green, red, or dark purple

Aerial roots grow in drought and eventually root into the soil

Aeonium arboreum 'Atropurpureum'

Purple rose tree
In summer sun, the green leaves turn a dark purple-red. Yellow flowers appear in late winter to spring. Use young plants to edge borders. Mature ones form large bushes.
H 3 ft (90 cm), S 4 ft (1.2 m). Min. 41˚F (5˚C).

Aeonium arboreum

Tree aeonium
An elegant sun-loving plant, this bears large clusters of small yellow flowers in spring. The stems turn brittle with age; remove the top-growth of a large plant and root several cuttings together to produce an instant new bush.
H 3 ft (90 cm), S 4 ft (1.2 m). Min. 41˚F (5˚C).

Aeonium tabuliforme

Saucer plant, dinner plate aeonium
When three years old, this species flowers and dies. Offsets rarely form, so keep several plants to cross-pollinate the yellow summer flowers and produce seedlings. The rosette is sometimes cristate, or crested, in shape. Protect this plant from hot sun.
H 2 in (5 cm), S 12 in (30 cm). Min. 41˚F (5˚C).

Rosettes of fleshy leaves
look like large flowers

Growing point in
center of rosette

Woody stem branches
to form a sparse bush

Aeonium haworthii

Pinwheel
This sun-loving plant offsets freely to form
a lush domed mound and is good for
miniature gardens when young. Some of
the older heads flower each spring, bearing
short spikes of creamy yellow blooms.
H 2 ft (60 cm), S 4 ft (1.2 m). Min. 36°F (2°C).

Aeonium arboreum 'Albovariegatum'

The rosettes of this large bushy cultivar
are at their best in summer, when they
become variegated and often flushed with
pink. The variegation may disappear in
winter temporarily. The plant grows a little
more slowly than the green-leaved species,
A. *arboreum*, but is otherwise similar.
H 3 ft (90 cm), S 4 ft (1.2 m). Min. 41°F (5°C).

Aeonium arboreum 'Schwartzkopf'

Black aeonium
So dark a purple that it appears almost
black, this cultivar retains its dramatic color
throughout the winter if placed in a bright
position. A striking edging for summer
borders, it has larger rosettes than
A. *arboreum* and is more robust.
H 3 ft (90 m), S 4 ft (1.2 m). Min. 41°F (5°C).

AGAVE

THE SUCCULENTS IN THIS GROUP take the form of stemless, or nearly stemless, rosettes, which vary from 6 in (15 cm) to 15 ft (5 m) across. Their leaves, each tipped with a sharp spine, tend to be blue-green in plants from colder climates and a soft gray-green in those from warmer areas. Once the rosette is mature – about five years for smaller species and up to 40 years for large ones – the growing point develops into a tall flower spike of many long-lasting, bell-shaped summer blooms, generally in shades of white, yellow, or green. The rosette usually dies after producing small, dry berries, leaving several younger offsets to grow on. Native to a range of habitats in the Americas and the West Indies, from coasts to mountains, these 450 or more sun-loving species are also known as American aloes.

Agave americana 'Variegata'

Century plant
Distinguished by yellow-edged leaves that grow up to 5 ft (1.5 m) long, this is a fine focal plant for both bedding and containers. Its large creamy flowers, which are fragrant, are borne on a 6–25 ft (2–7.5 m) stem after 20–30 years.
H 5 ft (1.5 m), S 12 ft (3.7 m). Min. 32˚F (0˚C).

HEIGHT AND SPREAD

A. utahensis *A. pumila* *A. parviflora* *A. victoria-reginae*	*A. parryi* *A. stricta*	*A. americana* 'Variegata'	

12 in/30 cm
6 in/15 cm
0 in/0 cm
INDOORS: 5 years' growth

12 in/30 cm
6 in/15 cm
0 in/0 cm

12 in/30 cm
6 in/15 cm
0 in/0 cm

12 in/30 cm
6 in/15 cm
0 in/0 cm
OUTDOORS: 10 years' growth

2 ft/60 cm
12 in/30 cm
0 in/0 cm

4 ft/1.2 m
2 ft/60 cm
0 in/0 cm

Sharp terminal spine ——————

Agave utahensis

Utah agave
This small to medium-sized plant has spiky leaves, which can be gray-, blue-, or deep green. Yellow blooms appear after 8–10 years. It is one of the hardiest *Agave* species.
H 12 in (30 cm), S 2 ft (60 cm). Min. 23˚F (-5˚C).

Agave parryi

Mescal agave
Clusters of creamy yellow flowers appear on a 12 ft (3.7 m) spike when this large plant is about 20–30 years old. It is a neat, broad-leaved rosette.
H 2 ft (60 cm), S 4 ft (1.2 m). Min. 32˚F (0˚C).

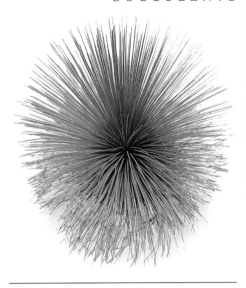

Agave pumila

Recently introduced into cultivation as a miniature form, this slow-growing species eventually achieves a moderate size. It has not yet been seen in flower.
H 15 in (38 cm), S 2 ft (60 cm). Min. 36°F (2°C).

Agave parviflora

Little princess agave
White markings and pale fibers curling from the leaf edges contrast with the deep green leaves of this small species, making it a popular pot plant. Green flowers, which are usually self-fertile if pollinated, appear on a 4–6 ft (1.2–2 m) spike after seven years.
H 6 in (15 cm), S 9 in (23 cm). Min. 36°F (2°C).

Agave stricta

This is one of the few *Agave* species whose rosette does not die after flowering: it develops a short trunk, which branches to form new growing points. The first spike of white flowers is produced after 10 or 15 years, followed by another every 5–10 years. The plant becomes prostrate and offsets freely to form a large spreading clump.
H 2 ft (60 cm), S 5 ft (1.5 m). Min. 36°F (2°C).

Broad white stripes show pattern left by tightly furled leaves of young rosette

Agave victoria-reginae

Queen Victoria century plant, royal agave
An elegant, domed rosette of short, broad leaves, strikingly edged and patterned in white, led to this species' early popularity in cultivation. Young plants have stiff leaves, but on older plants the tips curve inward to form a ball. Cream flowers appear after 20–30 years when the slow-growing plant is 2–3 ft (60–90 cm) in diameter. Some forms offset freely; others remain solitary.
H 12 in (30 cm), S 2 ft (60 cm). Min. 36°F (2°C).

ALOE

ALOE SPECIES, WHICH ARE WIDESPREAD from Arabia to South Africa, range from a 1 in (2.5 cm) stemless rosette to a 30 ft (9 m) tree. The 300 or so species are often confused with *Agave* (see pp. 106–7) but differ in several ways. The *Aloe*, unlike the *Agave*, flowers annually and its rosette is formed by leaves that grow, rather than unfurl, from the center. Long flower stems bearing clusters of small, long-lasting, tubular blooms which can be red, orange, green, or sometimes yellow, appear mostly in winter and spring. The small oval berries are green. Larger species thrive in sun, while smaller ones need shade; a few are dormant in summer.

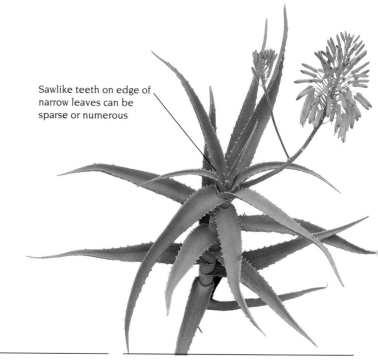

Sawlike teeth on edge of narrow leaves can be sparse or numerous

HEIGHT AND SPREAD

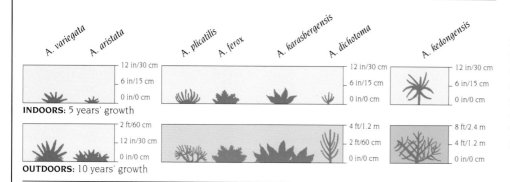

A. variegata A. aristata
A. plicatilis A. ferox A. karasbergensis A. dichotoma A. kedongensis

INDOORS: 5 years' growth

OUTDOORS: 10 years' growth

Aloe kedongensis

Branching and offsetting freely to make large, dense, bushy clumps, this fast-growing, sun-loving species is easy to propagate, even from cuttings as long as 6 ft (2 m). Its leaves may vary in breadth and length. The plant flowers freely, when still quite small, over a long period during the warmer months and produces well-spaced blooms on solitary stems.
H and S 3.7 m (12 ft). Min. 7°C (45°F).

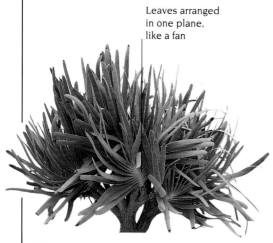

Leaves arranged in one plane, like a fan

Aloe plicatilis

Fan aloe
This sun-loving *Aloe* eventually forms a large, unusually shaped bush or tree, which is dormant in summer. Its sparse orange or red flowers appear from spring to summer.
H and S 10 ft (3 m). Min. 45°F (7°C).

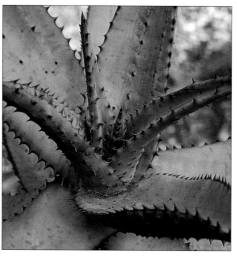

Aloe ferox

Older plants of this very variable, large, single-stemmed *Aloe* usually have fewer spiny leaves. In spring, a branched flower spike of dense orange-red blooms appears. This sun-lover tolerates dry cold.
H 15 ft (5 m), S 6 ft (2 m). Min. 36°F (2°C).

Aloe variegata

Partridge-breasted aloe, tiger aloe, kanniedood aloe
The spring blooms can be salmon to scarlet. The small rosette, when young, is slow to produce offsets; it spirals with age.
H 9 in (23 cm), S 2 ft (60 cm). Min. 45°F (7°C).

Aloe karasbergensis

The leaves of this stemless, clumping plant vary from a pale, greenish white to mauve and are patterned with lighter stripes or rows of spots. Once it grows to 18 in (46 cm) in diameter, the plant bears well-spaced, pale pink to strawberry-red flowers on tall stems in summer. It grows best in sun.
H and S 12 ft (3.7 m). Min. 45°F (7°C).

Aloe aristata

Lace aloe
Long, soft, slender thorns on the leaf edges give this freely clumping species its lacy appearance. When the plant is dormant or dry, its rough leaves curve inward into a small ball. Orange-red flowers are borne on a 3 ft (90 cm) stem in spring to early summer. The plant does well in sun or shade, and tolerates a light frost if kept dry.
H 6 in (15 cm), S 3 ft (90 cm). Min. 36°F (2°C).

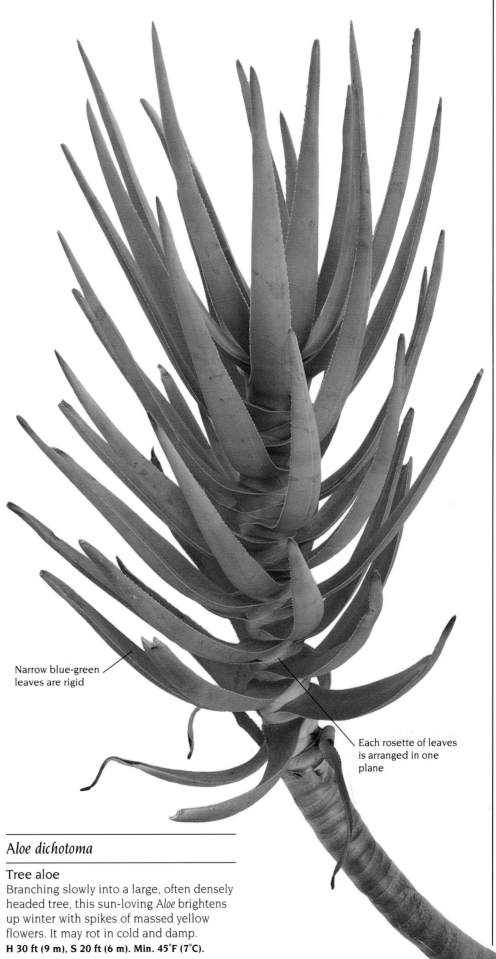

Narrow blue-green leaves are rigid

Each rosette of leaves is arranged in one plane

Aloe dichotoma

Tree aloe
Branching slowly into a large, often densely headed tree, this sun-loving *Aloe* brightens up winter with spikes of massed yellow flowers. It may rot in cold and damp.
H 30 ft (9 m), S 20 ft (6 m). Min. 45°F (7°C).

BRACHYSTELMA

THESE SUCCULENTS HAVE small to large underground tubers and deciduous climbing foliage that dies back in dry periods. They bear small, oddly shaped flowers and horned seedpods. There are about 100 variable species, mostly from southern Africa and India, but new ones are still being discovered, since they are visible in the wild only briefly each year while in growth. These challenging, slow-growing plants, which are sensitive to damp cold and dry heat, thrive in a gritty planting mix if the tuber is planted flush with the surface.

Long curved petals are united at the tips

HEIGHT AND SPREAD

B. barberae
- 12 in/30 cm
- 6 in/15 cm
- 0 in/0 cm

INDOORS:
5 years' growth

B. barberae
- 12 in/30 cm
- 6 in/15 cm
- 0 in/0 cm

OUTDOORS:
10 years' growth

Brachystelma barberae

The appeal of this plant lies in its bizarre appearance. Clusters of carrion-scented, maroon to chocolate-colored flowers appear on the large tuber's new growth between spring and early summer. The short bushy stems have tiny oval leaves. While in active growth, this plant prefers full sun.
H 1 in (2.5 cm), S 8 in (20 cm). Min. 50°F (10°C).

CARALLUMA

Erect ridged stems

Favorable conditions produce blood-red flowers on new growth

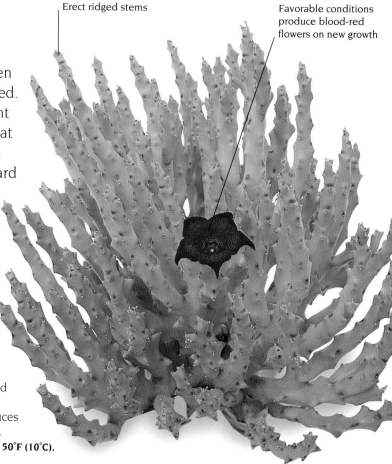

THE STRANGE FLESHY FLOWERS of this group of about 100 variable species are mostly star-shaped and often patterned, ranging from purple, black, or yellow to red. They open in summer or autumn, usually at the plant base. The angular stems have rudimentary leaves that resemble spines. In the wild, in Africa and India, the clump grows like a mushroom ring, spreading outward as the center dies. In cultivation, this process affects the whole plant if it is cold and damp, so renew plants from cuttings each year or plant in hanging baskets for better air circulation.

HEIGHT AND SPREAD

C. socotrana
- 12 in/30 cm
- 6 in/15 cm
- 0 in/0 cm

INDOORS:
5 years' growth

C. socotrana
- 12 in/30 cm
- 6 in/15 cm
- 0 in/0 cm

OUTDOORS:
10 years' growth

Caralluma socotrana

Sculptural, coral-like stems give this small succulent a strange look. The short stems branch and become prostrate; they sometimes turn brown and appear dehydrated. The plant enjoys sun or shade and produces twin-horned, papery seedpods.
H 6 in (15 cm), S 2 ft (60 cm). Min. 50°F (10°C).

CEROPEGIA

WIDESPREAD IN THE WILD from Africa to the Far East, this variable genus of over 150 species, which are mostly small and shade-loving, is constantly being expanded. Many have stems that can clamber up other plants. The tuberous-rooted species are deciduous; others may die back partly in drought or a dry winter. They often need warmth to grow well and flower over long periods, producing a large number of strangely shaped, mottled blooms. Twin-horned seedpods follow.

LENGTH AND SPREAD

	C. woodii	C. rendallii	C. sandersonii
INDOORS: 5 years' growth	12 in/30 cm / 6 in/15 cm / 0 in/0 cm		8 ft/2.4 m / 4 ft/1.2 m / 0 in/0 cm
OUTDOORS: 10 years' growth	4 ft/1.2 m / 2 ft/60 cm / 0 in/0 cm		8 ft/2.4 m / 4 ft/1.2 m / 0 in/0 cm

Brown to green creeping or trailing stems

Small fleshy leaves

Flower shape and color can vary

Tubular flowers with a bulbous base and united petals

Slender trailing or creeping stems

Ceropegia rendallii

This variable species has deciduous twining stems that bear lasting summer flowers and small seedpods. The underground tuber slowly forms a clump. It likes diffuse sun or shade but rots in cold damp conditions.
Tuber: S 2 in (5 cm), stems: L 3¹/2 ft (1.1 m). Min. 50°F (10°C).

Ceropegia sandersonii

Fountain flower, parachute plant
A few times each summer, this fleshy-rooted species bears a profusion of large, usually cone-shaped flowers, with parachute-like green canopies. They appear along the rough stems and last a few days.
L and S unlimited. Min. 50°F (10°C).

Ceropegia woodii

Heart vine, rosary vine
The leaves are very variable in shape and color, ranging from gray-green to purplish brown. Heart-shaped pairs are the prettiest and the most common. Mauve-pink hairy flowers appear in summer.
L and S unlimited. Min. 41°F (5°C).

CONOPHYTUM

THESE TINY CARPETING PLANTS are composed of a pair of swollen leaves; each leaf is partly joined to form two ears or fully united to look like a pea. In early summer, the leaves become dormant, withering into a papery sheath that protects a newly developing leaf pair. The new leaves burst through in autumn and variously hued daisylike blooms later emerge from the leaf fissure. This unusual growth cycle demands careful watering. These sun-loving, slow-growing succulents from South Africa and Namibia take 20–30 years to reach 6 in (15 cm) across. Recently, the 400 or more species were amalgamated into about 100 species.

Daisylike flowers range from white to purple

HEIGHT AND SPREAD

INDOORS: 5 years' growth

OUTDOORS: 10 years' growth

C. minutum
C. taylorianum v. ernianum
C. truncatum
C. bilobum

12 in/30 cm
6 in/15 cm
0 in/0 cm

12 in/30 cm
6 in/15 cm
0 in/0 cm

Conophytum minutum

Dainty, freckled green heads cluster into a neat, ball-shaped mound. This very variable species usually has cone-shaped leaf heads and can take up to 20 years to fill a 3 in (8 cm) pot.
H 1 in (2.5 cm), S 4 in (10 cm). Min. 43°F (6° C).

Leaf heads are slightly domed or flat at the top

Conophytum taylorianum v. ernianum

The gray-green leaf heads, which are usually almost square with two short ears, spread to form a relatively large mat. This succulent flowers well, producing small, pink to mauve blooms.
H 3 in (8 cm), S 15 in (38 cm). Min. 43°F (6°C).

Conophytum truncatum

Usually green with darker spots, the leaf heads of this variable species are flattened on top and have a sunken fissure. The flowers open in the evening and have spidery petals in shades of salmon, straw, or ivory.
H 1 in (2.5 cm), S 7 in (18 cm). Min. 43°F (6°C).

Conophytum bilobum

This species is very variable and has many synonyms. One of the largest in its genus, it has rabbit-eared leaf heads that may be up to 2 in (5 cm) tall. The plant, which is rarely dormant in summer, produces abundant, yellow or copper-colored flowers.
H 3 in (8 cm), S 7 in (18 cm). Min. 43°F (6°C).

COTYLEDON

EXTREMELY DIVERSE IN FORM, this slow- to moderately fast-growing group of African succulents includes tiny knobbly plants and large bushes. The foliage, sometimes hairy in texture, can be white or silvery to greenish yellow or brown. These plants flower well, producing spikes of long-lasting, bell-shaped blooms, which range from white or pale yellow to burnt orange and crimson. The dustlike seed is contained in dry papery capsules. Some of the 60 or so species prefer sun; others thrive in shade.

Withered flower stems

Cotyledon buchholziana

Brown stems, which are slim, tubular, and upright, make this small, sun-loving plant distinctive. The leaves appear only briefly after the autumn flowers, which are solitary, long-lasting, and rust or purple. This slow-growing species is prone to rot if it is damp.
H 6 in (15 cm), S 15 in (38 cm). Min. 43°F (6°C).

HEIGHT AND SPREAD

C. buchholziana *C. ladismithensis* *C. undulata*

12 in/30 cm
6 in/15 cm
0 in/0 cm
INDOORS: 5 years' growth

12 in/30 cm
6 in/15 cm
0 in/0 cm

12 in/30 cm
6 in/15 cm
0 in/0 cm
OUTDOORS: 10 years' growth

2 ft/60 cm
12 in/30 cm
0 in/0 cm

Leaf shape and size can vary

Young upright stems

Cotyledon undulata

Silver ruffles, silver crown
These handsome leaves have a delicate silvery bloom and are sometimes edged with scarlet. Orange to red flowers are borne on long stems. If the plant is grown outdoors, the leaves blush purple under their silvery bloom in summer. After a few years, this sun-loving bush tends to sprawl untidily, so renew it from cuttings.
H 2 ft (60 cm). S 4 ft (1.2 m). Min. 45°F (7°C).

Leaves crinkled on upper edges

Cotyledon ladismithensis

Cub's paws, bear claws
The fleshy leaves have three or more teeth at the tip, are often hairy, and can be tan-colored. In summer, mustard to greenish brown flowers cluster on the short stems. This small bush can be semiprostrate.
H 12 in (30 cm), S 2 ft (60 cm). Min. 43°F (6°C).

CRASSULA

WITHIN THIS LARGE GENUS from Madagascar and Africa are many commonly cultivated fleshy-leaved succulents. The 350 or so species are very diverse; some are only 1 in (2.5 cm) tall when fully grown, whereas others become 15 ft (5 m) trees. The plants can be solitary or clumping, slow or fast growing, sun or shade loving, and easy or difficult to care for. They are often dormant in summer, then bear clusters of small starry flowers on the stem tips from late autumn to early spring. These mostly white, pink, or red blooms are long lasting and provide good winter color. The seedpods are minute.

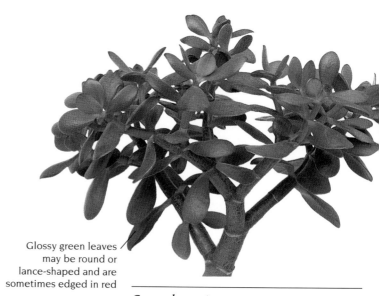

Glossy green leaves may be round or lance-shaped and are sometimes edged in red

Crassula ovata

Jade plant, money plant, Chinese rubber plant
If well fed and watered in summer, this large bush or small tree produces dense clusters of white flowers from late autumn to midwinter. An evergreen succulent, it sheds its old leaves in spring, when it benefits from pruning to keep it in shape.
H 15 ft (5 m), S 5 ft (1.5 m). Min. 41°F (5°C).

HEIGHT AND SPREAD

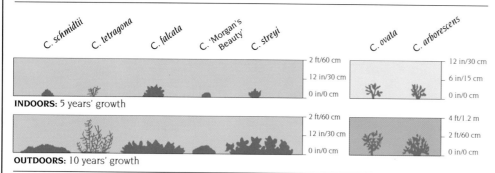

INDOORS: 5 years' growth

OUTDOORS: 10 years' growth

C. schmidtii   *C. tetragona*   *C. falcata*   *C. 'Morgan's Beauty'*   *C. streyi*   *C. ovata*   *C. arborescens*

2 ft/60 cm / 12 in/30 cm / 0 in/0 cm   12 in/30 cm / 6 in/15 cm / 0 in/0 cm

2 ft/60 cm / 12 in/30 cm / 0 in/0 cm   4 ft/1.2 m / 2 ft/60 cm / 0 in/0 cm

Crassula arborescens

Silver dollar plant
In sun, the round blue leaves of this large species have red margins. They are also thick and waxy; prune the bush regularly to prevent them from weighing down the brown stems. Pink flowers appear in late autumn.
H 10 ft (3 m), S 4 ft (1.2 m). Min. 41°F (5°C).

Crassula schmidtii

Ideal as a winter-flowering pot plant, this small variable species has tiny leaves, often with red spots, and bright pink to red flowers. It quickly forms a mat; clip it after flowering to keep it tidy. This plant thrives in light shade but not in winter dampness.
H 4 in (10 cm), S unlimited. Min. 41°F (5°C).

Crassula tetragona

When young, this small, upright, sun-loving bush with glossy, needlelike leaves looks like a conifer and is a good choice for miniature displays. Small clusters of white flowers appear in autumn. Prune after flowering to keep its spreading form neat.
H 2 ft (60 cm), S unlimited. Min. 41°F (5°C).

Sweetly scented flowers
open in late summer

Silver-gray,
propeller-shaped
leaves

Crassula falcata

Propeller plant, scarlet paintbrush
Frothy masses of small red flowers sit on top of the long stems of this sun-loving species. The stems eventually form a prostrate spreading clump. New shoots then grow from the plant base and the stem tips; use these shoots as cuttings and discard old plants.
H 9 in (23 cm), S 10 ft (3 m). Min. 41°F (5°C).

Crassula 'Morgan's Beauty'

The winter flowers of this slow-growing hybrid are some of the prettiest in the genus, contrasting well with its small mound of dense silver foliage. In winter, water the plant sparingly and split up large clumps to avoid rot. It likes sun or shade.
H 5 in (13 cm), S 3 ft (90 cm). Min. 50°F (10°C).

Crassula streyi

The dramatic contrast of its differently colored leaf surfaces make this a beautiful focal plant. When it is grown in shade, its glossy leaves become a rich deep green on the upper surfaces and wine-red on the undersides. In sun, the foliage becomes dull and muted in color. Clusters of small white flowers appear in autumn. The prostrate stems slowly form a low clump.
H 12 in (30 cm), S 6 ft (2 m). Min. 50°F (10°C).

CYPHOSTEMMA

SOME SPECIES IN THIS GENUS have been grown in Germany for over 400 years. These medium-sized to large African succulents have a woody caudex, or swollen trunk (see p. 10), from which a leafy stem grows each summer, sometimes quite late in the season. After 10–20 years, clusters of tiny, long-lasting, greenish yellow flowers are borne on stalks that emerge at the stem tip. Related to the grapevine, the plants produce inedible, grapelike fruits. Many of the 20 or so slow-growing, sun-loving species exude white latex droplets, which are often mistaken for an insect infestation, from the undersides of the leaves.

Cyphostemma juttae

This succulent is one of the larger species. With age, its thick tubular trunk develops a few branches near the crown, eventually forming a large bush. It is common in cultivation, but can be difficult to grow since it dislikes cold and high humidity. The fruits become red when ripe.

H 6 ft (2 m), S 12 in (30 cm). Min. 50°F (10°C).

HEIGHT AND SPREAD

C. juttae   C. bainesii

12 in/30 cm
6 in/15 cm
0 in/0 cm
INDOORS: 5 years' growth

2 ft/60 cm
12 in/30 cm
0 in/0 cm
OUTDOORS: 10 years' growth

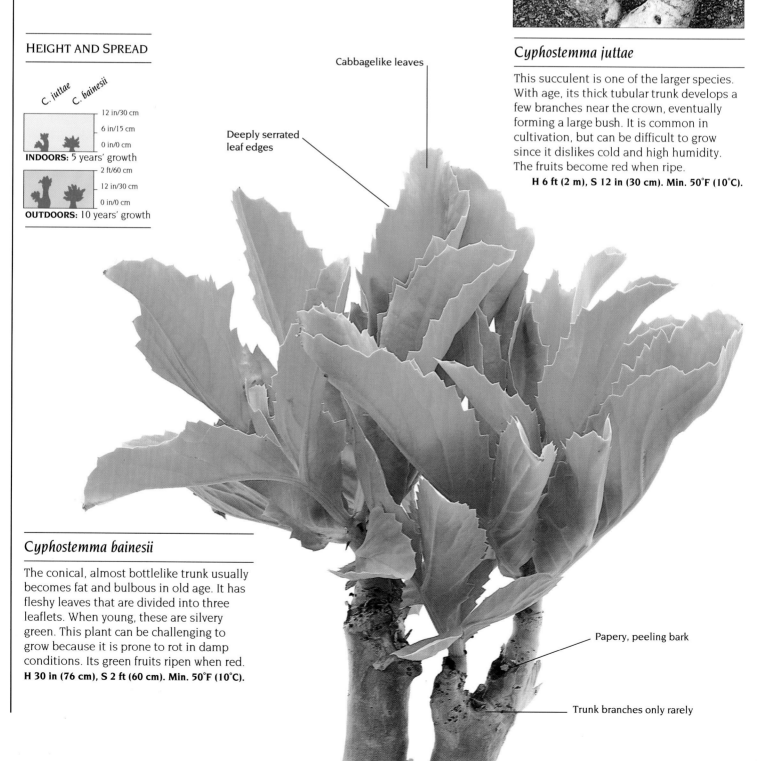

Cabbagelike leaves

Deeply serrated leaf edges

Papery, peeling bark

Trunk branches only rarely

Cyphostemma bainesii

The conical, almost bottlelike trunk usually becomes fat and bulbous in old age. It has fleshy leaves that are divided into three leaflets. When young, these are silvery green. This plant can be challenging to grow because it is prone to rot in damp conditions. Its green fruits ripen when red.
H 30 in (76 cm), S 2 ft (60 cm). Min. 50°F (10°C).

DUDLEYA

THE LEAVES OF THESE mainly small rosettes often have a silvery bloom, which is more pronounced in winter. In summer, small, long-lasting, starry flowers, which are mostly yellow, appear on long, sometimes prostrate stems. These sun-loving plants are best kept dry in winter. The 40 or so solitary or clump-forming species are very variable and hybridize freely in the wild in the US and Mexico.

HEIGHT AND SPREAD

| D. hassei | D. brittonii | D. pulverulenta |

INDOORS: 5 years' growth
- 12 in/30 cm
- 6 in/15 cm
- 0 in/0 cm

OUTDOORS: 10 years' growth
- 12 in/30 cm
- 6 in/15 cm
- 0 in/0 cm

Dudleya hassei

This spiky rosette reaches up to 5 in (13 cm) in diameter and branches freely to form large, coral-like clumps. Its white flowers are borne on 12 in (30 cm) stems, which grow from the sides of the rosette. This plant's open habit makes it less prone to rot than many other *Dudleya* species.
H 9 in (23 cm), S 3 ft (90 cm). Min. 45°F (7°C).

Silvery white leaves are usually narrow and tapering

Dudleya brittonii

Silver dollar plant
Generally a startling silver-white, this solitary rosette resembles a flower. Masses of pale yellow flowers are borne on 3 ft (90 cm) stems.
H 15 in (38 cm), S 30 in (76 cm). Min. 50°F (10°C).

Fleshy, often tapering leaves tightly packed at the center

Powdery bloom

Relatively slow-growing rosette carried on a short stem

Dudleya pulverulenta

The tightly packed rosette of this small species may be shaded silver-gray to pure white. It branches slowly to form a relatively dense clump of prostrate stems. Unusually for this genus, the succulent bears scarlet flowers, which are carried on flower stems that may be up to 5 ft (1.5 m) long. Protect the plant from winter cold and high humidity to guard against the risk of rot.
H 7 in (18 cm), S 30 in (76 cm). Min. 50°F (10°C).

ECHEVERIA

MOST OF THE ROSETTE-SHAPED SUCCULENTS in this large group are from Mexico. The 150 or so species vary in shape and size and are green to blue, red, purple, or pink. They are greener when in active growth in spring or summer and become richly colored during dormancy. Some have tall stems, others are stemless. Tall spikes of small, long-lasting, bell-shaped flowers, which are often bicolored in hues of gold, orange, and red, are produced from the rosette. Small, dry berries follow. In each season of the year, there are some *Echeveria* in flower. A few species are very challenging, but the thousands of hybrids are often beautiful and easy to grow. Generally sun-loving, *Echeveria* are more compact and intensely colored when grown outdoors, but they also make good house plants for a bright position. Many species tolerate dry cold, but may rot if it is damp.

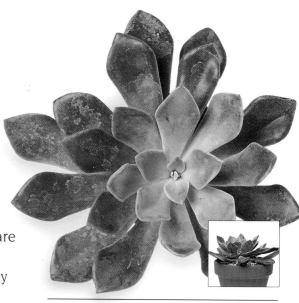

Echeveria fimbriata

The late summer flowers of this erect, bushy plant are either red and orange or red and yellow. Its foliage is usually purplish green.
H 2 ft (60 cm), S 3 ft (90 cm). Min. 41°F (5°C).

HEIGHT AND SPREAD

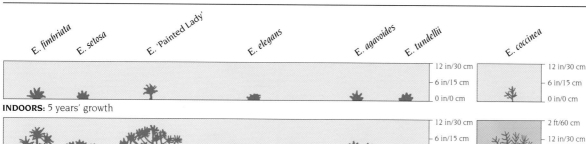

E. fimbriata E. setosa E. 'Painted Lady' E. elegans E. agavoides E. tundellii E. coccinea

12 in/30 cm
6 in/15 cm
0 in/0 cm

INDOORS: 5 years' growth

12 in/30 cm
6 in/15 cm
0 in/0 cm

2 ft/60 cm
12 in/30 cm
0 in/0 cm

OUTDOORS: 10 years' growth

Echeveria setosa

Mexican firecracker
The summer flowers of this small, variable, clumping plant are bright yellow and red. Prone to rot and scorch, it needs dry shade.
H 5 in (13 cm), S 3 ft (90 cm). Min. 45°F (7°C).

Echeveria 'Painted Lady'

This spreading, bushy hybrid has red blooms in summer and often pronounced leaf markings. It forms a prostrate clump with age and should be divided every few years.
H 15 in (38 cm), S unlimited. Min. 41°F (5°C).

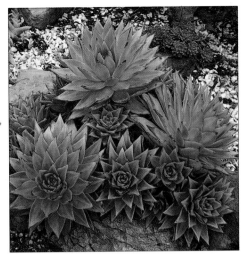

Echeveria coccinea

The abundant, reddish yellow, spring flowers of this bushy, narrow-leaved species last well when cut. Upright at first, its stems become prostrate and root into the soil to form a spreading mound.
H 2 ft (60 cm), S 3 ft (90 cm). Min. 41°F (5°C).

Echeveria elegans

This species is a good choice for formal summer bedding. It acquires a pink hue in full sun and pale yellow flowers appear in summer. The usually small but fast-growing parent offsets to form a mat of rosettes.
H 3 in (8 cm), S unlimited. Min. 41°F (5°C).

Echeveria agavoides

Wax agave, molded-wax agave
Grown for its variable but pretty foliage, this large stemless rosette offsets readily to form impressive clumps. In full sun, the usually pale gray-green leaves blush red. Its reddish summer flowers are tiny.
H 10 in (25 cm), S 3 ft (90 cm). Min. 41°F (5°C).

Downy hairs are more pronounced on young rosettes and stems

Echeveria tundellii

The downy, soft blue rosette offsets and develops into a small mound, which, in summer, provides a contrast to arching stems of brilliant flame-red and yellow flowers. Rosettes begin to flower when they are only 1 in (2.5 cm) in diameter.
H 5 in (13 cm), S 2 ft (60 cm). Min. 41°F (5°C).

Flower color is typical of Echeveria species

EUPHORBIA

THIS HUGE GROUP OF SHRUBS and perennials includes about 1,200 slow- to fast-growing succulent species, mainly from tropical and subtropical areas. They range from small, cactuslike plants to bushy or treelike ones and are mostly sun-loving. Their tiny flowers lack petals and sepals but are often enclosed by brightly hued, long-lasting leaf bracts. Both male and female plants are needed to produce the green seedpods. *Euphorbia*, known as spurge or milkweed, must be handled with gloves because they have a milky sap that irritates skin and can cause blindness. To stop the flow of sap from a "bleeding" plant, immerse it in warm water.

Squat globular body

HEIGHT AND SPREAD

E. obesa E. francoisii E. decaryi E. horrida E. grandialata E. neohumbertii E. milii

12 in/30 cm — 6 in/15 cm — 0 in/0 cm
2 ft/60 cm — 12 in/30 cm — 0 in/0 cm
INDOORS: 5 years' growth

12 in/30 cm — 6 in/15 cm — 0 in/0 cm
4 ft/1.2 m — 2 ft/60 cm — 0 in/0 cm
OUTDOORS: 10 years' growth

Euphorbia obesa

Basketball euphorbia, gingham golf ball, Hottentot's hut
Smooth-bodied, spineless, and usually olive-green, this succulent has pale green or mauve markings. The small, slow-growing body becomes slightly columnar with age. Tiny leaf bracts appear at the crown in summer. The plant, which does well in either sun or shade, needs a dry winter dormancy.
H 8 in (20 cm), S 5 in (13 cm). Min. 50°F (10°C).

Leaf bract

Thorns look like cactus spines

Euphorbia francoisii

The leaves may be dark green, white, or red, and vary greatly in shape. Yellow-green, kidney-shaped leaf bracts appear on the tips of the short prostrate stems in summer. This small species has a long taproot and spreads slowly by means of its underground stems.
H 5 in (13 cm), S 15 in (38 cm). Min. 50°F (10°C).

Euphorbia grandialata

The thorny angular stems are banded with pale green. They are upright at first, but branch at the base and form a large spreading bush relatively quickly. Tiny petalless flowers and coral-red leaf bracts are produced in summer. This species grows best in sun.
H 6 ft (2 m), S 8 ft (2.4 m). Min. 50°F (10°C).

Euphorbia neohumbertii

The erect stem has a handsome rosette of variable deciduous leaves. New growth from the banded, normally light brown stem is bright green. Leaf bracts, small and green with red tips, appear in spring while the stems are still bare. It does well in sun or shade, but not in cold.
H and S 2 ft (60 cm). Min. 50°F (10°C).

Euphorbia milii

Crown of thorns
Tiny white, gold, red, rose, or orange leaf bracts open periodically on new growth all year if the plant is kept moist and warm. In warmer climates, the thorny, fast-growing bush makes a good hedging plant. This variable species grows well in sun or shade.
H 6 ft (2 m), S 5 ft (1.5 m). Min. 55°F (13°C).

Euphorbia decaryi

Short upright stems with rosettes of variable leaves at their tips grow from slowly spreading underground stems. In summer, yellow-green and red leaf bracts appear at the stem tips. Protect this small shade-loving plant from cold and high humidity to guard against rot.
H 6 in (15 cm), S 2 ft (60 cm). Min. 50°F (10°C).

Upright stems may be gray to deep green

Ribs vary in number

Stem has powdery bloom

Euphorbia horrida

With deeply ribbed, swollen, columnar stems and long red thorns, this sun-loving plant looks like an offsetting cactus. Small purple leaf bracts appear on the upper ribs in summer. The stems occasionally branch.
H 4 ft (1.2 m), S 3 ft (90 cm). Min. 50°F (10°C).

FAUCARIA

THE FLESHY, BRIGHT GREEN LEAVES of these southern African plants are semicylindrical or triangular in shape and nearly all are tipped with soft short teeth, giving rise to their common name of tiger's jaws. The 30 or so sun-loving species often form small prostrate clumps. After only two years, large, stemless, bright yellow daisylike flowers grow from the center of each rosette in autumn and open in full sun. The plants start growing in late spring or in early summer and fall dormant after flowering. The green seedpods are woody when ripe. To avoid risk of rot, take care not to overwater plants early in the year.

Stemless flowers

HEIGHT AND SPREAD

F. tuberculosa	F. tuberculosa
12 in/30 cm	12 in/30 cm
6 in/15 cm	6 in/15 cm
0 in/0 cm	0 in/0 cm
INDOORS: 5 years' growth	**OUTDOORS:** 10 years' growth

Faucaria tuberculosa

Warty tiger's jaws
Strange "warts" – tiny white tubercles – stud the upper surfaces of the leaves, which are usually thick, short, and roughly triangular. The number of warts and teeth can vary considerably from plant to plant. The flowers are about 2 in (5 cm) wide.
H 4 in (10 cm), S 2 ft (60 cm). Min. 41°F (5°C).

FRITHIA PULCHRA

KNOWN AS PINK BABY'S TOES, the sole species in this genus forms a compact stemless rosette of fleshy leaves with flat translucent tips. When mature, the succulent is usually no more than 1 in (2.5 cm) tall and 5 in (13 cm) across. Masses of small, crimson to pink, daisylike flowers with white bases open in sun from late spring until autumn. Tiny brown fruits follow. This succulent usually lives for only five years but will slowly form offsets that can be used to propagate new plants. This frost-tender species needs sunny conditions and a minimum temperature of 41°F (5°C) to thrive.

Fleshy, toelike leaves with a rough gray skin

Leaf tips have "windows" to diffuse harsh sunlight

HEIGHT AND SPREAD

	12 in/30 cm	Does not live 10 years	12 in/30 cm
	6 in/15 cm		6 in/15 cm
	0 in/0 cm		0 in/0 cm
INDOORS: 5 years' growth		**OUTDOORS:** 10 years' growth	

GASTERIA

THESE COMPACT SUCCULENTS, known as ox tongues, form a distichous fan (two facing rows of upright fleshy leaves) when young, and some spiral into a rosette as they age. They usually have dark green leaves that are variously spotted, striped, or stippled white. Related to the *Aloe* (see pp. 108–9), they also have long-lasting, tubular flowers borne sparsely on long stems. Blooms that are mostly orange or red with yellow-green tips appear in spring. Mature plants flower until winter. Their green seedpods ripen to brown. The 75 or so species, from southern and southwestern Africa, grow in sun or shade.

The pendant flowers have a swollen middle, known as a gastro, or belly

Small flowers open in succession from the bottom of the stem

HEIGHT AND SPREAD

G. fuscopunctata · G. armstrongii · G. obtusa · G. batesiana

12 in/30 cm
6 in/15 cm
0 in/0 cm

INDOORS: 5 years' growth

2 ft/60 cm
12 in/30 cm
0 in/0 cm

OUTDOORS: 10 years' growth

Gasteria fuscopunctata

When it flowers, this succulent produces elegant, arching sprays of dainty, pendant flowers. The pointed leaves grow up to 12 in (30 cm) or more, making this species one of the largest in its genus, so it is most suitable for a large collection or a spacious position. The spiky rosette is dark green and is patterned with sparse brownish spots. A slow-growing plant, it eventually develops into a clump.

H 2 ft (60 cm), S 3 ft (90 cm). Min. 41°F (5°C).

Flower spikes grow from near the center of the rosette

Leaves have rough skin

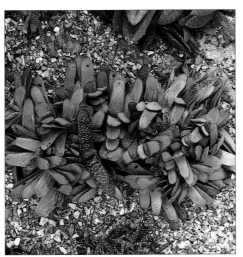

Gasteria armstrongii

Each small fan is formed of a few thick leaves, which are normally rough and tongue-shaped. The leaves vary considerably in size and shade of green from plant to plant. This succulent forms a low clump.

H 9 in (23 cm), S 2 ft (60 cm). Min. 41°F (5°C).

Gasteria obtusa

When still young, the small, fan-shaped plant offsets freely to form large clumps. The leaves vary widely; they can be spotted gray or green and, occasionally, variegated with bands of white, cream, or yellow.

H 8 in (20 cm), S 3 ft (90 cm). Min. 41°F (5°C).

Gasteria batesiana

Generally dark green with lighter bands or spots, the leaves of this species are also dagger-shaped and concave on their upper surfaces. They are arranged in a tight rosette, which offsets fairly readily in cultivation to form large clumps.

H 6 in (15 cm), S 3 ft (90 cm). Min. 41°F (5°C).

GIBBAEUM

THE FLESHY LEAVES OF THESE compact carpeting plants from the Cape of South Africa range from pea-shaped to long and fingerlike. They are often arranged in pairs of unequal length, with the longer leaf being slightly hooked at the tip. White to violet-red, daisylike flowers are produced near the stem tips in spring and sometimes in autumn. Their small green seedpods are woody when ripe. The 20 or so species grow best in sun. Water them well in autumn for a show of flowers; at other times water sparingly.

2 in (5 cm) wide flowers

HEIGHT AND SPREAD

G. velutinum   G. album   G. heathii   G. petrense

12 in/30 cm
6 in/15 cm
0 in/0 cm

INDOORS: 5 years' growth

12 in/30 cm
6 in/15 cm
0 in/0 cm

OUTDOORS: 10 years' growth

Gibbaeum velutinum

Asymmetrical paired leaves provide a contrast to relatively large flowers that vary from white to lavender or red. These are borne continuously from spring through to autumn.
H 5 in (13 cm), S 3 ft (90 cm). Min. 41°F (5°C).

Some leaves have hooked tips

Gibbaeum album

Each pair of downy white leaves on this neat slow-growing species forms a swollen, almost globular head. The heads divide after flowering and eventually spread to create a low knobbly mound. Not as free-flowering as other species in the genus, this succulent bears white blooms. The plant is prone to rot if it is overwatered.
H 4 in (10 cm), S 9 in (23 cm). Min. 41°F (5°C).

Gibbaeum heathii

In cultivation, this species forms dense mounds of soft, pealike heads. These proliferate into low carpets that are comparatively large for the genus. The flowers, in various shades of cream and rose, usually appear only in favorable outdoor situations. Although this succulent is moderately easy to grow, it requires protection from prolonged wet or damp conditions in order to guard against rot. G. *heathii* is quite widespread in the wild.
H 2 in (5 cm), S 3 ft (90 cm). Min. 41°F (5°C).

Gibbaeum petrense

Although it has very small heads, which are composed of pairs of thick triangular leaves only ½ in (1 cm) long, this species spreads into large, pale gray-green carpets that can trail over banks or walls. The flowers are produced more readily than in other *Gibbaeum* species and may be pink to reddish violet.
H 2 in (5 cm), S 3 ft (90 cm). Min. 41°F (5°C).

GRAPTOPETALUM

THIS GENUS FROM ARIZONA AND MEXICO is related to *Echeveria* (see pp. 118–9). The 12 species have green, blue, or gray rosettes, and some are speckled. Their small, upward-facing, starry flowers are long lasting, fairly large and shaded white to red. They appear most on long stems in spring to winter. Tiny seedpods follow. *Graptopetalum* prefer bright light, but some can suffer scorch in hot sun.

Often slate-gray leaves may vary in shape

HEIGHT AND SPREAD

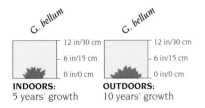

G. bellum | G. bellum

12 in/30 cm
6 in/15 cm
0 in/0 cm
INDOORS:
5 years' growth

12 in/30 cm
6 in/15 cm
0 in/0 cm
OUTDOORS:
10 years' growth

Graptopetalum bellum

Outstanding for its long-lasting, clear red, spring flowers borne on short stems, this species makes a good house plant. With age, it offsets to form clumps. Although it needs moderate summer watering, it rots in cold and damp, or very wet conditions.
H 4 in (10 cm), S 30 in (76 cm). Min. 50°F (10°C).

x GRAPTOVERIA

THESE INTERGENERIC HYBRIDS are crosses between the genera of *Graptopetalum* (see above) and *Echeveria* (see pp.118–9). In the wild, the species from both genera vary hugely according to the habitat, so the many hybrids and cultivars bred from them are difficult to identify correctly. They do, however, retain the basic characteristics common to both parent groups. Cuttings that are taken from the same plant but grown under different conditions produce dissimilar plants.

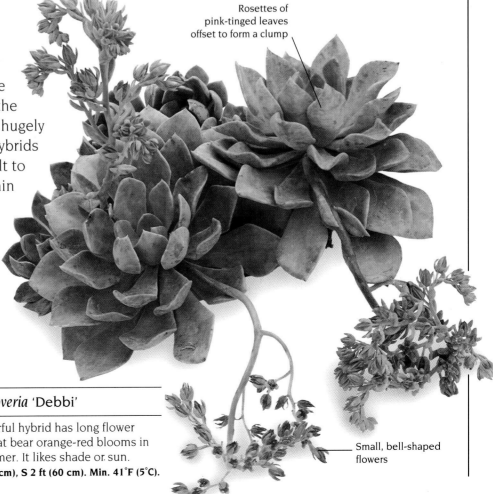

Rosettes of pink-tinged leaves offset to form a clump

Small, bell-shaped flowers

HEIGHT AND SPREAD

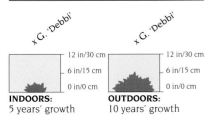

x G. 'Debbi' | x G. 'Debbi'

12 in/30 cm
6 in/15 cm
0 in/0 cm
INDOORS:
5 years' growth

12 in/30 cm
6 in/15 cm
0 in/0 cm
OUTDOORS:
10 years' growth

x *Graptoveria* 'Debbi'

This colorful hybrid has long flower spikes that bear orange-red blooms in late summer. It likes shade or sun.
H 6 in (15 cm), S 2 ft (60 cm). Min. 41°F (5°C).

HAWORTHIA

THIS GENUS OF SOUTHERN AFRICAN rosette-shaped succulents currently includes up to 80 small species. They are hugely variable in form, resulting in a confusing number of names. Leaf shapes and markings vary, but a pattern of raised white spots is common. Many species take on red to orange hues while dormant in hot weather, then regain their green color when they start to grow in cooler weather. The long-lasting clusters of small white flowers appear from spring to autumn on long, thin stalks and are followed by green berries. These plants prefer diffuse sun or shade and offset freely into spreading clumps.

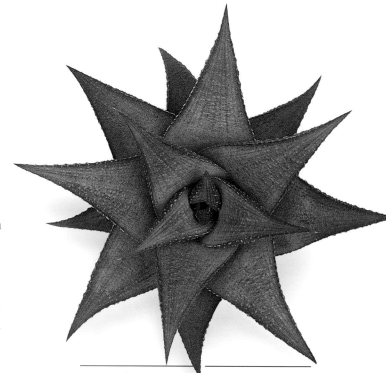

Haworthia venosa

This particularly variable species displays a range of fine foliage. The broad, triangular, sometimes stippled leaves may be olive-green to purple-brown and their upper surfaces are often crisscrossed with transparent markings. Both stemless and short-stemmed forms readily produce underground stems, which form new plants some distance from the parent.
H 4 in (10 cm), S 12 in (30 cm). Min. 41°F (5°C).

HEIGHT AND SPREAD

H. venosa   *H. attenuata v. clariperla*   *H. cymbiformis*   *H. truncata*   *H. coarctata v. adelaidensis*   *H. pumila*

	12 in/30 cm
	6 in/15 cm
	0 in/0 cm

INDOORS: 5 years' growth

	12 in/30 cm
	6 in/15 cm
	0 in/0 cm

OUTDOORS: 10 years' growth

Haworthia attenuata v. *clariperla*

Zebra plant
The numerous raised white dots on the leaves of this plant, often wrongly named H. *fasciata*, sometimes merge into stripes.
H 3 in (8 cm), S 3 ft (90 cm). Min. 41°F (5°C).

Haworthia cymbiformis

In full sun, the soft, semitransparent leaves of this robust variable succulent turn slightly orange. The rosette offsets rapidly in shade to form a low spreading mat.
H 3 in (8 cm), S 3 ft (90 cm). Min. 41°F (5°C).

Haworthia truncata

Cut window plant
These fat leaves resemble stepping stones. They are variable, slow growing and have opaque "windows" at the tips (see p. 11).
H 2 in (5 cm), S 15 in (38 cm). Min 41°F (5°C).

Large white dots emboss
incurving leaves

Haworthia coarctata v. adelaidensis

This plant is one of the few species in its
genus to form such striking clumps of tough,
leafy columns. Normally dark green,
it turns a rich purple-red in full
sun. The leaves are often
stippled with bands of
white spots.
**H 6 in (15 cm), S 15 in (38 cm).
Min. 41˚F (5˚C).**

Stem surrounded
by tightly packed,
usually scalelike leaves

Haworthia pumila

Pearly dots
Although *pumila* means small and this plant
was once thought to be a small A*loe* (see
pp. 108–9), in fact it has the largest rosette
of the *Haworthia* genus as well as a sturdy
flower stem. The rosette offsets with age.
H 6 in (15 cm), S 12 in (30 cm). Min. 41˚F (5˚C).

Leaves curve in
toward stem tip

Compact upright clump
formed by stem
branching at base

HOODIA

THESE SMALL SPINY SUCCULENTS are from southern Africa and are known as African hats. The 20 or so species form clumps of short, upright, sometimes branching stems in muted greens. Bizarre flowers, which are large, flat, and saucerlike, and mottled dark yellow, brown, or red, appear freely near the stem tips in summer. Twin-horned seedpods follow. Cultivating these slow-growing plants can be difficult; they need temperatures of at least 50°F (10°C) in sun or shade and tend to rot in winter dampness or shrivel if too dry.

HEIGHT AND SPREAD

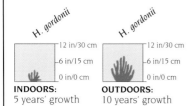

INDOORS:
5 years' growth

OUTDOORS:
10 years' growth

Hoodia gordonii

If kept warm and correctly watered, this is one of the least difficult *Hoodia* species to grow. It has pale green to purple, branching stems with short woody tubercles that are sometimes pointed. This succulent readily forms a clump. The straw-colored to brown flowers can vary in shape.
H and S 12 in (30 cm). Min. 55°F (13°C).

HUERNIA

THE UPRIGHT BRANCHING STEMS of these mostly small plants slowly spread into large mats. The 60 or so species from southern and eastern Africa often have flowers that look like carrion to attract pollinating insects. The long-lasting, star-shaped blooms, with deep cups and twin-horned seedpods, cluster at the bases of new stems from summer to autumn. These plants are challenging to grow, but tolerate sun or shade.

HEIGHT AND SPREAD

INDOORS: 5 years' growth

OUTDOORS: 10 years' growth

Huernia zebrina

Lifebuoy flower, owl's eyes
This is one of the few *Huernia* species with an annulus, or distinct raised ring, on the flower, which can be greenish to sulfur-yellow with maroon markings.
H 6 in (15 cm), S 15 in (38 cm). Min. 50°F (10°C).

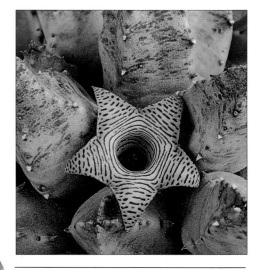

Huernia striata

Striking flowers, with their characteristic star-shaped petals, nestle at the base of the angular mottled stems. These blooms are pale green to yellow-brown, with dark purple stripes and often a small, black, central cup. This small *Huernia* species has short, blue-green, slightly toothed stems that spread slowly to form a carpet.
H 6 in (15 cm), S 15 in (38 cm). Min. 45°F (7°C).

Sharp, evenly spaced teeth

Huernia thuretii

The flowers of this small succulent can differ greatly but they are most often buff-colored with blood-red spots or stripes. Initially angular, the upright stems sometimes branch so that the plant's compact clump gradually spreads to form a low mat. The stems vary in color from a dull green to reddish purple.

H 6 in (15 cm), S 15 in (38 cm). Min. 50°F (10°C).

JATROPHA

IN THIS LARGE GROUP of about 175 species, there are only about 20 succulents. These succulents are very diverse in form, ranging from leafy, bushy plants to swollen-trunked trees. They can be slow or fast growing and are found throughout the world, mostly in tropical regions in sun or shade. They usually tolerate a minimum temperature of 50°F (10°C), and can be easy or difficult to cultivate. Related to the *Euphorbia*, or spurge (see pp. 120–21), they have similar flowers; these are usually tiny, grouped in threes, and enclosed by cup-shaped, colored leaf bracts. The green fruits can be pea- to walnut-sized.

HEIGHT AND SPREAD

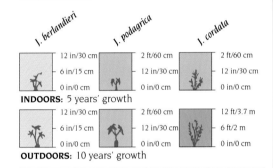

J. berlandieri	J. podagrica	J. cordata
12 in/30 cm	2 ft/60 cm	2 ft/60 cm
6 in/15 cm	12 in/30 cm	12 in/30 cm
0 in/0 cm	0 in/0 cm	0 in/0 cm

INDOORS: 5 years' growth

12 in/30 cm	2 ft/60 cm	12 ft/3.7 m
6 in/15 cm	12 in/30 cm	6 ft/2 m
0 in/0 cm	0 in/0 cm	0 in/0 cm

OUTDOORS: 10 years' growth

Large, bright green leaves have three lobes

Peeling bark can be light brown to gray-green

Swollen stem

Short annual stems with blue-green foliage

Jatropha berlandieri

The small, round caudex, or swollen trunk, produces many long-lasting spikes of poppy-red flowers from the tips of its short stems in summer. Green, pealike berries follow. This plant is slow-growing, does well in sun or shade, but tends to rot in cold damp.

H 6 in (15 cm), S 8 in (20 cm). Min. 50°F (10°C).

Jatropha cordata

Tree jatropha

This sun-loving succulent forms a bush or a swollen-trunked tree and is fairly easy to cultivate. Its five-lobed leaves and small, long-lasting, summer flowers appear near the ends of the smooth shiny branches.

H 30 ft (9 m), S 12 ft (3.7 m). Min. 50°F (10°C).

Jatropha podagrica

Interesting as a pot plant because of its swollen stem, this species slowly becomes a large branching tree. Given warmth and sun, it grows easily and blooms almost constantly in summer and autumn, bearing clusters of scarlet flowers at the stem tips.

H 5 ft (1.5 m), S 2 ft (60 cm). Min. 55°F (13°C).

KALANCHOE

THE 200 SPECIES IN THIS GENUS are widespread in subtropical and tropical countries throughout the world. They vary greatly, from small leafy succulents to huge treelike plants. Species and hybrids are equally suitable as house plants; many are grown for their decorative, often hairy foliage and some of the trailing species are excellent in hanging baskets. The mostly bell-shaped, long-lasting flowers vary in color from white, yellow, or orange to brown, red, or purple. They appear at the stem tips mainly in early spring, but also occasionally in autumn. Small, brown, dry seedpods appear after flowering. These succulents are sometimes fast-growing and many are easy to cultivate in sun or shade, but several species cannot tolerate low temperatures.

Kalanchoe beharensis

Felt bush, elephant's ears
Large, olive- to gray-green leaves with velvety bronze hairs give this sun-loving plant its common names. The slender stems quickly grow into a large bush or tree. Minute, yellow-green flowers appear in spring on mature plants only. Plantlets, which form on the stalks of cut leaves (see p. 155), grow easily into new plants.
H 12 ft (3.7 m), S 7 ft (2.1 m). Min. 45°F.(7°C).

HEIGHT AND SPREAD

K. rhombopilosa K. tomentosa K. fedtschenkoi 'Variegata' K. blossfeldiana 'Flaming Katy' K. x kewensis K. tubiflora K. beharensis

INDOORS: 5 years' growth
12 in/30 cm — 6 in/15 cm — 0 in/0 cm
4 ft/1.2 m — 2 ft/60 cm — 0 in/0 cm
4 ft/1.2 m — 2 ft/60 cm — 0 in/0 cm

OUTDOORS: 10 years' growth
12 in/30 cm — 6 in/15 cm — 0 in/0 cm
4 ft/1.2 m — 2 ft/60 cm — 0 in/0 cm
8 ft/2.4 m — 4 ft/1.2 m — 0 in/0 cm

Leaves usually spotted dark red

Leaves are generally pale blue-green

Darker leaf tips vary from reddish to golden or dark brown

Kalanchoe rhombopilosa

Flat whorls of gray-green to white leaves adorn short upright stems that, with age, form a small prostrate bush. It bears tiny, greenish yellow spring flowers. A hard knock can defoliate this fragile plant, but its leaves root easily. Plant in sun or shade.
H 6 in (15 cm), S 15 in (38 cm). Min. 45°F (7°C).

Kalanchoe tomentosa

Panda plant, plush plant, pussy ears
Grown for its soft felty leaves rather than its tiny summer flowers, this bushy species is an ideal house plant when young. It thrives in sun or shade. Grow new, neater plants from cuttings after three years or so.
H 2 ft (60 cm), S 4 ft (1.2 m). Min. 45°F (7°C).

Leaf edges are tinged red in bright shade

Aerial roots

Kalanchoe fedtschenkoi 'Variegata'

South American air plant, aurora borealis
This fast-growing, spreading bush has variegated leaves and clusters of dusty pink spring flowers. It grows best in shade.
H 2 ft (60 cm), S unlimited. Min. 45°F (7°C).

Kalanchoe blossfeldiana 'Flaming Katy'

In open ground, this dwarf hybrid eventually forms a dense spreading bush of often red-edged, glossy leaves. Small flowers appear in winter or early spring if there is less than 12 hours of daylight. This shade-loving plant is often forced and sold in flower as a house plant all year round.
H and S unlimited. Min. 50°F (10°C).

Kalanchoe x *kewensis*

When young, this elegant hybrid forms a bush of upright stems. In spring, vivid pink flowers appear, which contrast well with the deep green, antlerlike leaves. Like many other bushy *Kalanchoe*, it becomes untidy with age and is best grown anew from cuttings. It thrives in sun or shade.
H 2 ft (60 cm), S 3 ft (90 cm). Min. 45°F (7°C).

Plantlets grow at the leaf tips and are easily shed to form new plants

Leaves can be blotched pink, purple, gray, or greenish brown

Hairless central stem branches after flowering, eventually becoming prostrate

Kalanchoe tubiflora

Mother of thousands
A starburst of long tubular leaves, each with a frill of plantlets, grows from the central upright stem. The numerous plantlets are very robust, whether in sun or shade, and will even take root in carpets or fabric. Once the plant reaches its mature size, dense clusters of orange-red to purple flowers are produced in early spring.
H 2 ft (60 cm), S unlimited. Min. 41°F (5°C).

LAMPRANTHUS

MASSES OF VIVIDLY HUED, daisylike blooms in almost any color but blue make these ice plants, or Livingstone daisies, excellent ground cover in frost-free areas. There are more than 60 mostly South African species. Whether bushy, creeping, or trailing, they readily adapt to and stabilize arid soil. Some flower over long periods between spring and autumn; others have a short flowering season. The blooms grow near the stem tips and need sun to open. Fleshy fruits, which are woody when ripe, soon follow. There are countless hybrids and forms of this fast-growing succulent. Although some species tolerate light frost, they can rot if it is cold and damp.

HEIGHT AND SPREAD

L. haworthii   L. spectabilis   L. aurantiacus

12 in/30 cm   12 in/30 cm
6 in/15 cm   6 in/15 cm
0 in/0 cm   0 in/0 cm
INDOORS: 5 years' growth

2 ft/60 cm   4 ft/1.2 m
12 in/30 cm   2 ft/60 cm
0 in/0 cm   0 in/0 cm
OUTDOORS: 10 years' growth

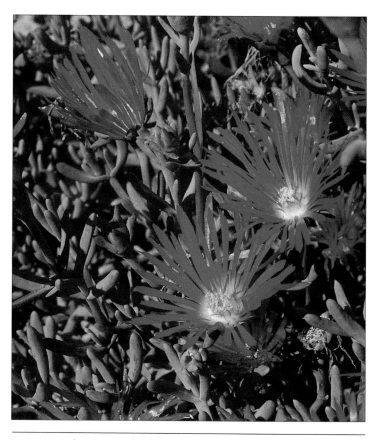

Lampranthus spectabilis

Well worth growing for its long flowering season, this sun-loving, prostrate bush produces brilliant, white to purple flowers, which are about 2 in (5 cm) across, throughout spring. The succulent's narrow tubular leaves are gray-green.

H 2 ft (60 cm), S unlimited. Min. 36°F (2°C).

Lampranthus haworthii

In spring, this spectacular succulent is entirely smothered by large, bright pink, magenta, or purple flowers, which are about 2 in (5 cm) across. More blooms appear occasionally during the summer. Its candelabra-like leaves are blue-green. This plant does best in sun and is a good choice for frost-free gardens or for tubs. It quickly spreads sideways, forming a domed bush.

H 2 ft (60 cm), S unlimited. Min. 36°F (2°C).

Lampranthus aurantiacus

The vivid orange flowers are about 2 in (5 cm) in diameter and are produced in profusion in spring. This sun-loving bush has upright, then prostrate, stems and blue-green tapering leaves.

H 2 ft (60 cm), S unlimited. Min. 41°F (5°C).

LITHOPS

THE TINY SUCCULENTS that belong to this fascinating South African genus consist of united pairs of swollen leaves and are known as living stones or pebble plants. Most of the 60 species vary widely in color and in intensity of patterning. In the heat of summer, they become semidormant. Then in early autumn, white or yellow daisylike flowers grow from the leaf fissure. Small fleshy seedpods follow. After a winter rest, *Lithops* burst into growth in late spring. These slow-growing sun-lovers do not tolerate incorrect watering or poor light.

HEIGHT AND SPREAD

L. salicola
L. pseudotruncatella
v. pulmonuncula
L. aucampiae
L. karasmontana

12 in/30 cm
6 in/15 cm
0 in/0 cm
INDOORS: 5 years' growth

12 in/30 cm
6 in/15 cm
0 in/0 cm
OUTDOORS: 10 years' growth

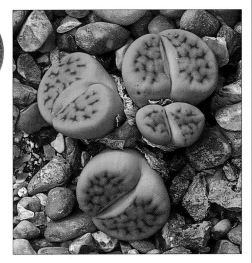

Pure white daisylike blooms open in afternoon sun

Pairs of leaves form a small clump

Flower bud

Lithops salicola

Only one other *Lithops* species has mostly slate-gray leaf heads with gray patterning. This variable succulent is one of the taller *Lithops* and its leaf heads, atypically for the genus, stand well above the soil surface.
H 2 in (5 cm), S 9 in (23 cm). Min. 36°F (2°C).

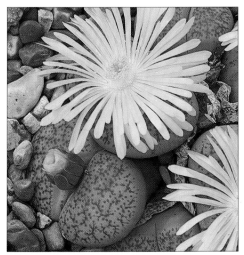

Lithops pseudotruncatella
v. *pulmonuncula*

Young plants have a shallow slit across the finely marked, round or oval leaves. Uneven in size and mostly flat-topped, the gray or brown leaves sit almost flush with the soil.
H 1 in (2.5 cm), S 9 in (23 cm). Min. 36°F (2°C).

Lithops aucampiae

The gray-brown leaf heads, up to 2 in (5 cm) across, are large for *Lithops* and flat-topped. One leaf in each pair is usually smaller than the other. The plant forms a small clump. Its flowers open in sun.
H 1 in (2.5 cm), S 9 in (23 cm). Min. 36°F (2°C).

Lithops karasmontana

This species is very variable: the leaf heads may be blue-gray to brown and many have muted markings. The flat-topped leaf heads often have one leaf smaller than the other. The flowers are white.
H 1 in (2.5 cm), S 9 in (23 cm). Min. 36°F (2°C).

MONADENIUM

ORIGINALLY, THIS GROUP came mostly from eastern and southern tropical Africa. Like *Euphorbia* (see pp. 120–21), the plants have tiny true flowers surrounded by small leaf bracts. The bracts are often hooded, are shaded white, cream, pink, or red, and appear in spring, summer, or autumn on young growth. Small green berries follow. Some of the 50 slow- to fast-growing species have underground tubers and annual leafy growth; others form small bushes, and several are large and treelike. With a few exceptions, *Monadenium* species are challenging to grow; most require high temperatures in sun or shade.

Long-lasting leaf bracts

Slim stem up to 18 in (46 cm) long

Tubercles are diamond-shaped

HEIGHT AND SPREAD

M. ritchiei

M. guentheri

M. rhizophorum v. stoloniferum

M. magnificum

M. lugardae

12 in/30 cm
6 in/15 cm
0 in/0 cm

12 in/30 cm
6 in/15 cm
0 in/0 cm

INDOORS: 5 years' growth

12 in/30 cm
6 in/15 cm
0 in/0 cm

4 ft/1.2 m
2 ft/60 cm
0 in/0 cm

OUTDOORS: 10 years' growth

Monadenium ritchiei

The strange knobbly look of the stem is due to its geometric tubercles. The stem often becomes prostrate and branches to form a mound. Its stubby spines are brown. Small fleshy leaves, which are usually darker green on the upper surface, appear on new growth and are followed by bracts in summer. This plant soon rots if overwatered.
H 12 in (30 cm), S 4 ft (1.2 m).
Min. 55°F (13°C).

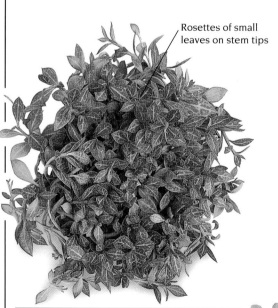

Rosettes of small leaves on stem tips

Monadenium guentheri

New growth briefly bears variable fleshy leaves. The stem has long hexagonal tubercles and becomes prostrate in habit, branching into a dense clump. In summer, long-lasting hooded bracts, which are greenish white with purple spots, appear on the stem tips.
H 12 in (30 cm), S 4 ft (1.2 m).
Min. 50°F (10°C).

Monadenium rhizophorum v. stoloniferum

This plant forms small sparse clumps from underground stems; its top-growth also roots in the soil. Pale green summer bracts, spotted green or red, grow at the stem tips. This shade-lover needs a dry dormancy.
H 3 in (8 cm), S unlimited. Min. 50°F (10°C).

Stem branches at base

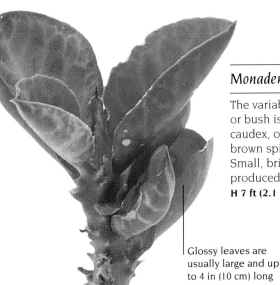

Monadenium magnificum

The variable foliage of this fast-growing tree or bush is borne on an angular stem with a caudex, or swollen base (see p. 10). Red-brown spine clusters grow on the stem. Small, bright scarlet, long-lasting bracts are produced near the stem tips in summer.
H 7 ft (2.1 m), S 4 ft (1.2 m). Min. 50°F (10°C).

Glossy leaves are usually large and up to 4 in (10 cm) long

Thickness of stem can vary

Monadenium lugardae

The succulent stems bear rosettes of foliage and form fine clumps. In summer, hooded pale green bracts grow near the stem tips. The plant rots in cold, damp conditions.
H 2 ft (60 cm), S 3 ft (90 cm). Min. 50°F (10°C).

PACHYPHYTUM

THESE MEXICAN SUCCULENTS have small to medium-sized, sometimes stemless rosettes of fleshy leaves, in shades of green, blue, orange, red, or purple. Related to *Echeveria* (see pp. 118–19), the 12 or so species produce arching spikes of long-lasting, pendant flowers enclosed by bell-shaped sepals. Tiny seedpods follow the flowers in spring, summer, or autumn. *Pachyphytum* species are slow-growing and prefer either sun or shade.

HEIGHT AND SPREAD

P. oviferum

P. viride

12 in/ 30 cm
6 in/15 cm
0 in/0 cm

12 in/30 cm
6 in/15 cm
0 in/0 cm

INDOORS: 5 years' growth

12 in/30 cm
6 in/15 cm
0 in/0 cm

2 ft/60 cm
12 in/30 cm
0 in/0 cm

OUTDOORS: 10 years' growth

Pachyphytum viride

Rosettes of green, purple-red, or orange leaves are carried on a slow-growing upright stem that is relatively tall. The plant eventually forms a clump and grows well in sun or shade. Greenish white flowers with wine-red petals are borne on arching spikes in spring and early summer.
H and S 2 ft (60 cm). Min. 45°F (7°C).

Pachyphytum oviferum

Sugar almond plant, pearly moonstones
The powdery, often pinkish blue rosettes of leaves resemble sugared almonds. They grow along short clumping stems. Arching spikes of flowers with powdery, gray-green sepals and red petals appear in spring and early summer. The plant prefers sun.
H 6 in (15 cm), S unlimited. Min. 43°F (6°C).

PACHYPODIUM

THESE WIDELY VARIABLE succulents are closely related to *Adenium* (see p. 103). They usually have swollen bases or trunks, which are gray to brown and spiny. Some of the 12 species from southern Africa and Madagascar take 25 years to reach 5 in (13 cm) in diameter, while others quickly soar to 30 ft (9 m). All but the treelike species are deciduous. Trumpet-shaped flowers, which are white, red, or yellow appear at the stem tips in different seasons. Twin-horned seedpods follow. Challenging to grow, these frost-tender sun-lovers are very prone to rot. The rarer, slow-growing species are often grafted onto P. *lamerei*.

HEIGHT AND SPREAD

P. *namaquanum*   P. *rosulatum*   P. *succulentum*   P. *lamerei*

12 in/30 cm
6 in/15 cm
0 in/0 cm
INDOORS: 5 years' growth

12 in/30 cm
6 in/15 cm
0 in/0 cm

2 ft/60 cm
12 in/30 cm
0 in/0 cm
OUTDOORS: 10 years' growth

4 ft/1.2 m
2 ft/60 cm
0 in/0 cm

Pachypodium namaquanum

Half man, ghost-man
Rare in the wild, this palmlike plant is now available in cultivation. Its solitary, erect brown stem with long pointed spines tilts its head towards the sun. In warm climates, the large but slow-growing stem produces flowers after 10–15 years. Small red-brown blooms appear on the plant crown in spring. In colder climates, flowers rarely emerge and the plant needs pampering to survive the winter without rotting.
H 5 ft (1.5 m), S 9 in (23 cm). Min. 50°F (10°C).

Spines are reddish brown

Short sharp spines

Swollen stem ranges from long and slender to short and squat

Pachypodium rosulatum

Both the leaves and the large grayish trunk vary in shape. The trunk is swollen from an early age and slowly forms a head of slim branches. Open-faced canary-yellow flowers appear in late winter and in early spring, before the plant comes into leaf.
H 5 ft (1.5 m), S 3 ft (90 cm). Min. 55°F (13°C).

Pachypodium lamerei

Madagascar palm
If given warmth and care, this treelike species reaches a flowering size of 4 ft (1.2 m) in ten years. In summer, it bears fragrant flowers, which are white with a gold throat. After flowering, the stems branch. The spines are long, gray, and pointed.
H 20 ft (6 m), S 6 ft (2 m). Min. 50°F (10°C).

Pachypodium succulentum

This variable species usually has a swollen, half-buried stem topped with slender but bushy branches. Small, trumpet-shaped, white to crimson or pink flowers are produced quite freely towards the stem tips during spring and summer. The succulent is relatively easy to grow.
H 5 ft (1.5 m), S 6 ft (2 m). Min. 45°F (7°C).

PEDILANTHUS

ALTHOUGH WIDESPREAD IN THE CARIBBEAN and from the southern US to northern South America, these 12 bushy species, known as rickrack plants, are closely related to *Euphorbia* (see pp. 120–21). They differ from *Euphorbia* mainly in their flowers, which are enclosed by small leaf bracts shaped like a bird's head and are green, red, or brown. Except for *P. tithymaloides* and its forms, *Pedilanthus* succulents are seldom cultivated.

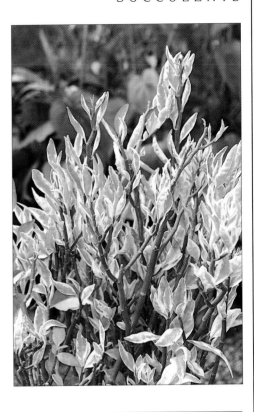

HEIGHT AND SPREAD

P. tithymaloides 'Variegata'

12 in/30 cm	8 ft/2.4 m
6 in/15 cm	4 ft/1.2 m
0 in/0 cm	0 in/0 cm
INDOORS: 5 years' growth	**OUTDOORS:** 10 years' growth

Pedilanthus tithymaloides 'Variegata'

Redbird flower
With its zigzagging stems and white or pink variegated foliage, this cultivar makes a fine pot plant. Tiny greenish flowers and red to yellow bracts appear near the stem tips from summer to autumn. The small fruits are green. The plant dislikes harsh sun and cold, damp conditions.
H 9 ft (2.7 m), S 5 ft (1.5 m). Min. 55°F (13°C).

SANSEVIERIA

THESE BOWSTRING HEMP PLANTS from tropical Africa are very variable. Their rosettes of leaves, usually dark green and fleshy, differ in size and shape and are often variegated. Like the *Agave* (see pp. 106–7), each rosette dies after flowering. Spikes of pale, often scented flowers and white to orange berries appear from spring to autumn. The 60 species grow well in sun or shade if sparingly watered. Fine border plants in warm areas, they are also good in wire-mesh hanging baskets, where their underground stems push through to form a cascade of rosettes.

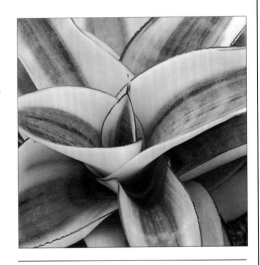

Sword-shaped leaves usually have silvery bands and a broad yellow or cream border

HEIGHT AND SPREAD

S. trifasciata 'Golden Hahnii'   *S. trifasciata* 'Laurentii'

12 in/30 cm	4 ft/1.2 m
6 in/15 cm	2 ft/60 cm
0 in/0 cm	0 in/0 cm
INDOORS: 5 years' growth	

12 in/30 cm	4 ft/1.2 m
6 in/15 cm	2 ft/60 cm
0 in/0 cm	0 in/0 cm
OUTDOORS: 10 years' growth	

Sansevieria trifasciata 'Golden Hahnii'

Golden bird's nest
Each rosette is no more than 12 in (30 cm) across, but it offsets to make large clumps. Protect its variegated leaves from hot sun.
H 6 in (15 cm), S unlimited. Min. 55°F (13°C).

Sansevieria trifasciata 'Laurentii'

Mother-in-law's tongue, snake plant
In good summer light, tall spikes of pale green flowers and orange berries appear. This plant grows best in a small pot.
H 4 ft (1.2 m), S unlimited. Min. 55°F (13°C).

SEDUM

THE SEVERAL HUNDRED stonecrop plants include slow-
to fast-growing succulents from all over the world.
Most hardy species are small bushes or carpeting
plants and make good, albeit invasive, ground cover.
The tender species are more fleshy and diverse,
ranging from small rosettes to large bushes. Free-
flowering, *Sedum* mostly bear flat-topped clusters of
starry, long-lasting, white, gold, or red flowers and
tiny seedpods at the stem tips. Tender species bloom
in spring; hardy ones in summer and autumn. These
pale to blue-green plants like sun or shade.

Stems may shed
their leaves in
dry conditions

LENGTH/HEIGHT AND SPREAD

S. nussbaumeranum *S. furfuraceum* *S. kamtschaticum* *S. spathulifolium* 'Cape Blanco' *S. morganianum* *S. acre* *S. frutescens*

12 in/30 cm
6 in/15 cm
0 in/0 cm
INDOORS: 5 years' growth

2 ft/60 cm
12 in/30 cm
0 in/0 cm

12 in/30 cm
6 in/15 cm
0 in/0 cm
OUTDOORS: 10 years' growth

4 ft/1.2 m
2 ft/60 cm
0 in/0 cm

Tiny red flowers

Sedum kamtschaticum

In winter, this mat-forming succulent sheds
most of its abundant, slightly toothed
leaves. A skeleton of bare stems with only
small rosettes of leaves at the tips remains.
The golden or orange flowers are produced
in summer and autumn.
H 3 in (8 cm), S unlimited. Min. -30°F (-35°C).

Sedum spathulifolium 'Cape Blanco'

Although it grows quite well in shade, this
small carpeting plant has leaves of a darker
purple and silver hue in full sun. It is good
for growing in rock gardens and wall
crevices. The summer flowers are yellow.
H 2 in (5 cm), S unlimited. Min. 5°F (-15°C).

Sedum morganianum

Burro's tail, donkey's tail
Pale, powdery green leaves clothe the long
pendant stems so that they appear plaited.
Light pink to scarlet flowers cluster at the
stem tips in spring. This shade-loving plant
needs careful watering to guard against rot.
L 9 ft (2.7 m), S unlimited. Min. 45°F (7°C).

Sedum nussbaumeranum

Golden sedum
In shade, the leaves at the stem tips are pale greenish yellow but in sun they are rust in color. The spring flowers are bright white.
H 9 in (23 cm), S unlimited. Min. 41°F (5°C).

Sedum furfuraceum

Tight clusters of variable, dark green to purple leaves grow at the tips of the creeping stems. The leaves are very dark if grown in the full sun that this small, slow-growing plant prefers. It has pale pink spring flowers.
H 3 in (8 cm), S 3 ft (90 cm). Min. 41°F (5°C).

Sedum acre

Biting stonecrop, common stonecrop
Ideal for planting in crevices or in paths, this dwarf creeping plant flowers freely in summer, producing innumerable short-stemmed heads of tiny golden flowers. Its leaves vary in shape and size. The plant is very easy to grow in sun or shade, but can become invasive if unchecked.
H 1 in (2.5 cm), S unlimited. Min. -40°F (-40°C).

Very small leaves are shed in periods of drought

Sedum frutescens

Tree sedum
A good natural bonsai, this bush sheds its lower branches when dormant. It bears clusters of tiny white flowers in late spring.
H 5 ft (1.5 m), S 3 ft (90 cm). Min. 45°F (7°C).

Peeling skin

Swollen trunk

SEMPERVIVUM

THESE SMALL HARDY ALPINES, or houseleeks, from northern Africa and Europe, make fine rock garden and pot plants. Their neat rosettes of leaves offset freely in spring to form a spreading carpet. In free-draining and exposed conditions, many turn red or violet in midsummer while semidormant. Each rosette, when a few years old, bears a tall, long-lasting spike of starry, pink summer flowers and tiny dry seedpods, then dies. The 35 species of this sun-loving succulent hybridize prolifically, so it is difficult to identify unnamed plants.

HEIGHT AND SPREAD

S. *arachnoideum* S. 'Emerson's Giant' S. 'Oddity' S. 'Bellot's Pourpre'

			12 in/30 cm
			6 in/15 cm
			0 in/0 cm

INDOORS: 5 years' growth

			12 in/30 cm
			6 in/15 cm
			0 in/0 cm

OUTDOORS: 10 years' growth

White filaments

Compact rosettes are 1 in (2.5 cm) or less in diameter

Sempervivum arachnoideum

Cobweb houseleek

The only species with "cobwebs," which stretch from the leaf tips over the crown, this species is very common and variable in the wild. Most marked in summer, the cobweb filaments may disappear in winter.
H 1 in (2.5 cm), S 2 ft (60 cm). Min. 5°F (-15°C).

Sempervivum 'Emerson's Giant'

In summer, the pointed, scalelike leaves of this symmetrical rosette turn from green to a reddish purple color.
H 1 in (2.5 cm), S 2 ft (60 cm). Min. 5°F (-15°C)

Sempervivum 'Oddity'

Grown from a chance seedling in the US, this hybrid is valued for its unusual, quill-like leaves, tipped violet in summer, which make it look like an *Echeveria* (see pp. 118–19). It is not known to have flowered.
H 1 in (2.5 cm), S 2 ft (60 cm). Min. 5°F (-15°C).

Sempervivum 'Bellot's Pourpre'

The tightly furled leaves of this hybrid become suffused with red that becomes a rich purple in the hot summer sun. Like all *Sempervivum* with hairy or downy leaves, it needs protection from winter dampness.
H 1 in (2.5 cm), S 2 ft (60 cm). Min. 5°F (-15°C).

SENECIO

THIS HUGE GENUS OF OVER 1,000 species includes about 100 very slow-to fast-growing succulents, which are mainly from Africa and India. Grown for their decorative foliage, they are very diverse and range from small sticklike plants to large bushes. The flowers, borne on long stems in spring, summer, or autumn, resemble white or red brushes or golden daisies. They are usually long lasting. Most *Senecio* species are fairly easy to grow although some from Madagascar need warmth.

Cocoon-shaped leaves thickly covered with silvery white hairs

HEIGHT AND SPREAD

S. haworthii   S. rowleyanus   S. stapeliiformis   S. articulatus

INDOORS: 5 years' growth

OUTDOORS: 10 years' growth

Senecio haworthii

Cocoon plant
There are several forms of this sun-loving species. Mature plants eventually form a large sprawling bush. They also lose their lower leaves, so renew them from 3 in (8 cm) stem cuttings every few years (see p. 156). Cultivated plants seldom bear the yellow, daisylike flowers that grow in the wild.
H 12 in (30 cm), S 3 ft (90 cm). Min. 41°F (5°C).

Senecio articulatus

Candle plant
If watered freely its jointed stems grow very fast and long, but this species is best grown in poor, dry soil to form a compact knobbly plant. The summer-dormant succulent bears tiny, long-lasting, foul-smelling, cream flowers in autumn. It likes sun or shade.
H 3 ft (90 cm), S unlimited. Min. 41°F (5°C).

Senecio rowleyanus

String of beads
Fine trailing stems, studded with pealike, often bluish leaves, make this fast-growing sun-lover a good choice for hanging baskets. Long-lasting, cup-shaped heads of tiny white flowers, scented like hyacinths, appear near the stem tips in autumn.
H and S unlimited. Min. 41°F (5°C).

Senecio stapeliiformis

Belisha beacon plant
The variable stems grow from underground creeping stems, and are mottled green with spinelike leaves on the ribs. Long-lasting scarlet flowers appear on short stalks in summer. This plant, which likes sun or shade, can be invasive.
H 6 in (15 cm), S unlimited. Min. 41°F (5°C).

STAPELIA

FLESHY, FIVE-PETALED, FOUL-SMELLING blooms give these African succulents the name of starfish flowers or carrion plants. Sometimes huge, and mustard to maroon in hue, the summer flowers usually appear at the base of new stems; twin-horned seedpods follow. Most of the 100 slow- to fast-growing species form clumps of short, green or brown, angular stems, which briefly bear vestigial leaves along the ribs. After a few years, the older stems in the center of the clump die back. In cooler climates, rot then sets in, so the plant should be renewed from cuttings each year. *Stapelia* like sun or light shade and thrive in hanging baskets, but cannot tolerate prolonged drought or cold, damp conditions.

HEIGHT AND SPREAD

S. gettleffii *S. flavirostis* *S. grandiflora* *S. variegata*

12 in/30 cm
6 in/15 cm
0 in/0 cm

INDOORS: 5 years' growth

12 in/30 cm
6 in/15 cm
0 in/0 cm

OUTDOORS: 10 years' growth

Petals fringed
with tiny hairs

Flower stalks
grow near base
of new stem

Angular stems
have four ribs

Vestigial leaves
on ribs of new stems
look like spines

Stapelia gettleffii

Splendid yellow flowers, which vary in form, are decorated with narrow, caramel-brown to purple bands. They are about 6 in (15 cm) across, and are carried on velvety green stems. In strong sun, the stems become tinged with red. This species is one of the easiest in the genus to grow.
H 10 in (25 cm), S unlimited. Min. 50°F (10°C).

Stapelia flavirostis

This species, which is closely related to *S. grandiflora*, has longer hairs at the petal edges and variable stems. The flowers are up to 4 in (10 cm) wide and are colored rust to pale purple with bands of ocher.
H 10 in (25 cm), S unlimited. Min. 50°F (10°C).

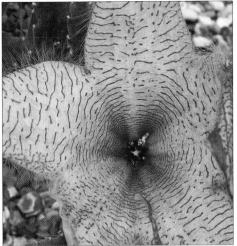

Stapelia grandiflora

Giant toad plant
Purple-brown or pale yellow flowers, up to 10 in (25 cm) wide, appear on chunky erect stems, which have tiny hairs. The stems make good grafting stocks (see pp. 158–9).
H 12 in (30 cm), S 5 ft (1.5 m). Min. 50°F (10°C).

Stapelia variegata

Mostly spotted or striped purple, the flowers are 3 in (8 cm) wide. The short, slender, robust stems of this widely grown species are green or blue-green and become tinged red in sun or drought.
H 4 in (10 cm), S 3 ft (90 cm). Min. 45°F (7°C).

TESTUDINARIA

THE STATUS OF THIS GROUP OF FIVE deciduous species from southern Africa and Mexico as a distinct genus is in dispute. Each plant has a slow-growing woody caudex (see p. 10), or tuber, which sits below or on the soil surface in sun or shade. Dormant for half the year, it produces fast-growing, climbing or twining stems with fine leaves. This top-growth dies back at the season's end. Tiny yellow flowers appear along the upper stems of older plants.

HEIGHT AND SPREAD

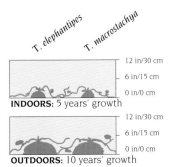

T. elephantipes   *T. macrostachya*

| 12 in/30 cm |
| 6 in/15 cm |
| 0 in/0 cm |
INDOORS: 5 years' growth

| 12 in/30 cm |
| 6 in/15 cm |
| 0 in/0 cm |
OUTDOORS: 10 years' growth

Testudinaria elephantipes

Plant this "elephant's foot" with its base below the soil to avoid dehydration, and water it well in spring to break its dormancy.
Tuber: H 2 ft (60 cm), S 3 ft (90 cm), foliage: L 15 ft (5 m). Min. 50°F (10°C).

Hemispherical caudex

Foliage normally grows from autumn until spring

Testudinaria macrostachya

Tortoise plant
Almost identical to *T. elephantipes*, this plant has slightly larger leaves and a flatter tuber.
Tuber: H 2 ft (60 cm), S 3 ft (90 cm), foliage: L 15 ft (5 m). Min. 50°F (10°C).

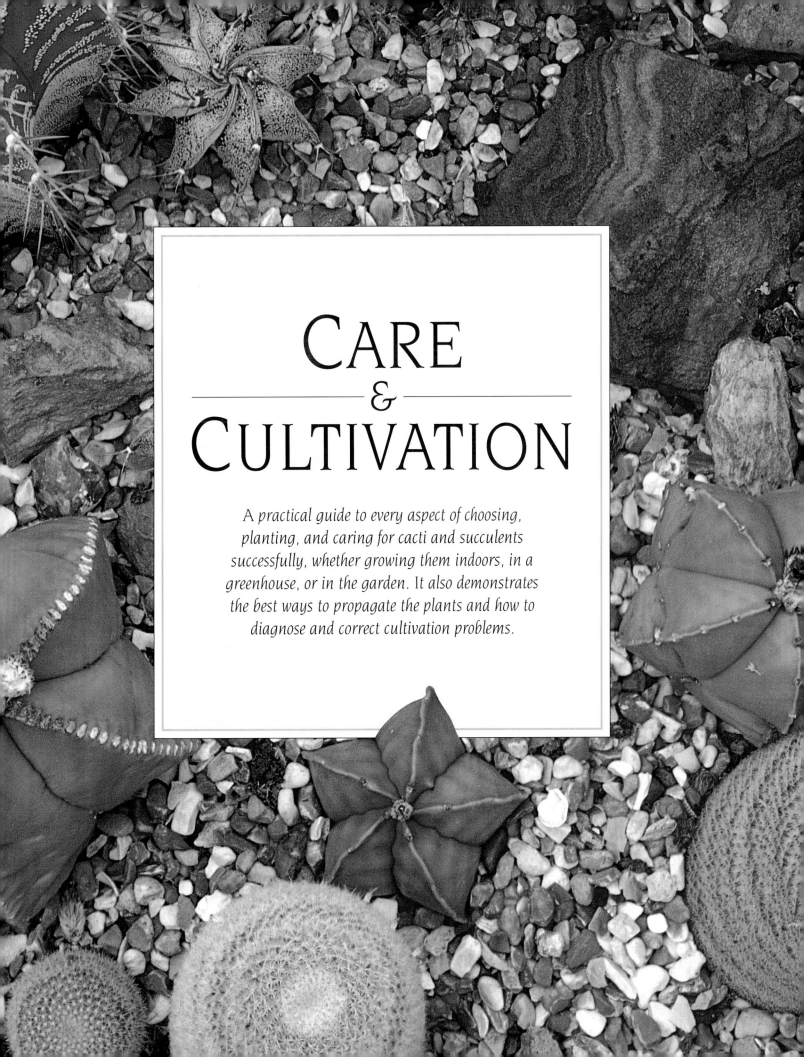

CARE
&
CULTIVATION

*A practical guide to every aspect of choosing,
planting, and caring for cacti and succulents
successfully, whether growing them indoors, in a
greenhouse, or in the garden. It also demonstrates
the best ways to propagate the plants and how to
diagnose and correct cultivation problems.*

EQUIPMENT AND MATERIALS

MOST GENERAL GARDENING EQUIPMENT is perfectly adequate for growing cacti and succulents; but there are a few items, shown here, that are especially useful. Gritty potting mixes and soils, as well as top-dressings, provide the free drainage in which these plants thrive. When propagating new plants, a few pots or seed trays on a windowsill are sufficient for most purposes. If you have a conservatory or greenhouse, install a circulatory or extractor fan or an automatic vent-opener to keep it well ventilated. In temperate or cool climates, some form of greenhouse heating is necessary for the winter.

CULTIVATION TOOLS

High-quality tools are always worth the extra initial expense because they are durable and easy to use. A few items are invaluable for handling spiny cacti, particularly those with very fine or barbed spines. Use thick gloves, a paper collar, a cloth wad, or barbecue tongs to guard against becoming attached to a cactus. Remove any spines that do become embedded with tweezers. Pat the skin with adhesive tape to strip out bristles, or soak the affected part in hot soapy water.

FOLDING PRUNING SAW
This is essential for pruning large plants, especially at an awkward angle or in a confined space. The blade folds into the handle so that the saw can fit easily into a pocket.

ALL-PURPOSE KNIFE
This is useful for all cutting jobs except heavy pruning.

RETRACTABLE-BLADE KNIFE
With its thin sharp blade, this is a good alternative for grafting to the all-purpose knife.

Square-edged, lower anvil blade

Sharp, thin-edged upper blade

Safety catch

PRUNERS
Used for pruning and taking cuttings, anvil pruners are preferable to those with a scissor action, which may not always make a clean cut, especially on woody stems. Left-handed people may find anvil pruners easier to handle than those with a scissor action.

GLOVES
Suede or leather gloves provide protection when handling spiny or thorny plants. Heavy-duty vinyl gloves are more flexible, but they can be uncomfortable in hot weather.

NARROW-BLADED TROWEL
The narrow blade makes this trowel convenient when digging between plants or in confined spaces.

DIBBER
Use this to make holes in planting mix when inserting seedlings or cuttings.

WIDGER
If lifting seedlings and cuttings, use this to avoid damaging their roots.

WIDE-BLADED TROWEL
Use this to dig in open or raised beds, plant up large containers or window boxes, and when mixing up planting mixes.

SPOON
A large spoon makes a good mini-trowel for use in small spaces.

HAND HOE
This type of hoe is useful for weeding in small areas and between closely spaced plants.

MINIMUM-MAXIMUM THERMOMETER
By recording the highest and lowest temperatures, this type of thermometer can help to find the most suitable site for a plant. It may also indicate why a plant has suffered some types of damage.

MOISTURE METER
The only accurate way to measure moisture content throughout a container or bed is with a meter. Water only when the meter indicates that the soil is dry. A meter is essential whenever watering should be kept to a minimum.

SEED TRAY
Used for growing seedlings or rooting cuttings, this should be 1¹/₂–2¹/₂ in (4–6 cm) deep to stop the potting mix from drying out too quickly.

Terracotta label | Reusable plastic label

Scratch-and-write label

Pot is deeper than it is wide | Pan is wider than it is deep

BRUSHES
A very fine paintbrush is essential for pollination. A larger soft brush is useful for removing grit, dirt, and cobwebs from spiny plants without damaging them.

PLANT LABELS
Use labels to identify plants. This is very important when propagating.

POT AND PAN WITH SAUCERS
Small, full-depth pots or larger shallow pans are suitable for most cacti and succulents. Plastic pots are more robust than terracotta ones and plants in them need less watering. Drip saucers are useful indoors.

POTTING MIXES AND TOP-DRESSINGS

Soilless potting mix

Commercial cactus potting mix

Pea-sized pebbles

Soil-based potting mix

Peat

Small gravel

Crushed stone

Many potting mixes can be used with cacti and succulents but only a few basic types are really necessary. Commercial cactus potting mixes are available but it is cheaper to make your own. For indoor plants, seedlings, or cuttings, mix two parts commercial soilless potting mix with one part ¹/₄ in (6 mm) washed grit. For outdoor containers or raised beds, make a soilless mix from three parts peat or wood bark and one part ¹/₄ in (6 mm) washed grit; use equal parts of peat and grit for small containers that do not drain easily. Add more grit if needed to improve drainage and a balanced fertilizer according to the supplier's instructions. Do not use sand since it clogs the mix and stops drainage.

Soil-based potting mixes are good for both indoor and outdoor use, but can compact if allowed to dry out. A good mix is three parts of sterilized, fibrous soil, one part peat moss, and one part ¹/₄ in (6 mm) washed grit, enriched with balanced fertilizer.

Any display is enhanced by a top-dressing that completely covers the soil. Top-dressings also reduce soil erosion and water splashmarks on the plants, conserve moisture, and suppress weeds. Use a top-dressing in a size and color appropriate to the container or bed. Local stone is best, although pumice, perlite, or pea-sized beach pebbles may also be suitable. Do not use crushed limestone, which increases the soil's alkalinity, because the top-dressing must be inert.

BUYING AND PLANTING

AS WITH OTHER PLANTS, the first steps in growing cacti and succulents successfully are to choose healthy plants and then to establish them in a position that suits their cultural needs (see pp. 150–51). For an indoor display of cacti and succulents, a position near a sunny window is fine. The greenhouse or conservatory, however, is the best place to house a large collection because it offers bright, even light and easily regulated temperature and humidity.

Plants in containers can be placed outdoors in summer once the temperature averages 70°F (21°C). A permanent outdoor planting is possible in areas that are virtually frost-free, and many hardy succulents can be planted outdoors even in cold climates. Epiphytes and other shade-loving plants, which need special growing conditions, do well in natural shade in warm areas. Wherever plants are sited, ensure that they have a good start by planting them correctly.

BUYING PLANTS

Supermarkets, florists, and garden centers generally stock cacti and succulents that are easy to grow. They do, however, offer only a limited choice. A specialist cactus nursery or a local cactus show will have a much larger and more interesting variety of plants on sale.

Some cactus nurseries and botanic gardens have permanent collections. It is well worth visiting one or two of these in order to see what mature specimens of cacti and succulents look like and how to display them effectively.

Even distribution of brightly colored, undamaged spines

Plump, well-shaped stem

Regular overall shape

Waxy, evenly colored skin

HEALTHY PLANTS
Choose unblemished plants that display signs of new growth. A well-presented plant in fresh, weed-free potting mix shows that the grower has looked after it well.

Deformed leaf indicates insect damage or disease

Mix is old, weed-ridden, and too low in the pot

UNHEALTHY SUCCULENT
Symptoms of poor growth are often more visible in succulents than in cacti. Avoid plants that show signs of disease or pests, that have few or pale leaves and spindly growth, or that are potbound or in poor potting mix.

Uneven growth indicates poor care

Plant is lopsided because of poor root system

CACTUS IN POOR CONDITION
Do not buy cacti that show signs of pests, diseases, or uneven growth. Check that the skin is not dull and the spines are not damaged.

PLANTING INTO CONTAINERS

Mostly shallow-rooted, succulents and cacti do not require a great depth of soil. Plants less than 6 in (15 cm) across are best grown in pots that are about 1 in (2.5 cm) wider than the plants; larger plants require a pot 2–4 in (5–10 cm) wider than their diameter. For pots up to 3½ in (9 cm) across or for very tall plants, full-depth pots are best. Otherwise, use half pots, known as pans, which are 3–6 in (8–15 cm) deep.

When planting into individual pots, follow the process shown (right). For details on how to plant into different types of container, see pp. 46–51. Make sure that all outdoor containers have drainage holes and line the bottoms with material such as turface or gravel.

When growing plants together in one container, choose plants with similar cultural needs and growing seasons. Many slow-growing succulents do well when planted with desert cacti, but can be swamped by fast-growing succulents. Plant *Lithops* on their own because their watering needs and growth cycle (see p. 133) differ from those of other plants.

1 If necessary, wrap a paper collar around the plant or wear gloves as protection against the spines. Gently ease the plant out of its pot and tease out the roots.

3 Fill in with potting mix to within ½ in (1 cm) of the pot's rim, while holding the cactus with the paper collar. Then gently firm in the plant, with a widger if needed.

2 Line a clean, suitably sized pot with fresh cactus potting mix. Position the plant so that the top of its root ball is ½ in (1 cm) below the pot's rim.

4 Using a spoon, carefully cover the potting mix with a top-dressing of ¼ in (6 mm) small washed grit. Allow the plant to settle and water lightly after 3–4 days.

PLANTING IN A BED

In frost-free areas, cacti and succulents can be planted in any sunny location, as long as the soil is very free-draining and not too alkaline or acid, and there is shelter from strong winds. In climates that occasionally suffer near-freezing temperatures, plant next to a sunny wall to provide extra protection. To ensure good drainage in a greenhouse or an area where the annual rainfall exceeds

25 in (635 mm), build a raised bed or a raised sloping mound with a suitable soil or potting mix (see p. 151). Applying a top-dressing to the bed (see p. 147) also aids drainage and hinders erosion.

When planting, allow enough space between the plants for future growth. Harden off indoor plants for a few days in the shade before planting outdoors. For a summer planting, prepare a bed or gravel-filled trough and plunge plants in terracotta pots in it up to their rims.

PLANTING IN WALL CREVICES

Some small creeping succulents native to rocky habitats, such as certain *Sedum* species, shrubby *Mesembryanthemum*, or *Crassula*, grow well even in the shallow soil of a wall crevice. Seedlings and rooted cuttings are easiest to plant into crevices and quickly establish.

With the aid of a widger, scrape out some soil from the crevice. While supporting the plant with one hand, gently ease in the plant's roots. Fill in with a little new soil with the widger and firm the plant in position.

1 Clear the top-dressing from the planting area. Dig a hole big enough for the root ball. Ease the plant from its pot, wearing gloves if need be, and tease out the roots.

2 Place the plant in the hole at the same depth as it was in its pot. Spread out the roots. Fill in and firm the soil; replace the top-dressing. Water after 3–4 days.

PLANT NEEDS

IT IS OFTEN ASSUMED that cacti and succulents need little or no care because they come from deserts. In fact, their basic cultural needs are similar to those of other plants, except that cacti and succulents require less water and most are sensitive to cold. Although they can tolerate a great deal of neglect, they are likely to retreat into dormancy and look unattractive. If given appropriate levels of light, water, warmth, and nutrients, however, as well as a suitable growing medium, these plants will grow well and, since most flower on new growth, should bloom every year.

Cacti and succulents are broadly divisible into desert plants, which like dry sun, and jungle plants, which prefer moist shade. All need warmth, a free-draining soil, and feeding in their growing season. For details of individual plant needs, refer to the relevant entries in the Plant Catalog (pp. 56–143) and the Plant Selection Lists (pp. 165–6).

LIGHT

When mature, most cacti and succulents need full sun, so they are best grown outdoors in warm climates that have a minimum temperature of 61°F (16°C), in a sunny position such as a windowsill or in a greenhouse. In summer, the greenhouse may need some shading to prevent plants from being scorched. Until they become acclimatized to the strong sun, cover young plants moved outdoors with shading fabric for a few days. Greenhouses receive more light if their roof ridge runs from east to west, less if the ridge runs north to south.

Jungle plants prefer the bright shade found beneath a tree, under a greenhouse bench, or by a shady window. In warm climates, a permanent shade house with a slatted, solid, or net roof, and open or adjustable sides, reduces the light by up to 50 percent.

When cacti and succulents are dormant, which is usually in winter, they tolerate lower light levels. Where winter sun is weak, however, place even the shade-loving plants in a bright position. Natural daylight can be supplemented by artificial lights that have wavelengths adjusted to plant needs. The distance between a plant and the lights is often critical, so follow the manufacturer's instructions. Indoors, position a mirror behind a plant to provide an even light.

A few cacti, such as *Schlumbergera*, and some succulents, for example *Crassula*, are so light sensitive that they do not flower unless the days are shorter than 12 hours. Artificial light can suppress flowering, so keep the plants in a little-used room until they come into bud.

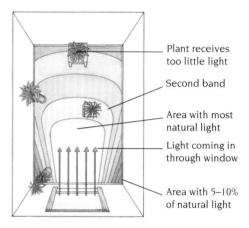

Plant receives too little light

Second band

Area with most natural light

Light coming in through window

Area with 5–10% of natural light

LIGHT DISTRIBUTION IN A ROOM
Light levels diminish rapidly away from the window. In the second band (above), it may be half as bright as in front of the window and too dark for most cacti and succulents. The darkest areas are beside the window and at the back of the room.

TEMPERATURES

Most cactus species and some succulents are sensitive to temperature as well as light. They are generally dormant in winter and are in active growth in the summer, but extreme heat or cold can also induce dormancy at any time of the year. The plants will then remain dormant until the temperature returns to an appropriate range for growth.

In the wild, cacti and succulents survive a wide variety of temperature ranges. *Sempervivum* may be covered in snow in winter; plants from the Andes, such as *Oreocereus*, tolerate fierce sun and night frosts; others, like *Epiphyllum*, live in constantly hot, steamy jungles. In cultivation, most cacti and succulents do well indoors, although they will appreciate being moved outdoors into the fresh air in summer. In winter, in a centrally heated house, move dormant plants to a position with a temperature of 50–59°F (10–15°C). In cooler climates, remove plants from windowsills that may become very cold at night to protect them from suffering any damage.

Temperatures in a greenhouse should be kept between 50–90°F (10–32°C) for most cacti and succulents. Excessive heat can scorch the plants, especially those near the roof. In very hot weather, shade the greenhouse with blinds or apply greenhouse shading to the glass. Good, draft-free ventilation is essential for healthy plant growth and to reduce humidity, which can cause rot in many cacti. This applies even in winter if the internal temperature is 61°F (16°C) or more. Tropical cacti and succulents will not thrive unless they are given warmer conditions; they need a temperature range of 70–90°F (21–32°C).

A few cacti and succulents tolerate outdoor temperatures as low as 32°F (0°C) for short periods, but only grow well in a minimum of 41°F (5°C). In areas where the winter temperature falls below freezing regularly, grow plants outdoors in summer in containers or plunge them in their pots into seasonal beds. Before cold weather arrives, move them under cover. To protect plants from occasional frosts in normally frost-free areas, cover them with bags, newspaper, or plastic. Columnar plants are very vulnerable. If cold damage occurs, it tends to attack only soft new growth, which can be cut out.

GROWING MEDIA

Although able to survive in solid clay or pure sand, cacti and succulents will be much healthier and more vigorous if grown in a soil or potting mix that is open in texture and free-draining, yet retains moisture. For pot plants and small beds, always use a gritty potting mix (for details, see p. 147); garden soil is likely to harbor pests and diseases.

Outdoors, it is useful to assess the soil and prepare it before planting. Most cacti and succulents like a slightly acid soil (pH 5.5–6.5). If the soil is very acid, dig in ground limestone. To make soil more acid, add plenty of peat, compost, flowers of sulfur or an acidifying chemical according to the supplier's instructions. Regular use of fertilizers also keeps soil slightly acid.

If the soil is sandy, add one part peat or well-rotted compost to three parts soil to aid moisture retention. Add one part small washed grit or pea-sized pebbles to three parts of the improved soil to help keep it open.

Heavy clay drains very poorly and planting holes can be waterlogged in rain, so build a raised bed at least 6 in (15 cm) above soil level to create a free-draining site, but do not position it over an impermeable base. Fill the bottom with 2 in (5 cm) of drainage material such as gravel or rubble. Cover it with old carpet or newspaper to stop soil from clogging it up. Fill the bed with gritty topsoil or potting mix and firm, giving the surface a slight slope for good drainage.

WATER

Probably the most common cause of death in cultivated succulents and cacti is overwatering, which rots the plants. No matter how experienced the grower, a moisture meter (see p. 147) is the only sure way to gauge accurately how dry or wet the compost or soil is. Do not water until the gauge shows almost dry. Most cacti and succulents survive long droughts, so if in doubt, don't water them. Cacti and succulents need some water when in active growth (usually in spring and summer) and little or no water while dormant (mainly in winter).

In spring and autumn, water plants every 1–2 weeks; plants in small pots may need more frequent watering. In summer, allow the soil or potting mix nearly to dry out between waterings. Do not overwater plants since most are dormant in hot weather. They are unable to take up water and, if left in wet potting mix, rot from the roots up. This may not be instantly apparent, but the plants will collapse when cooler weather arrives. In winter, in areas where the temperature does not fall below 50°F (10°C), water the plants sparingly from time to time to stop the roots from drying out; in cooler regions, stop watering.

Water a large collection of plants overhead with a hose or automatic greenhouse spray system. Do this either early in the morning or late in the day so that the plants can absorb the water, and surplus moisture on the leaves or stems, which could scorch them, can evaporate before the sun becomes too hot. With a few pot plants, it is more convenient to stand the pots in water until the potting mix surface is moist; then allow the pots to drain.

Outdoor plantings, pots, and window boxes, especially those with a top-dressing, retain moisture longer than those under cover. The watering routine will depend on local conditions.

Jungle plants often need high humidity. To maintain this under cover, mist-spray occasionally. Other cacti and succulents prefer a dry atmosphere.

NUTRIENTS

Cacti and succulents are hungry plants that need regular feeding during the growing season with a balanced range of minerals. These include nitrogen (N) for vigorous top-growth, potassium (K) to encourage flowers and fruit, and phosphorus (P), for good root growth, as well as all the minor, or trace, elements. In the wild, cacti and succulents can absorb whatever minerals are in the soil only when they are dissolved in rain or dew. As a result of the sporadic and unbalanced availability of minerals, many cacti and succulents only just survive in the wild, whereas, with regular feeding, they flourish in cultivation.

Fertilizers may be organic or inorganic and are available in powder, granular, liquid, or solid form. The advantage of inorganic fertilizers is that their chemical content is consistent. Some of the organic fertilizers such as seaweed are rich in trace elements required for healthy growth; others can be deficient in some of the trace elements, so it may be necessary to supplement such fertilizers with extra minerals.

Cacti and succulents require feeding in two stages. Add a powder or granular fertilizer to the potting mix at planting time or during the annual renovation of a permanent bed.

Thereafter, apply either liquid or solid fertilizers throughout the growing season, generally in spring and summer, to allow the plants' new growth to ripen in autumn. Fertilize summer-dormant plants, such as *Testudinaria*, in spring and autumn while they are in active growth. Add the fertilizer with routine waterings, half as often as the plant is watered, but no more than twice a month for desert plants or once a week for jungle species.

Cacti and succulents respond well to liquid fertilizers consisting of 15 percent nitrogen, 15 percent potassium, 30 percent phosphorus, and all the trace elements. Use at half the normal strength. Tomato fertilizers can be used on cacti and succulents, but should be applied at half the normal strength recommended for use with tomatoes. Fertilizers that are deficient in nitrogen cause stunted growth in cacti and succulents after prolonged use. Cacti that are overfed with nitrogen grow thin and do not flower well, while succulents produce spindly growth.

KEEPING PLANTS HEALTHY

CACTI AND SUCCULENTS should survive quite well if their basic requirements are met (see pp. 150–51), but a little attention will keep them healthy and looking their best. Check the plants once or twice a month and, when necessary, clean off the dust or tidy up the spines. Cacti and succulents also benefit from occasional pruning to keep them in shape and, if grown in containers, from repotting every few years.

PRUNING

To look attractive and grow well, most succulents and some cacti, particularly epiphytes (see pp. 10–11), benefit from some shaping and restriction of their growth, to make them bushier and more compact. The other purpose of pruning is to remove any unproductive growth that may impair the vigor of the plant.

Prune shrubby succulents at the start of the growing season, winter-flowering succulents in summer, and epiphytic cacti such as E*piphyllum* after flowering.

Always use clean, sharp pruning tools (see p. 146) to avoid infecting the plant through ragged cuts. Cut back shrubby plants just above a shoot or outward-facing bud, leaving no stub that could become diseased. Some creeping or mounding plants look healthier if old foliage beneath the new growth is removed. Cut back the longest stems of trailing plants that have outgrown their hanging baskets to encourage new bushier growth near the base.

Eventually, plants that have been regularly pruned will become woody; use some of the prunings to root as cuttings to replace the old plant.

PRUNING AN EPIPHYTIC CACTUS

1 Cut back top-heavy stems that have branched from the tip. Use anvil pruners to make a clean straight cut across the parent stem just below the leaf joint.

2 Stunted stems are unlikely to flower. Remove these and any old or diseased stems at the base of the plant, again cutting straight across the stem.

3 To stop dieback occurring, prune out stubs, or dead stem ends; cut straight across the healthy part of each stem.

Scar tissue from old pruning cut

4 Prune back old stems that have flowered to new young shoots, making an angled cut that runs above and parallel to the leaf vein that feeds the young shoot.

BEFORE PRUNING
An overgrown plant looks unattractive, is less vigorous, and is susceptible to pests and diseases.

5 After pruning, the plant may look a little shorn but it will quickly produce strong new flowering shoots and a much more elegant shape.

REPOTTING

All plants must be repotted periodically to allow for root growth; otherwise, they become potbound and their growth is checked. How often depends mainly on the plants' growth rate, but all container-grown plants need repotting every two or three years to renew their potting mix even if they have not yet outgrown their pots. The potting mix in a pot will slowly compact, making it difficult for water and air to circulate to the plant roots; over time, watering also creates mineral imbalances in the potting mix.

The best time to repot is at the beginning of the growing season. Choose a clean, new pot that is large enough in relation to the overall size of the plant in order to accommodate its new root growth (see Planting into Containers, p. 149). Most cacti and succulents, except tall-growing plants, are shallow-rooted so use pans rather than full-depth pots.

Examine the plant roots and control any pests (see p. 160). Plants that have not been repotted for years and those kept too wet or dry may have very poor roots, so take care not to overwater after repotting until new roots develop.

If using the same sort of potting mix as in the old pot, lightly break up the root ball to help the roots grow out into the new mix. If repotting into a different type, remove as much of the old mix as possible. The process is then the same as for planting into a container. Do not water the plant for a week or any damaged roots may rot. If the plant is very spiny, use the method shown below.

When teasing out the root ball, take care not to damage the fine feeding roots

REPOTTING A POTBOUND PLANT
Prepare the plant for repotting by gently teasing out its compacted root ball, letting the old potting mix fall away. Cut out any excessively long, old, or damaged roots.

REPOTTING A VERY SPINY CACTUS

1 Use a pot at least ½ in (1 cm) larger than the plant. Scrub it with slightly soapy water and place a little potting mix in the base. Use another pot as a proxy plant and position it in the center of the larger pot.

Proxy pot is exactly the same size as the existing one

2 Fill in between the pots with more potting mix to within ½ in (1 cm) of the rims. Firm it well and remove the smaller pot, so that it leaves its impression in the fresh potting mix.

3 Wear gloves as protection against the spines, if needed. Place the plant on its side and ease off the old pot. Remove the old potting mix from the top of the root ball and tease out the roots a little. Prune out dead roots. Control any pests or diseases.

4 Hold the plant by its root ball over the prepared new pot. Gently drop the plant into place and straighten it, if necessary. Top up with more potting mix, pushing it under the plant with a dibber; firm lightly. Cover with ½ in (1 cm) of top-dressing.

PLANT HYGIENE

Good hygiene maintains both the appearance and vigor of plants. House plants and outdoor plants in hot areas with low rainfall tend to become dusty; clean spiny plants with a soft brush (see p. 47) or spray nonhairy plants thoroughly with a hose or a mist-sprayer. If the plant is very dirty, spray it with a teaspoon of liquid soap in 1 pint (600 ml) of water.

Deadhead plants after flowering, unless they have decorative seedpods, and remove unsightly foliage. To prevent disease, cut out any damaged areas of cactus stems with sharp pruners or a knife, leaving a smooth clean wound surface that can heal easily.

Remove dead leaves or shoots, which harbor pests and diseases. Pull off leaves from rosette-shaped succulents or, with thumb and forefinger, pinch out shoots above a healthy joint.

PROPAGATION

PROPAGATING MOST CACTI and succulents is rewarding, easy, and inexpensive. It is also the only way to obtain new plants of endangered species. Taking cuttings or dividing a plant often gives the quickest results and is a reliable means of reproducing hybrid plants. Raising plants from seed is slower but yields many new plants and makes it possible to cultivate new forms. Very slow-growing plants or difficult ones that need high temperatures are best grafted so that they grow into good-sized plants in only a few years. For details on which methods suit individual plants, see the Plant Selection Lists (pp. 166–7).

RAISING FROM SEED

Dry seed is available commercially but for best results use fresh seed. Allow the seedpods to ripen on the plants and collect the seed. Squash the wet seed from fleshy fruit onto a paper towel and leave the seed to dry. Sieve dry seed to remove any chaff that could cause rot. It is best to sow seed toward the end of winter so that the seedlings are as large as possible by the following winter.

SOWING SEED: Choose a 2 in (5 cm) pot, a 2 in (5 cm) deep seed tray, or a 5 in (13 cm) pan, according to the quantity and size of the seed. When watering the potting mix, add a fungicide to keep the seedlings from damping off (see p. 161).

1 Fill a pot almost to the brim with cactus potting mix and firm. Scatter the seed evenly over the surface (see inset). Stand the pot in tepid water until the potting mix surface is moist; then allow to drain. Cover thinly with small washed grit.

2 Label the pot and place it in a plastic bag or propagator. Leave in bright shade at a minimum temperature of 66°F (19°C), or 70–81°F (21–27°C) to speed germination.

PRICKING OUT: After the seed germinates (within 2–4 weeks), move the seedlings out of the plastic bag or propagator. Grow on at 50°F (10°C) in a bright airy site, but not in sun, which can scorch them. Wait a few months to a year to prick them out; new roots can easily be damaged and if so, growth is checked. Plant seedlings less than 1 in (2.5 cm) wide in a tray, and larger ones in pots.

2 Gently separate each seedling from the clump, saving as much old potting mix as possible with the roots. Cactus seedlings have very soft spines and can be handled safely without gloves but avoid touching the delicate roots.

Plant the seedling at the same depth as it was in the old pot

3 Almost fill some 2 in (5 cm) or 2½ in (6 cm) pots with cactus potting mix. Plant one seedling in each pot and firm gently. Top-dress with a thin layer of small washed grit and label. After 3–4 days, water with a fungicide solution, diluted as recommended by the supplier.

1 Prick out seedlings only when they begin to crowd each other or the potting mix begins to cake. Use a widger to ease out a clump of seedlings with their potting mix. Take care not to damage the young roots.

CROSS-POLLINATION

Many cacti and succulents cannot fertilize their own flowers. To produce seed, pollen must be transferred from the flowers of one plant to another. This is done outdoors by wind, insects, bats, or birds, but under cover, plants must be cross-pollinated by hand. Pollinating two plants of the same species results in new plants similar to the parents.

Before cross-pollinating a flower, isolate it or place a bag over it to protect it from contamination by pollen from other plants. Always label seed with details of its parentage because it takes several years for a new plant to flower.

To create new hybrid forms, transfer pollen from a flower of one species to a bloom of a different species in the same genus. Remove all the unripe stamens on the pollinated (female) flower to be sure of the hybrid's parentage.

1 When the male anthers are ripe and laden with pollen, dab them gently with a small clean paint-brush until it is covered in pollen.

2 Transfer the pollen on the brush to the female stigma of a flower on another plant of the same species.

Stigma

Anther

Stamen

TAKING CUTTINGS

Cuttings provide a quick and easy means of propagating cacti and succulents, especially hybrids, which do not produce similar offspring from seed. Most plants can be increased from stem cuttings or stem sections, and some succulents also reproduce from leaf cuttings. The best time to take cuttings is when a plant starts into active growth, which for most species is in spring. To reduce the risk of rot or disease setting in, dust wounds with a rooting hormone mixed with a fungicide such as sulfur. Allow the cuttings to heal and form a callus before they are inserted into pots. In summer, this may take only two days, but in winter it can take several months, depending on the type of plant.

LEAF CUTTINGS: Succulents such as *Gasteria* and some *Haworthia* root readily from leaf cuttings in 3–12 weeks. An alternative to rooting leaf cuttings in potting mix is to use a pot filled with only one-third mix and topped with two-thirds fine grit. Moisture evaporates from the mix to encourage rooting, while the grit stops the leaf from rotting.

1 Carefully pull a young healthy leaf away from the parent plant or cut it off at the base with a clean sharp knife. Leave the leaf cutting (see inset) in a bright, warm, dry place for a day or two until a callus has formed over the wound.

2 Fill a small pot with cactus potting mix to within 1 in (2.5 cm) of the rim. Sit the cutting in the top of the potting mix and firm in. Fill the pot with small washed grit to keep the cutting upright.

3 Set the labeled pot in partial shade at a minimum of 64°F (18°C). Keep the potting mix slightly damp. When the new plantlets appear, separate and pot them up.

BUDDING LEAVES

The leaves of succulents such as *Crassula*, *Echeveria*, and *Kalanchoe* can be easily pulled from the stem, together with a bud at the base of the leaf stalk. The bud is then stimulated to form new roots and plantlets. *Echeveria* leaves growing from a flower stem usually come off more easily than those growing from the main rosette.

Remove a healthy leaf and leave in a slightly humid, shady place. Plantlets should form in 3–6 months (see above). When they are large enough, separate them and pot them up singly in 2 in (5 cm) pots of cactus potting mix.

TAKING CUTTINGS

STEM CUTTINGS: Most succulents, except for caudiciform species (see p.10), can be propagated by stem cuttings. Take cuttings in spring at the end of the dormant period (or autumn for winter-flowering plants). Long cuttings fail because they wilt before they can root. To stop the flow from stems that bleed when cut, dip them in water. Take cuttings from rosette-shaped plants by pulling a young rosette cleanly from the parent, then trim the stem to a length less than the rosette's width. Keep potted-up cuttings in an airy place in bright shade at temperatures of 64–75°F (18–24°C). Mist-spray with water periodically to keep moist.

Parent plant should be healthy and vigorous

Cut straight across stem

1 Choose a healthy, sturdy stem whose removal will not disfigure the plant. With a sharp knife, cut the stem just above a bud or shoot. Do not leave a stub.

2 Trim the stem so that the cutting is 2–4 in (5–10 cm) long. Remove any lower leaves, if necessary, so that the stem is clean at the base. Leave the cutting in a warm dry place for a couple of days until a callus forms over the wound.

3 Fill a small pot one-third full of cactus potting mix. Cover with some small washed grit. Stand the cutting in the center of the pot. Fill in the pot with more grit and firm. The cutting should root in 2–6 weeks.

STEM SECTIONS: Many cacti, including epiphytic species (see pp. 10–11), can be economically propagated from a section of stem. Very slow-growing plants are not usually good subjects for sections because they tend to rot.

The length of the stem section depends on the plant. Cuttings from very tall columnar cacti can be 3 ft (90 cm) or more in length, but bear in mind that if the parent is fast-growing, very large cuttings will soon outgrow an indoor position. Padlike jointed stems should be severed from the parent at a joint and a single pad used as a cutting.

Take stem sections at the end of their dormancy, which is usually in spring. Once planted, keep them slightly damp in a bright shady place at a temperature of 64–75°F (18–24°C). The sections should root from the stem base in 3–12 weeks, depending on the plant and season. Sections taken in spring that fail to root by autumn can take up to a year to do so. Keep these dry in winter.

Clean sharp knife

1 Cut a flat stem to a suitable length: 9 in (23 cm) sections are easy to handle and root rapidly. Sever a columnar stem at a point in proportion to its diameter (see inset). Leave in a warm dry place until it calluses. Use the smallest pot the section will stand up in without falling over and fill it one-third full of cactus potting mix.

2 Cover the potting mix with a thin layer of small washed grit and stand the stem section on it. Add grit up to the rim to support the section (above). Place each section as it would naturally grow, with the end that was nearest the parent stem in the pot (right). Label the section and stake it, if necessary.

DIVISION

In this technique, a vigorous plant is divided into several pieces, each of which has either its own roots or a growing point. It is a simple and quick way to obtain new plants of a good size. Cacti and succulents that readily form stem or tuberous offsets lend themselves to this technique; some clump-forming species are also suitable. Usually, the best time to divide these types of cacti and succulents is at the beginning of the growing season in spring or early summer.

Some species of succulents that have swollen rootstocks can be increased by cutting off segments in winter while the plants are dormant. Before potting up the divided pieces, allow any cut surfaces to form a callus as a protection against infection by rot and other diseases.

Water all newly divided plants sparingly until they have become well established and show signs of active growth; otherwise, their stems may rot in the damp potting mix.

CLUMPING OFFSETS: Succulents such as *Haworthia* and *Gasteria* and some cacti, such as *Mammillaria* and *Echinopsis*, produce many offsets in a dense clump. Mature offsets, which have begun to form their own roots, can be detached from the parent to grow into new plants. Once they have been potted up, leave the offsets at a minimum temperature of 64°F (18°C) in sun or bright shade, according to the plant's needs. Water sparingly until new growth appears.

If the offsets are tightly packed, it is easier to remove the parent clump from its pot or to dig it up, so that the offsets can be teased apart at the roots. Leave small offsets; they will grow much more quickly if still attached to the parent.

1 With a widger, carefully dig out an offset from around the base of the plant. Pull it away gently or cut across the joint with a clean sharp knife. Dust the wound with fungicide and allow it to callus for a few days.

2 Almost fill a suitably sized pot with cactus potting mix. Insert the offset into the potting mix at the same depth as it was before and firm gently. Top-dress with small washed grit and label the pot.

OFFSET TUBERS: Some succulents such as *Senecio* and *Ceropegia* have tuberous roots and form offset tubers just below soil level around the parent. These can be gently detached or severed with a knife and grown on. Allow any cut surfaces to callus for a few days before planting the offsets. When they begin to produce new top-growth, pot the offset tubers on or, in warm climates, plant them out.

1 Clear away any top-dressing, then dig carefully with a widger in the potting mix to locate an offset tuber. If necessary, sever it from the main tuber, using a clean sharp knife. Lift it out of the pot, taking care to protect any top-growth and new roots that have developed.

2 Leave the offset in a warm dry place to callus. If the offset has roots, plant it in a pot of cactus potting mix. (If it has no roots, use a pot filled with one-third potting mix and two-thirds small washed grit.)

3 Cover the potting mix thinly with small washed grit. Label the pot. Place it in shade or bright light, according to the plant, at a temperature of 64°F (18°C). Leave for a few days. Water sparingly until the plant is established.

Top-growth of parent plant

Young roots on offset

DIVISION

DIVISION OF ROOTSTOCKS: This is used for a few clumping plants at the start of the growing season. It ensures that new plants from variegated cultivars of species such as *Sansevieria trifasciata* do not revert to the unvariegated form. Some *Sedum* and caudiciform succulents (see p. 10) have a swollen rootstock with several growing points. When the plant is dormant, cut the rootstock or tuber into pieces, each with its own growing point. Dust the cuts with commercial fungicide and allow to callus. Divisions of shrubby plants callus in days but those of caudiciform plants take a few weeks. Pot up each section and grow on in conditions that suit the plant's needs.

1 Dig up the parent plant or remove it from its container. Using a strong sharp knife, cut the rootstock into sections, each with at least one healthy growing point and some vigorous roots.

2 Cut out any part of the stock that is old and woody or damaged. Dust the cut surfaces with fungicide and allow to callus. Replant each section in a pot of cactus potting mix. Water after a few days.

GRAFTING

This process, used mainly to increase cacti, involves uniting a scion, or cutting, from one species with the rootstock or stock, or base, of a more vigorous one. When grafted, many slow-growing and difficult species are easier to cultivate and bring into flower, and their growth rate can be increased by ten times. With practice and healthy plants, a 90 percent success rate is possible. The choice of split, flat, or side grafting depends on the plant. Graft cacti at the start of the growing season from midspring to early summer for best results.

SPLIT GRAFTING: This is suitable for cacti with slim, leaflike stems, such as *Schlumbergera* and other epiphytes, and some slender-stemmed succulents. It is also a good way to create a standard plant – one with a treelike appearance.

1 With a sharp knife, remove 1 in (2.5 cm) from the top of a healthy stock. Make a vertical cut 1/2–3/4 in (1–2 cm) deep into the stem (see inset), ensuring that the cut passes through the central core tissue.

2 To create a scion, select a length of healthy stem from the parent plant, about one or two sections long if it is a *Schlumbergera*. Make a straight clean cut through the leaf joint.

3 Pare away the bottom 1/2 in (1 cm) of the stem section, carefully removing the skin from both sides to form a tapered scion. If necessary, trim the scion to the same diameter as the stock.

4 Gently insert the prepared scion (see inset) into the slit at the top of the stock. Check that the central core tissue of the scion is in close contact with that of the stock. The more snugly the scion and stock fit, the more likely the graft will succeed.

5 Secure the two parts in position with a sharp, straight cactus spine or a clean needle. Then bind the graft firmly with raffia. Leave in a bright airy situation, at a temperature of least 50°F (10°C), for about four weeks until new growth is visible.

FLAT GRAFTING: Similar to split grafting but even easier, flat grafting can be used to propagate most types of cacti, including the brightly colored neon cacti, which lack chlorophyll, and mutant cristate, or crested, forms.

Choose a healthy vigorous stock with a diameter similar to or a little larger than that of the intended scion; *Echinopsis* species, particularly those from the former genus *Trichocereus*, are a good choice. When preparing the graft, ensure your hands and the equipment are clean and take care not to touch either of the cut surfaces; they are very vulnerable to infection by fungal disease until the graft unites. Both the water-storing tissue and the central transport tissue, or core,

of the scion and stock must be in contact for a successful graft, so if the diameters of the two plants are different, the scion may need to be positioned off-center on the stock.

A gentle, even pressure must be maintained for about two weeks to hold the scion and the stock together while the graft unites. A convenient method for grafts of small pot plants is to use two wide rubber bands. With taller pot plants or cacti that are growing in a bed, take two lengths of string and weight them at the ends, then drape them at right angles over the scion. If the cacti are spiny, cut a couple of strips from old nylon stockings; stretch them at right angles over the scion and hook the ends onto spines on either side of the stock.

1 With a clean sharp knife, cut horizontally through the stock about 1 in (2.5 cm) below the growing point. Remove the top. Check that some central core tissue is clearly exposed; if not, slice off another thin portion of the stock until the core is visible.

2 Bevel the edges of the cut, removing ¼ in (6 mm) of skin from all around the stock. This prevents the hard skin from holding the scion off the stock when the fleshy stock tissue shrinks after grafting.

3 Cut through the scion at the base. Bevel ¼ in (6 mm) of skin from around the cut edge of the scion (see inset). Place the cut surfaces of the scion and stock together so that their central core tissues touch.

4 Firmly rotate the scion to remove any air pockets. Secure the stock and scion in position with a pair of rubber bands. Place the grafted plant in a bright airy situation (but not in full sun) at a minimum temperature of 50°F (10°C).

5 If the graft is successful, the scion and stock should unite in about two weeks. Then feed and water as normal. Once there are signs of active growth – in about four weeks – remove the rubber bands.

SIDE GRAFTING

This is ideal for grafting very slender-stemmed plants, such as *Echinopsis chamaecereus*, which often have a very small central core. Cut the stock and scion obliquely, rather than horizontally, to expose more of the central core tissue and improve the chance of a successful union. Press the cut surfaces together, ensuring that both types of tissue overlap, and secure with one or two clean needles or cactus spines. Bind the graft with raffia, nylon stocking strips, or rubber bands and, if necessary, support it with a thin stake and twine. Then treat the plant in the same way as a flat graft.

PLANT PROBLEMS

IF THEY ARE GROWN in appropriate conditions and properly cared for, cacti and succulents should remain healthy and vigorous and be no more prone to cultivation problems or attack from diseases or pests than any other type of plant. Inspect cacti and succulents now and then, perhaps when watering them, so that you can spot signs of trouble early on. Any symptoms or pests can then be treated before they become established and seriously affect the plant. Keep newly purchased succulents or cacti isolated for about two weeks before placing them with other plants. This allows any diseases or pests to become apparent and be controlled before they have a chance to spread. When applying pesticides, fungicides, or other treatments, always follow the manufacturer's instructions for use.

PESTS

Pests can be controlled by chemical insecticides or, in greenhouses, often by natural predators specific to each pest. Systemic insecticides are absorbed into the plant sap, poisoning any insects that feed on the plant, and are more efficient than a contact application. Use a systemic insecticide 2–3 times in the growing season as a preventative measure. The waxy skin of many succulents and cacti repels moisture, so water with a solution to drench the roots. If an infestation appears, use the insecticide weekly for 3–4 weeks.

In addition to the pests shown here, cacti and succulents may be attacked by rodents and caterpillars, which nibble fleshy plants, and birds, which eat berries and steal woolly spines for nests. Roots are also eaten by root mealybugs, which leave powdery white deposits along the roots. To save an infested plant, stand its root ball in a bath of soapy insecticide, then allow it to drain. Sciarid fly larvae, which look like tiny white worms, and microscopic nematodes, which leave galls on the roots, destroy the roots and base of a plant. Treat sciarid flies with an insecticide and prevent nematodes from spreading by discarding the plant, its potting mix, and pot.

VINE WEEVILS
Resistant to most chemicals, these increasingly troublesome brown beetles nibble leaves and their fat white larvae eat roots and burrow into stems, causing the plant to collapse and die. When repotting, look out for tunnels in the potting mix. If any exist, replace the mix.

MEALYBUGS
An infested plant is covered in tiny, woolly white nests and sticky honeydew. The insects look like pale waxy sowbugs. Treat with either a systemic or soapy contact insecticide or, in temperatures over 70°F (21°C), introduce the predator ladybug *Cryptolaemus montrouzieri*.

SPIDER MITES
Brown dots are a sign of spider mite attack on young growth. The tiny, yellow, red, or brown mites resemble ground pepper, thrive in dry hot greenhouses, and spin fine webs. Increase the humidity or use the predator mite *Phytoseiulus persimilis* in temperatures over 70°F (21°C).

SCALE INSECTS
Control these small, brown, moundlike insects with systemic insecticide. They usually appear on the stems and lower leaves of an indoor or greenhouse plant, and migrate up the stem. Plant growth is then checked and the sticky honeydew can encourage sooty mold.

WHITEFLIES
These white, mothlike insects excrete honeydew on which sooty mold thrives, especially on soft-leaved succulents such as *Euphorbia*. Use an insecticidal spray or soap or, in the green-house, the wasp *Encarsia formosa*. This preys on young nymphs, which blacken when they die.

SLUGS AND SNAILS
These feed on leaves and fleshy stems, leaving unsightly holes and telltale slimy traces. They prefer damp shady places, so they often attack epiphytes. To eradicate persistent offenders, scatter slug pellets between the plants or apply a preparation based on metaldehyde.

DISEASES

Cacti and succulents suffer mainly from fungal diseases. Fungal spores abound in the atmosphere and attack plants in damp or wet conditions, especially in a shady spot with similar daytime and nighttime temperatures. Some fungi actually grow through the plant skin. Most problems occur in late spring and autumn when condensation from cold nights fails to evaporate from plants if the next day is overcast.

In addition to the diseases shown below, overwatering or damp conditions cause root or stem rot (treat as for basal stem rot) and damping off in seedlings, which makes them wilt and die. Avoid the latter by sowing seed thinly and lightly spraying the potting mix with a copper sulfate solution, which can also be used to treat white powdery mildew in dry conditions.

CULTURAL DAMAGE

Although pests and diseases do affect cacti and succulents, the plants are much more likely to suffer physical damage caused by incorrect feeding and watering or adverse growing conditions, for example inappropriate light, temperature, soil, or humidity. A plant that is grown in an unsuitable position may produce unattractive distorted leaves or stems. Healthy growth can be retarded and permanent physical damage may result, which can lead to insect infestation, disease, or even the death of the plant.

If a plant fails to flower once it has reached a size at which flowering normally begins, check carefully that the plant is being grown in an appropriate environment and that all its basic requirements have been met (see pp.150–51).

FUNGAL LEAF SPOT
Usually brown or gray, the spots may merge and cause leaf drop. Minute fungal sporeheads develop where water droplets lie on the leaf, leaving sunken brown scars. Discard all infected leaves; treat the plant with copper sulfate and, under cover, improve ventilation.

SOOTY MOLD
Caused by a soilborne fungus, this sooty black mold attacks plants, especially seedlings, that are damaged, weakened by very wet conditions, or covered in honeydew. Discard infected seedlings and soil, treat plants with a systemic fungicide, and control any pests present.

SCORCH DAMAGE
Hot stuffy greenhouses, strong winds, or sudden bright sunshine on dewy plants can cause sunken brown patches where the tissue has collapsed. When moving plants to less sheltered positions, harden them off in shade or protect them with fabric or a flexible mesh.

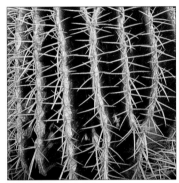

COLD DAMAGE
Plants subject for a long period to temperatures that are too low for them can suffer stem tip damage, scarring, or even stem collapse. Rot often then attacks the affected areas. Increase the temperature so that dead tissue can dry out. Alternatively, cut out all the damaged tissue.

CORKY SCAB
Brown, barklike spots that usually develop near the base of a stem are a result of past disease damage or poor cultivation. Do not confuse these spots with natural corking on very old plants. If growing conditions are improved, the spots should not reappear.

BASAL STEM ROT
Plants that are cold, damp, or have poor roots are prone to rot. Rot fungus penetrates rapidly from the skin into the tissue, turning them soft and black. Cut off sound pot plant stems for cuttings and discard the rest. Apply copper sulfate to permanent plantings.

ETIOLATION
Poor light, especially in warmth, as well as incorrect feeding, causes plants to become pale-skinned with elongated stems, or to have stunted leaves on spindly shoots. Healthy growth resumes once the plant is given sufficient light. Prune affected stems back to good tissue.

DROUGHT
If starved of water, leafy succulents shed their leaves, then start to die back from the stem tips or shed their branches, and eventually die. Watering usually reverses this process of decline. Cacti shrink into dormancy in a drought but rejuvenate rapidly once watered.

PLANT SELECTION LISTS

PLANTS FOR BEGINNERS

These include cacti and succulents that will stand some mistreatment. Many flower readily when only a few years old.

Adromischus, most species, including
  A. cooperi
  A. festivus
  A. maculatus
Aeonium, most species and hybrids, including
  A. arboreum
  A. haworthii
  A. tabuliforme
Agave, most species, including
  A. americana
  A. attenuata
Aloe aristata
  A. arborescens
  A. brevifolia
  A. ferox
  A. microstigma
  A. variegata
Aporocactus, most species and forms, including
  A. f. flagelliformis
Astrophytum ornatum
Cephalophyllum, most species and hybrids, including
  C. alstonii
  C. subulatoides
Cereus aethiops
  C. hildmannianus
  C. hildmannianus v. monstrose
  C. jamacaru
Ceropegia woodii
Cheiridopsis, most species, including
  C. candidissima
  C. pillansii
  C. purpurata
Cleistocactus hildegardiae
  C. strausii
  C. winteri
Cotyledon ladismithensis
  C. undulata
Crassula falcata
  C. ovata
  C. tetragona
Delosperma, most species, including
  D. minimum
  D. sutherlandii
  D. tradescantioides
Echeveria, most species, including
  E. agavoides
  E. derenbergii
  E. elegans
  E. harmsii
Echinocactus grusonii
Echinocereus cinerascens
  E. engelmannii
  E. scheeri
  E. stramineus
Echinopsis aurea
  E. backebergii
  E. chamaecereus, its forms and hybrids, including
    E. c. 'Fire Chief'
    E. c. 'Jubilee'
  E. densispina
  E. 'Forty-niner'
  E. huascha
  E. oxygona
Epiphyllum, most hybrids, including
  E. 'Carole'
  E. 'Fortuna'
  E. 'Hermossissimus'
  E. 'Jennifer Ann'
Euphorbia mammillaris
  E. milii
Faucaria, all species
Ferocactus, most species, including
  F. cylindraceus
  F. latispinus
  F. wislizeni
Frithia pulchra
Gasteria, most species, including
  G. armstrongii
  G. liliputana
  G. obtusa
  G. verrucosa
Gibbaeum petrense
Glottiphyllum, most species, including
  G. depressum
  G. oligocarpum
Gymnocalycium, most species, including
  G. andreae
  G. baldianum
  G. gibbosum
  G. horstii
  G. quehlianum
Haworthia, most common species, including
  H. attenuata
  H. cymbiformis
  H. obtusa
  H. reinwardtii
Kalanchoe, most species, including
  K. beharensis
  K. blossfeldiana
  K. daigremontiana
  K. pumila
  K. tomentosa
Lampranthus, most species, including
  L. citrinus
  L. haworthii
  L. spectabilis
Mammillaria, most species, including
  M. albilanata
  M. elongata
  M. zeilmanniana
Neoporteria curvispina
  N. subgibbosa
Opuntia ficus-indica
  O. lindheimeri
  O. neoargentina
Pachyphytum, all species and hybrids
Parodia concinna
  P. crassigibba
  P. herteri
  P. horstii
  P. leninghausii
  P. magnifica
  P. mammulosa
  P. ottonis
  P. scopa
Pereskia aculeata
Pleiospilos, most species, including
  P. bolusii
  P. nelii
  P. simulans
Rebutia, most species, including
  R. miniscula
  R. muscula
  R. senilis
Ruschia, most species, including
  R. crassa
  R. dualis
  R. macowanii
  R. mucronata
Schlumbergera, most hybrids, including
  S. 'Gold Charm'
  S. 'Lilac Beauty'
  S. 'Marie'
  S. 'Sonja'
  S. 'White Christmas'
Sedum, most hardy species
  S. morganianum
  S. nussbaumeranum
Sempervivum, most species and hybrids, including
  S. arachnoideum
  S. 'Bellot's Pourpre'
  S. montanum
  S. tectorum
Senecio aizoides
  S. articulatus
  S. fulgens
  S. haworthii
S. rowleyanus
S. stapeliiformis
Stenocactus, most species, including
  S. multicostatus
  S. phyllacanthus
Thelocactus bicolor
  T. setispinus
Trichodiadema, most species, including
  T. densum
  T. mirabile
Weberbauerocereus johnsonii

PLANTS FOR THE ENTHUSIAST

These present a challenge to the gardener because they are uncommon in cultivation and are usually difficult to grow well, except in ideal conditions.

Adenia, all species
Adenium, all species
Alluaudia, all species
Ariocarpus, all species
Arrojadoa, all species
Astrophytum asterias
Brachystelma, most species, including
  B. barberae
  B. modestum
Caralluma, most species, including
  C. burchardii
  C. lutea
  C. mammillaris
  C. retrospiciens
Ceropegia, most species, including
  C. elegans
  C. juncea
  C. multiflora
  C. rendallii
  C. sandersonii
Copiapoa cinerea
Cotyledon buchholziana
Cyphostemma, all species
Discocactus, all species
Epithelantha, all species
Escobaria, most species, including
  E. aguirreana
  E. dasyacantha
  E lloydii
  E. minima
  E. missouriensis
  E. roseana
Euphorbia, most species, including
  E. decaryi
  E. lactea
  E. muirii
  E. obesa
Fouquieria, all species
Hoodia, all species
Huernia macrocarpa
Jatropha berlandieri
Leuchtenbergia principis
Mammillaria guelzowiana
  M. saboae
  M. theresae
  M. wrightii
Melocactus, most species, including
  M. bahiensis
  M. glaucescens
  M. matanzanus
  M. oreas
  M. salvadorensis
  M. zehntneri
Monadenium, most species
Neolloydia, all species
Pachypodium, most species, including
  P. bispinosum
  P. densiflorum
  P. lamerei
  P. namaquanum
  P. rosulatum
  P. succulentum
Parodia graessneri
  P. haselbergii
Pelecyphora, all species
Sarcocaulon, all species
Sclerocactus, all species
Stapelia, most species, including
  S. erectiflora
  S. flavirostis
  S. grandiflora
  S. revoluta
  S. variegata
Testudinaria elephantipes
  T. macrostachya
Trichocaulon, all species
Turbinicarpus, all species
Uebelmannia, all species

ARCHITECTURAL PLANTS

Because of their strong shapes, these plants make excellent focal points in a bed or a striking feature plant in a container.

Aeonium arboreum
  A. a. 'Atropurpureum'
A. haworthiii
Agave americana, its varieties and forms
  A. parryi
  A. stricta
  A. victoria-reginae

Aloe arborescens
A. dichotoma
A. ferox
A. plicatilis
A. ramosissima
Cephalocereus, all species
Cereus, all species
Cleistocactus, all species
Cotyledon undulata
Crassula arborescens
C. falcata
C. ovata
C. tetragona
Cyphostemma bainesii
C. juttae
Dudleya, all species
Echeveria, many species and
hybrids, including
E. coccinea
E. gibbiflora
E. 'Painted Lady'
E. pulvinata
E. secunda
Echinocactus grusonii
Echinocereus cinerascens
E. pentalophus
Echinopsis bridgesii
E. bruchii
E. calochlora
E. deserticola
E. huascha
E. scopulicola
E. thelogona
Espostoa, all species
Euphorbia candelabrum
E. cooperi
E. evansii
E. horrida
E. milii
Ferocactus cylindraceus
F. histrix
F. wislizeni
Fouquieria, all species
Jatropha cordata
Kalanchoe beharensis
Lampranthus, all species
Opuntia basilaris
O. lindheimeri
O. monacantha
O. neoargentina
O. pilifera
O. scheeri
O. tunicacta
Oreocereus, all species
Pachycereus, all species
Pachypodium geayi
P. lamerei
Parodia leninghausii
P. magnifica
Pedilanthus tithymaloides
Pereskia, all species
Pilosocereus, all species
Plumeria, all species and
hybrids
Sedum frutescens
S. spectabile 'Brilliant'
Senecio haworthii

GROUND COVER PLANTS

Forming low mats or bushy mounds, these are useful for covering the ground between large plants, either in the open garden or in greenhouse beds.

Carpobrotus, all species
Cephalophyllum, all species
Coleus, most succulent
species, including
C. arabicus
C. coerulescens
C. spicatus
Crassula, most species,
including
C. falcata
C. lactea
C. marginalis
C. multicava
Cyanotis somaliensis
Cylindrophyllum, most
species, including
C. comptonii
C. tugwelliae
Delosperma, all species
Drosanthemum, all species
Kalanchoe tubiflora
Lampranthus, most species,
including
L. aurantiacus
L. haworthii
L. pleniflorus
L. recurvus
L. spectabilis
Senecio citriformis
S. jacobsenii
S. kleiniiformis
S. rowleyanus

CLIMBING AND TRAILING PLANTS FOR SHADE

These plants usually prefer shady conditions and are good for covering walls and banks or for growing in hanging baskets.

Aporocactus flagelliformis
A. martianus
Aporophyllum, all hybrids
Ceropegia, most species,
including
C. ballyana
C. elegans
C. nilotica
C. rendallii
C. sandersonii
C. woodii
Cynanchum, most species,
including
C. aphyllum
C. marnieranum
C. perrieri

Disocactus, all species
Epiphyllum, most species and
some hybrids, including
E. anguliger
E. 'Communion'
E. crenatum
E. 'Fortuna'
E. laui
E. oxypetalum
E. 'Professor Ebert'
E. 'Reward'
E. 'Space Rocket'
Harrisia, most species,
including
H. adscendens
H. gracilis
H. hahniana
H. martinii
H. pomanensis
H. tortuosa
Heliocereus, most species,
including
H. aurantiacus
H. cinnabarinus
H. schrankii
H. speciosus
Hylocereus, all species
Lepismium, all species
Rhipsalis, most species,
including
R. baccifera
R. cereuscula
R. hadrosoma
R. micrantha
R. oblonga
R. teres
Sarcostemma, most species,
including
S. aphyllum
S. australe
S. vanlessenii
S. viminale
Schlumbergera, most species
and hybrids, including
S. 'Christmas Charm'
S. 'Gold Charm'
S. 'Joanne'
S. 'Lilac Beauty'
S. russelliana
S. truncata
Selenicereus, all species
Senecio rowleyanus

PLANTS FOR A GREENHOUSE COLLECTION

Many groups of plants, including large but very slow-growing species, are suitable for growing in pots or small beds.

Small greenhouses

Adromischus, all species
Aeonium, all species
Agave parviflora
A. victoria-reginae

Aloe aristata
A. variegata
Aporocactus, all species and
hybrids
Ariocarpus, all species
Astrophytum, all species
Caralluma, all species
Cephalocereus senilis
Cereus hildmannianus
C. hildmannianus v.
monstrose
Ceropegia, most species,
including
C. dichotoma
C. woodii
Cleistocactus strausii
C. winteri
Conophytum, all species
Copiapoa, all species
Coryphantha, all species
Cotyledon ladismithensis
C. undulata
Crassula, most species,
including
C. deceptor
C. ovata
C. tetragona
Cyphostemma bainesii
C. juttae
Dudleya, all species
Echeveria, all species and
hybrids
Echinocactus grusonii
Echinocereus, all species
Echinopsis backebergii
E. chamaecereus and its
hybrids
E. oxygona
Epiphyllum, most hybrids,
including
E. 'Fortuna'
E. 'Hollywood'
E. 'Jennifer Ann'
Espostoa, all species
Euphorbia decaryi
E. horrida
E. mammillaris
E. obesa
Faucaria tuberculosa
Ferocactus, most species,
including
F. cylindraceus
F. hamatacanthus
F. latispinus
Frithia pulchra
Gasteria, most species,
including
G. batesiana
G. liliputana
G. obtusa
G. verrucosa
Gibbaeum, all species
Graptopetalum, all species
and hybrids
Gymnocalycium, all species
Haworthia, all species
Huernia, all species

Jatropha berlandieri
J. podagrica
Kalanchoe, most species,
including
K. blossfeldiana
K. pumila
K. tomentosa
Leuchtenbergia principis
Lithops, all species
Mammillaria, all species
Matucana, all species
Neoporteria, all species
Oreocereus, all species
Pachyphytum, all species and
hybrids
Parodia, all species
Rebutia, all species
Schlumbergera, all species and
hybrids
Sedum frutescens
S. furfuraceum
S. morganianum
Senecio haworthii
S. rowleyanus
S. stapeliiformis
Stapelia, all species
Stenocactus, all species
Testudinaria elephantipes
Thelocactus, all species
Weberbauerocereus johnsonii

Large greenhouses

Agave americana 'Variegata'
A. stricta
Aloe dichotoma
A. ferox
A. kedongensis
A. plicatilis
Carnegiea gigantea
Cephalocereus senilis
Cereus aethiops
C. hildmannianus
C. hildmannianus v.
monstrose
C. validus
Cleistocactus strausii
Crassula arborescens
C. ovata
Cyphostemma bainesii
C. juttae
Echinocactus grusonii
Echinopsis bruchii
E. calochlora
E. deserticola
E. scopulicola
Espostoa lanata
E. melanostele
Euphorbia milii
Ferocactus cylindraceus
F. wislizeni
Jatropha cordata
Kalanchoe beharensis
Lampranthus aurantiacus
L. haworthii
L. spectabilis
Opuntia neoargentina
O. tunicata

Oreocereus celsianus
  O. trollii
Pachycereus schottii
  P. schottii v. monstrose
Pachypodium lamerei
Pedilanthus tithymaloides
Pereskia aculeata
Pilosocereus leucocephalus f. palmeri
Selenicereus grandiflorus
  S. spinulosus
Testudinaria elephantipes
  T. macrostachya
Weberbauerocereus johnsonii

INDOOR POT PLANTS
Many small plants are especially suitable for small indoor displays; most flower easily.

Adenium obesum
Aeonium tabuliforme
Agave parviflora
  A. victoria-reginae
Aloe aristata
  A. bakeri
  A. variegata
Astrophytum, all species
Cephalocereus senilis
Cereus hildmannianus v. monstrose
Ceropegia woodii
Cleistocactus strausii
Conophytum, all species
Copiapoa hypogaea
Cotyledon undulata
Crassula 'Morgan's Beauty'
  C. ovata
  C. schmidtii
  C. tetragona
Echeveria, most species and hybrids, including
  E. affinis
  E. agavoides
  E. fimbriata
  E. 'Painted Lady'
  E. shaviana
Echinocactus grusonii
Echinocereus rigidissimus v. rubrispinus
  E. subinermis
Echinopsis backebergii
  E. chamaecereus
  E. chamaecereus f. lutea
  E. densispina
  E. 'Forty-niner'
  E. oxygona
Espostoa, all species
Euphorbia mammillaris
  E. milii
  E. obesa
Faucaria tuberculosa
Ferocactus cylindraceus
Frithia pulchra
Gasteria obtusa
Gibbaeum album

Graptopetalum bellum
Gymnocalycium baldianum
  G. bruchii
  G. mihanovichii 'Red Top'
  G. quehlianum
Haworthia, most species, including
  H. angustifolia
  H. arachnoidea
  H. attenuata
  H. cooperi
  H. venosa
Kalanchoe tomentosa
  K. tubiflora
Lithops, all species
Mammillaria, most species, including
  M. bocasana
  M. candida
  M. hahniana
  M. prolifera
  M. rhodantha
  M. schiedeana
Melocactus matanzanus
Neoporteria, most species, including
  N. clavata
  N. curvispina
  N. napina
  N. subgibbosa
  N. villosa
Oreocereus, all species
Pachyphytum oviferum
Pachypodium lamerei
Parodia, all species
Rebutia, all species
Sansevieria, most species, including
  S. caulescens
  S. cylindrica
  S. grandis
  S. intermedia
  S. parva
  S. trifasciata and forms
Schlumbergera, most species and hybrids, including
  S. abendrothii
  S. bicolor
  S. delicatus
  S. 'Ilona'
  S. 'Norris'
  S. russelliana
  S. truncata
  S. 'Westland'
Sedum furfuraceum
  S. daigremontianum
  S. morganianum
  S. nussbaumeranum
Sempervivum 'Oddity'
Senecio haworthii
  S. rowleyanus
  S. stapeliiformis
Stapelia flavirostis
  S. grandiflora
  S. variegata
Stenocactus, all species
Thelocactus, all species

FREE-FLOWERING PLANTS
If grown from seed or cuttings, most of these plants will provide a good display of flowers in under five years.

Aloe aristata
  A. variegata
Aporocactus, all species and hybrids
Astrophytum capricorne
  A. ornatum
Bergeranthus, most species
Bowiea, all species
Carruanthus, all species
Cephalophyllum, most species, including
  C. alstonii
  C. regale
  C. subulatoides
Cleistocactus strausii
  C. winteri
Coleus, most succulent species, including
  C. coerulescens
  C. spicatus
Conophytum, most species, including
  C. bilobum
  C. cupreatum
  C. ectypum
  C. minutum
  C. taylorianum
  C. wettsteinii
Crassula, most species, including
  C. falcata
  C. lactea
  C. marginalis
  C. multicava
  C. nealeana
  C. perfoliata
Cyanotis somaliensis
Delosperma, most species, including
  D. ashtonii
  D. lydenburgense
Drosanthemum, most species, including
  D. bicolor
  D. hallii
  D. speciosum
  D. tuberculiferum
Dudleya, most species and hybrids, including
  D. brittonii
  D. pulverulenta
Echeveria, most species and hybrids, including
  E. derenbergii
  E. harmsii
  E. nodulosa
  E. pulvinata
  E. setosa
  E. spectabilis

Echinocereus chloranthus
  E. knippelianus
  E. scheeri
Echinopsis backebergii
  E. chamaecereus
  E. densispina
  E. oxygona
Epiphyllum, most hybrids, including
  E. 'Baby'
  E. 'Best of All'
  E. 'Fantasy'
  E. 'King Midas'
  E. 'Thunder Cloud'
Euphorbia milii
Faucaria, all species
Frithia pulchra
Gasteria, most species, including
  G. batesiana
  G. liliputana
  G. obtusa
  G. verrucosa
Glottiphyllum, all species
Graptopetalum, most species and hybrids
Gymnocalycium, most species, including
  G. baldianum
  G. bruchii
  G. mihanovichii
  G. quehlianum
Haworthia, most species, including
  H. attenuata
  H. cuspidata
  H. glabrata
  H. reinwardtii
  H. tessellata
Jatropha podagrica
Kalanchoe, most species and hybrids, including
  K. citrina
  K. figueiredoi
  K. 'Flaming Katy'
  K. grandiflora
  K. manginii
  K. pumila
  K. 'Tessa'
Lampranthus, most species, including
  L. amoenus
  L. curvifolius
  L. haworthii
  L. magnificus
  L. roseus
  L. spectabilis
Lewisia, most species and hybrids, including
  L. cotyledon
  L. rediviva
Lithops, most species, including
  L. aucampiae
  L. karasmontana
  L. lesliei
  L. salicola

Mammillaria, most species, including
  M. elongata
  M. magnimamma
  M. matudae
  M. spinosissima
Opuntia neoargentina
Pachyphytum, most species and hybrids, including
  P. hookeri
  P. oviferum
Parodia, most species, including
  P. crassigibba
  P. herteri
  P. ottonis
Pleiospilos, most species, including
  P. bolusii
  P. nelii
  P. simulans
Rebutia, most species, including
  R. aureiflora
  R. marsoneri
  R. minuscula
Rhipsalis, many species, including
  R. cereuscula
  R. crispata
  R. pilocarpa
  R. teres
Schlumbergera, most hybrids, including
  S. 'Bristol Princess'
  S. 'Lilofee'
  S. 'Marie'
  S. 'Sonja'
Sedum, most species, including
  S. adolphii
  S. kamtschaticum
  S. morganianum
  S. spectabile
Sempervivum, most species and hybrids, including
  S. arachnoideum
  S. montanum
  S. tectorum
Stapelia, most species, including
  S. flavirostis
  S. variegata
Stenocactus, most species, including
  S. multicostatus
  S. phyllacanthus
  S. vaupelianus
Thelocactus bicolor
  T. setispinus
Titanopsis
  T. calcarea
  T. schwantesii
Trichodiadema, most species, including
  T. densum
  T. mirabile

WINTER-FLOWERING PLANTS

When many other plants are dormant or look dull, these plants flower and provide winter color.

Aloe, many species, including
A. arborescens
A. bakeri
A. comosa
A. jacksonii
A. krapohliana
A. longistyla
A. microstigma
A. plicatilis
A. tenuior
A. thraskii
A. variegata
A. wickensii
Ceropegia woodii
Cotyledon ladismithensis
Crassula 'Blue Haze'
C. 'Morgans Beauty'
C. ovata
C. schmidtii
C. streyi
C. tetragona
Echeveria, many hybrids and species, including
E. coccinea
E. gibbiflora
E. grandifolia
E. montana
E. pulvinata
E. 'Pulvicox'
E. tenuis
E. 'Zahnii'
Kalanchoe blossfeldiana
K. tubiflora
Rhipsalis, many species, including
R. cereuscula
R. crispata
R. paradoxa
Schlumbergera, most species and hybrids, including
S. 'Joanne'
S. 'Lilac Beauty'
S. obtusangula
S. opuntioides
S. orrssichiana
S. truncata

PLANTS TO GROW IN DIFFERENT CLIMATES

Warm climates

These plants need an all-year minimum temperature of 61°F (16°C) to flourish.

Adenium obesum
Brachystelma barberae
Caralluma, most species, including
C. burchardii
C. dodsoniana
C. dummeri
C. hesperidum
C. joannis
C. longipes
C. lutea
C. mammillaris
C. pillansii
C. speciosa
C. turneri
Ceropegia, most species, including
C. aristolochioides
C. devecchii
C. dimorpha
C. distincta
C. lingaris
Cyphostemma, most species, including
C. bainesii
C. juttae
C. seitziana
C. uter
Didierea, all species
Discocactus, all species
Disocactus, all species
Echinocactus grusonii
Echinopsis chamaecereus f. lutea
Epiphyllum, most species, including
E. anguliger
E. cartagense
E. crenatum
E. grandilobum
E. oxypetalum
E. thomasianum
Euphorbia, many succulent species, including
E. aeruginosa
E. cooperi
E. cylindrifolia
E. decaryi
E. grandicornis
E. lophogona
E. milii
E. poissonii
E. sipolisii
E. susannae
E. tuberosa
Fouquieria, all species
Gymnocalycium mihanovichii 'Red Top'
Hoodia gordonii
Hoya, most species, including
H. coronaria
H. cinnamomifolia
H. imperialis
H. multiflora
Jatropha, most succulent species, including
J. cordata
J. gossypifolia
J. multifida
J. podagrica
J. tuberosa

Melocactus, all species
Monadenium, all species
Pachypodium, most species, including
P. brevicaule
P. densiflorum
P. lamerei
P. namaquanum
P. rosulatum
P. rutenbergianum
Pedilanthus tithymaloides
Pilosocereus, most species, including
P. floccosus
P. fulvilanatus
P. glaucochrous
P. leucocephalus
P. magnificus
P. royenii
Plumeria, all species and hybrids
Rhipsalis, most species, including
R. cereoides
R. crispata
R. elliptica
R. micrantha
R. pachyptera
R. pilocarpa
Sansevieria, most species, including
S. aethiopica
S. cylindrica
S. kirkii
S. raffillii
S. singularis
S. trifasciata
S. trifasciata 'Hahnii'
Stapelia, most species, including
S. acuminata
S. englerana
S. glanduliflora
S. longidens
S. longipes
S. schinzii
S. stultitioides

Temperate climates

Although they can withstand near-freezing temperatures for very short periods, these plants should be kept at a minimum temperature of 41°F (5°C).

Aeonium arboreum
A. arboreum 'Atropurpureum'
A. haworthii
Agave americana 'Variegata'
A. parryi
A. parviflora
Aloe aristata
Aporocactus flagelliformis
Cereus hildmannianus v. monstrose

Delosperma, most species, including
D. ashtonii
D. cooperi
D. hallii
D. litorale
D. parviflorum
D. taylorii
D. tradescantioides
Drosanthemum, most species, including
D. barwickii
D. bellum
D. bicolor
D. hallii
D. hispidum
D. speciosum
D. striatum
D. tuberculiferum
Echeveria elegans
Echinocereus, most species, including
E. cinerascens
E. engelmannii
E. reichenbachii
E. stramineus
E. triglochidiatus
E. viridiflorus
Gasteria, most species, including
G. batesiana
G. liliputana
G. maculata
G. nigricans
G. obtusa
G. verrucosa
Gibbaeum album
G. petrense
Haworthia attenuata
H. coarctata v. adelaidensis
H. cymbiformis
Lampranthus, most species and hybrids, including
L. amoenus
L. aurantiacus
L. haworthii
L. roseus
L. spectabilis
L. stipulaceus
Lewisia cotyledon and hybrids
L. tweedyi

Cold climates

A few species are hardy and can survive winter temperatures as low as 5°F (-15°C) if they are kept dry or are protected by a layer of snow.

Sedum, many hardy species, including
S. acre
S. album
S. cauticolum
S. ewersii
S. kamtschaticum

S. spectabile
S. spurium
Sempervivum, most species and hybrids, including
S. 'Alpha'
S. 'Apollo'
S. 'Bengal'
S. 'Commander Hay'
S. 'Darkie'
S. dolomiticum
S. 'Fame'
S. 'Grey Ghost'
S. 'Hayling'
S. montanum
S. 'Red Beauty'
S. 'Silver Spring'
S. tectorum
S. 'Wendy'

PLANTS THAT NEED CERTAIN LIGHT LEVELS

Full sun

These are desert plants that need dry conditions in full sun to thrive.

Adenium, all species
Agave, most species, including
A. americana
A. attenuata
A. ferox
A. filifera
A. horrida
A. lechuguilla
A. parrasana
A. parryi
A. striata
A. stricta
A. toumeyana
A. utahensis
A. xylonacantha
Aloe dichotoma
A. ferox
Ariocarpus, all species
Astrophytum, all species
Carnegiea gigantea
Cephalocereus, all species
Cleistocactus, all species
Conophytum, all species
Copiapoa, all species
Coryphantha, all species
Cyphostemma, all species
Echinocactus, all species
Echinocereus, most species, including
E. maritimus
E. nivosus
E. rigidissimus
E. triglochidiatus
Echinopsis, most species, including
E. calochlora
E. ferox
E. formosa
E. huascha

Echinopsis (cont.)
  E. *mamillosa*
  E. *oxygona*
Espostoa, all species
Euphorbia, most cactus-like
  species, including
  E. *candelabrum*
  E. *cooperi*
  E. *evansii*
  E. *grandicornis*
  E. *horrida*
Ferocactus, most species,
  including
  F. *alamosanus*
  F. *cylindraceus*
  F. *latispinus*
Gibbaeum, all species
Gymnocalycium baldianum
  G. *horstii*
  G. *saglionis*
Hoodia, all species
Jatropha berlandieri
  J. *cordata*
Lampranthus, all species
Leuchtenbergia principis
Lithops, all species
Mammillaria, most species,
  including
  M. *bombycina*
  M. *candida*
  M. *geminispina*
  M. *zeilmanniana*
Matucana, all species
Neoporteria, most species,
  including
  N. *curvispina*
  N. *islayensis*
  N. *subgibbosa*
Opuntia, most species,
  including
  O. *invicta*
  O. *leptocaulis*
  O. *lindheimeri*
  O. *neoargentina*
  O. *tunicata*
Oreocereus, all species
Pachycereus, all species
Pachypodium lamerei
  P. *namaquanum*
Parodia, most species,
  including
  P. *chrysacanthion*
  P. *magnifica*
  P. *penicillata*
Pilosocereus, all species
Rebutia, most species,
  including
  R. *canigueralii*
  R. *marsoneri*
  R. *steinbachii*
Sedum acre
  S. *frutescens*
  S. *furfuraceum*
Sempervivum, all species and
  hybrids
Senecio haworthii
Thelocactus, all species

Dry shade
These desert plants need
dry conditions in diffuse sun.

Adromischus, most species,
  including
  A. *festivus*
  A. *hallii*
  A. *maculatus*
Aeonium, most species,
  including
  A. *simsii*
  A. *tabuliforme*
Aloe antandroi
  A. *brevifolia*
  A. *humilis*
  A. *millotii*
  A. *thompsonii*
  A. *variegata*
Caralluma socotrana
Ceropegia, most species,
  including
  C. *africana*
  C. *bulbosa*
  C. *woodii*
Cotyledon ladismithensis
Crassula, most species,
  including
  C. *lactea*
  C. *lycopodioides*
  C. *schmidtii*
Echeveria, most species,
  including
  E. *carnicolor*
  E. *ciliata*
  E. *harmsii*
  E. *setosa*
Echinopsis chamaecereus f.
  lutea
Euphorbia decaryi
  E. *francoisii*
  E. *neohumbertii* and many
  other leafy species,
  including
  E. *cap-saintemariensis*
  E. *didiereoides*
  E. *leuconeura*
  E. *tuberculata*
Gasteria, all species
Graptopetalum bellum
x Graptoveria 'Debbi'
Haworthia, most species,
  including
  H. *attenuata*
  H. *batesiana*
  H. *cymbiformis*
  H. *reinwardtii*
  H. *translucens*
Huernia, most species,
  including
  H. *hystrix*
  H. *macrocarpa*
  H. *pillansii*
Kalanchoe, most species,
  including
  K. *blossfeldiana*
  K. *manginii*

  K. *porphyrocalyx*
  K. *pumila*
  K. *schumacheri*
Monadenium guentheri
  M. *rhizophorum* v.
  stoloniferum
Pedilanthus tithymaloides
Sansevieria trifasciata
  'Laurentii'
Sedum morganianum
Senecio rowleyanus
Stapelia, most species,
  including
  S. *gettleffii*
  S. *schinzii*
  S. *trifida*
  S. *variegata*

Moist shade
Jungle species require
shade and a humid
atmosphere.

Aporocactus flagelliformis
x Aporophyllum, most
  hybrids, including
  x A. 'Dawn'
  x A. 'Gigantea'
  x A. 'Sussex Flame'
  x A. 'Vivide'
Disocactus, all species
Epiphyllum, all species and
  hybrids
Heliocereus, all species
Hylocereus, all species
Rhipsalis, all species
Schlumbergera, all species
  and hybrids
Selenicereus, all species

PLANTS TO GROW FROM SEED
Many species can be
grown from seed, but
hybrids and cultivars will
not produce similar
offspring from seed.

Aloe, most species, including
  A. *ferox*
  A. *tenuior*
  A. *variegata*
Aloinopsis, all species
Astrophytum ornatum
Carpobrotus, all species
Cephalophyllum subulatoides
Cereus, all species
Cheiridopsis candidissima
  C. *pillansii*
  C. *purpurata*
Echinocactus grusonii
Echinocereus cinerascens
  E. *engelmannii*
  E. *pectinatus*
  E. *pentalophus*
  E. *reichenbachii*
  E. *scheeri*

Echinopsis ancistrophora
  E. *backebergii*
  E. *eyriesii*
  E. *huascha*
  E. *oxygona*
  E. *thelegona*
Faucaria, all species
Ferocactus, all species
Glottiphyllum, all species
Gymnocalycium, most
  species, including
  G. *baldianum*
  G. *gibbosum*
  G. *quehlianum*
Lampranthus, all species
Mammillaria, most species,
  including
  M. *albilanata*
  M. *bocasana*
  M. *discolor*
  M. *duoformis*
  M. *elongata*
  M. *magnimamma*
  M. *microhelia*
  M. *prolifera*
  M. *rhodantha*
  M. *zeilmanniana*
Matucana aureiflora
  M. *intertexta*
Neoporteria chilensis
  N. *jussieui*
  N. *villosa*
Oreocereus celsianus
  O. *trollii*
Parodia crassigibba
  P. *horstii*
  P. *magnifica*
  P. *ottonis*
Pilosocereus azureus
  P. *magnificus*
Rebutia, most species,
  including
  R. *aureiflora*
  R. *marsoneri*
  R. *minuscula*
Stenocactus, all species
Thelocactus bicolor
  T. *setispinus*

PLANTS TO PROPAGATE FROM CUTTINGS
This is a good way to
obtain identical offspring
from hybrids and cultivars.

Stem cuttings
Use this method for many
bushy succulents.

Aeonium, all species
Aloe, most branching species,
  including
  A. *arborescens*
  A. *kedongensis*
  A. *jacksonii*
Caralluma, all species

Ceropegia, most species,
  including
  C. *dichotoma*
  C. *sandersonii*
Cotyledon ladismithensis
  C. *orbiculata*
  C. *undulata*
Crassula, most species,
  including
  C. *falcata*
  C. *ovata*
Duvalia, all species
Echeveria, all species
Echinopsis, all species
Euphorbia, many species,
  including
  E. *flanaganii*
  E. *mammillaris*
  E. *pentagona*
  E. *triangularis*
Graptopetalum, all species
Hoya, all species
Huernia, all species
Kalanchoe, most species,
  including
  K. *beharensis*
  K. *eriophylla*
  K. *tomentosa*
Lampranthus, all species
Monadenium, all species
Senecio, most species,
  including
  S. *aizoides*
  S. *coccineiflorus*
  S. *haworthii*
Stapelia, all species
Trichodiadema, all species

Stem sections
All epiphytic cacti species
and hybrids and some
columnar cacti are suited to
this technique.

Aporocactus, all species
x Aporophyllum, all hybrids
Cereus, all species
Cleistocactus baumannii
  C. *hildegardiae*
  C. *icosagonus*
  C. *samaipatanus*
  C. *winteri*
Corryocactus, all species
Disocactus, all species
Echinopsis bridgesii
  E. *pachanoi*
  E. *spachiana*
Epiphyllum species and
  hybrids
Hatiora, all species
Heliocereus, all species
Hylocereus, all species
Lepismium, all species
Opuntia, all species
Pereskia aculeata
  P. *bleo*
  P. *grandifolia*

Pereskiopsis diguetii
  P. rotundifolia
Quiabentia verticillata
Rhipsalis, all species
Samaipaticereus corroanus
Schlumbergera, all hybrids
Selenicereus, all species
Tacinga funalis
Weberbauerocereus, all species

Leaf cuttings
Leafy succulents lend themselves to this technique.

Adromischus, all species
Cotyledon jacobseniana
  C. ladismithensis
  C. orbiculata
  C. tomentosa
  C. undulata
Crassula, many species, including
  C. anomala
  C. fragilis
  C. lactea
  C. liebuschiana
  C. macowaniana
  C. mesembryanthoides
  C. 'Morgan's Beauty'
  C. nealeana
  C. perforata
  C. rogersii
  C. rupestris
  C. schmidtii
  C. socialis
  C. susannae
  C. tecta
  C. watermeyeri
Echeveria, many species, including
  E. affinis
  E. agavoides
  E. amoena
  E. carnicolor
  E. ciliata
  E. derenbergii
  E. goldmanii
  E. nodulosa
  E. pulvinata
  E. rosea
  E. shaviana
  E. tenuis
Graptopetalum, all species
Kalanchoe, many species, including
  K. beauverdii
  K. daigremontiana
  K. eriophylla
  K. figueiredoi
  K. manginii
  K. marmorata
  K. orgyalis
  K. pinnata
  K. rhombopilosa
  K. rosei
  K. thyrsiflora

K. tomentosa
K. tubiflora
Pachyphytum, all species
Sedum, many species, including
  S. adolphii
  S. album
  S. anglicum
  S. comixtum
  S. hintonii
  S. nussbaumeranum
  S. pachyphyllum
  S. palmeri
  S. rubrotinctum
  S. rubrum
  S. stahlii

PLANTS TO PROPAGATE BY DIVISION
This method has a high level of success but it yields a fairly low number of new plants.

Clumping plants that produce offsets
Aloe albiflora
  A. bakeri
  A. bellatula
  A. brevifolia
  A. humilis
  A. jucunda
  A. millotii
  A. parvula
  A. rabaiensis
  A. rauhii
  A. thompsonii
  A. variegata
Crassula corallina
  C. lycopodioides
  C. marginalis
  C. marnierana
  C. multicava
  C. perforata
  C. schmidtii
  C. socialis
  C. teres
Echeveria agavoides
  E. amoena
  E. ciliata
  E. derenbergii
  E. elegans
  E. glauca
  E. runyonii
  E. setosa
  E. tenuis
  E. 'Zahnii'
Gasteria, most species, including
  G. acinacifolia
  G. armstrongii
  G. batesiana
  G. caespitosa
  G. liliputana
  G. maculata
  G. marmorata

G. minima
G. obtusa
G. verrucosa
G. zeyheri
Haworthia, most species, including
  H. arachnoidea
  H. attenuata
  H. batesiana
  H. coarctata
  H. cooperi
  H. cuspidata
  H. glauca
  H. herbacea
  H. limifolia
  H. reinwardtii
  H. retusa
  H. tessellata
Sedum acre
  S. dasyphyllum
  S. hirsutum
  S. humifusum
  S. kamtschaticum
  S. lydium
  S. maximowiczii
  S. spurium

Tuberous plants that produce offsets
Begonia incana
  B. natalensis
  B. shepherdii
Brachystelma, most species, including
  B. barberae
  B. cathcartense
  B. coddii
  B. foetidum
  B. modestum
  B. stellatum
Calibanus hookeri
Senecio coccineiflorus
  S. acaulis
  S. fulgens
  S. orbicularis
  S. oxyriifolius
  S. tropaeolifolius
  S. vallyi

Plants to divide at the rootstock
Sansevieria, all species and cultivars, including
  S. cylindrica
  S. grandis
  S. parva
  S. trifasciata 'Hahnii'
  S. thyrsiflora
Sedum, many species, including
  S. anacampseros
  S. cauticolum
  S. ewersii
  S. sieboldii
  S. spectabile
  S. tatarinowii
  S. telephium

PLANTS FOR GRAFTING
A specialized technique for slow-growing cacti or those requiring very warm temperatures. With succulents, graft the scions listed below only onto stocks of the same group.

Flat grafting

Cactus stocks
Cleistocactus samaipatanus
  C. winteri
Echinopsis, many species, including
  E. eyriesii
  E. oxygona
  E. pachanoi
  E. spachiana
  E. scopulicola
Hylocereus trigonus
  H. undatus
Myrtillocactus geometrizans
Opuntia, many species, including
  O. cochenillifera
  O. cylindrica
  O. ficus-indica
  O. robusta
Pereskiopsis diguetii (for small seedlings)

Cactus scions
Any species or hybrid cactus whose diameter is equal to or greater than its height, including
Ariocarpus, all species
Discocactus, all species
Melocactus, all species
Pediocactus, all species

Succulent stocks
Group 1
Euphorbia, many species, including
  E. canariensis
  E. candelabrum
  E. mammillaris
  E. resinifera
  E. submammillaris

Group 2
Ceropegia woodii (tuber)
Stapelia grandiflora

Group 3
Pachypodium lamerei
Nerium oleander

Succulent scions
Group 1
Euphorbia, all species

Group 2
Brachystelma, all species
Caralluma, all species

Group 2 (cont.)
Ceropegia, all species
Hoodia, all species
Huernia, all species
Stapelia, all species
Trichocaulon, all species

Group 3
Adenium, all species
Pachypodium, all species
Plumeria, all species

Split grafting and side grafting
Use these techniques for very slender, flat-stemmed, or columnar cacti.

Cactus stocks
Cleistocactus samaipatanus
  C. winteri
Harrisia 'Jusbertii'
Heliocereus speciosus
Selenicereus, all species

Cactus scions
Slender-stemmed cactus and seedlings, including
Ariocarpus seedlings
Austrocactus, all species
Echinocereus leucanthus
  E. schmollii
Echinopsis chamaecereus
  E. chamaecereus f. lutea
Peniocereus, all species

Epiphytic cactus stocks
Epiphyllum, any with thick triangular stems
Heliocereus speciosus
Hylocereus, all species
Selenicereus, all species

Epiphytic cactus scions
Aporocactus, any long-stemmed species to make standard "weeping" plants
x Aporophyllum, any long-stemmed hybrids to make standard "weeping" plants
Hatiora, all species
Schlumbergera, any species or hybrids to make standard "weeping" plants

Succulent stocks
Group 1
Adenia globosa
Group 2
Portulacaria afra

Succulent scions
Group 1
Adenia, all species
Group 2
Ceraria, all species

GLOSSARY

Words in *italics* within a definition have a separate entry.

AERIAL ROOTS Roots that grow from the plant stem above soil level; used to anchor the plant and, in *epiphytes*, for absorption of atmospheric moisture and nutrients.

ANNUAL 1. Living for only one season, applied to top-growth. 2. A plant that grows from seed, produces flowers and seed, and then dies in one growing season.

ANNULUS The raised ring around the center of a succulent flower.

ANTHER The part of a *stamen* that produces pollen, usually carried on a *filament*.

AREOLE The cushionlike *growing point*, actually a modified leaf bud, on a cactus from which grow its spines, leaves, side shoots, or flowers.

BLEEDING When sap or *latex* flows freely from a damaged stem.

BLOOM 1. A flower. 2. A waxy, white or bluish-white coating on stems, succulent leaves, or fleshy fruit.

BRACT A modified leaf at the base of a flower or flower cluster, which often protects the flower. Bracts can resemble normal leaves, appear small and scalelike, or be large, brightly colored, and look like flower petals.

CALLUS The protective tissue formed over a wound, for example, at the base of cuttings.

CAPSULE A dry seedpod that splits open when ripe to release its seeds.

CAUDEX The swollen water-storage tissue, usually composed of both root and stem of a succulent or woody plant.

CAUDICIFORM 1. Possessing a *caudex*. 2. With a swollen stem.

CEPHALIUM A densely spined crown, which produces the flowers and fruit. It is produced only by species of *Discocactus* or *Melocactus*.

CHLOROPHYLL The green pigment present in leaves or stems and used in *photosynthesis*.

CORKING Gradual ripening of stem from the base, to produce a barklike texture.

CROSS-POLLINATION See *pollination*.

CULTIVAR Contraction of "cultivated variety." Derived from a *species*, a variant selected or bred only in cultivation.

CUTTING A cut or detached section of a plant, either from a leaf or stem, or an entire leaf, that is used for propagation.

DAMPING OFF The rapid wilting and collapse of seedlings due to fungal attack on the seedling stem at soil level.

DIEBACK Progressive death of a stem from the tip due to damage or disease.

DIVISION A method of propagation in which a single plant or a clump is divided into several sections, each with its own roots and a *growing point*.

DORMANCY A temporary cessation of a plant's active growth and a slowing-down of its other functions, usually in winter, drought, or extreme heat or cold. Some succulents can produce flowers when otherwise dormant.

EPIPHYTE A plant that grows on the surface of another plant but is not a parasite. The plant obtains moisture and nutrients from the atmosphere, not the soil.

ERICACEOUS Applied to acid potting mix with a pH of 6.5 or less. It is generally used for lime-hating plants.

ETIOLATION Pale, sickly, excessive growth caused by insufficient light, incorrect feeding, or overcrowding.

FAMILY A grouping of related *genera*. For example, the family of Cactaceae contains about 140 genera.

FIBROUS ROOT A fine, densely branching root, which absorbs moisture and nutrients from the soil.

FILAMENT The threadlike stalk supporting an *anther*; together they form the *stamen*.

FLAT GRAFTING See *grafting*.

FLOWERHEAD A mass of tiny flowers, or florets, that looks like a single large flower.

FORCING The technique of bringing a plant into growth or flower ahead of its natural season, usually by providing it with extra warmth or controlling daylength.

FORM (f.) Cultivated or naturally occurring variant of a *species*, differing only slightly from the *species*.

GENUS (plural, *genera*) A category in plant classification ranked between *family* and *species*, denoting a group of plants with several common characteristics.

GLAUCOUS Possessing a smooth, blue-white, blue-green, or blue-gray *bloom*.

GLOCHIDS Barbed bristly *spines* or hairs, usually very fine and easily detached, on an *Opuntia* cactus.

GRAFTING A method of propagation in which an artificial union is made between different parts of two closely related plants; a *scion* from one is grafted onto a *stock* from another so that they grow into one plant. Methods include flat grafting, split grafting, and side grafting.

GROWING POINT The tip of a shoot from which new growth emerges.

HARDY Able to withstand most climatic conditions all year without protection, often qualified with a minimum temperature, for example, 5°F (-15°C).

HERBACEOUS A nonwoody plant in which the top-growth dies down to a *rootstock* at the end of the growing season.

HYBRID A plant produced by crossing two different *species* within a *genus* or two closely related genera (intergeneric hybrid).

HYBRIDIZATION The production, either in nature or in cultivation, of a *hybrid* by cross-pollination (see *pollination*).

INTERGENERIC HYBRID See *hybrid*.

LATEX The milky white sap that exudes or bleeds from damaged stems of some succulents, for example, *Euphorbia*.

LEAF BRACT See *bract*.

LEAF CUTTING A *cutting* composed of a single leaf.

LOAM A soil of medium texture, with equal parts of sand, silt, and clay, which is usually well-structured, fertile, and moisture-retentive but also free-draining.

OFFSET 1. A young plant produced by the parent, usually at its base; also known as an offshoot. 2. To produce offsets.

OVARY The base of the female portion of a flower that develops into a fruit after fertilization occurs.

PAN A shallow pot that is wider than it is deep, often used for potting established cacti and succulents.

PERENNIAL Living for at least three seasons.

pH The horticultural measure of the acidity or alkalinity of a soil or compost; pH 7 is neutral, below pH 7 is acid, and above pH 7 is alkaline. Cacti prefer a slightly acid soil.

PHOTOSYNTHESIS The production by a plant of compounds required for its growth, prompted by light acting on the plant's *chlorophyll*. Also needed in the process are water and carbon dioxide.

PINCHING OUT The removal of the *growing point* of a plant or its stems to induce the production of side shoots or more flower buds.

PLANTLET A new young plant, which usually arises from the site of a wounded leaf or stem or is naturally borne on the leaf margins, for example, in some *Kalanchoe*.

POLLINATION (also known as cross-pollination) The transfer of pollen from the *anther* to the *stigma* on the same or a different flower by gravity, wind, birds, bats, or insects in nature or by hand in cultivation.

PROPAGATOR A small case, usually heated, with a removable top of plastic or glass. It is used to provide a suitably moisture-retentive atmosphere for raising seedlings or rooting cuttings.

PSEUDOCEPHALIUM A growth of long, hairlike spines on one side of the upper stem of a columnar cactus, like a *cephalium*.

RIB A ridge on a cactus stem, usually vertical, that is formed from the skin.

ROOT BALL The root mass, together with its soil or potting mix, visible when a plant is lifted from its bed or taken from a pot.

ROOTSTOCK 1. A vigorous plant which provides the root system in *grafting*. Also known as a stock. 2. A plant's root system.

ROSETTE A group of leaves radiating from approximately the same point, often borne at ground level at the base of a very short stem, or at the tip of longer stems.

SCION A shoot or bud of one *species* which is united to the stock of another plant by *grafting*, for propagation.

SIDE GRAFTING See *grafting*.

SPECIES The unit of classification below a *genus*, denoting very closely related plants.

SPINE A modified leaf, which can be needlelike, barbed, curved, hairlike, or bristly.

SPLIT GRAFTING See *grafting*.

STAMEN The male reproductive organ in a flower, consisting of the *anther* and its supporting *filament*.

STANDARD A treelike cactus obtained by grafting a trailing or arching species, for example, *Schlumbergera*, onto a tall or columnar species.

STEM CUTTING A cutting taken from a portion of stem.

STIGMA The central part of the female portion of the flower that must receive pollen before fertilization can occur.

STOCK See *rootstock*.

STYLE The stalk that supports the *stigma* so that it is well placed to receive pollen.

SUCCULENT A plant with thick fleshy leaves and/or stems that are adapted to store water. This includes all cacti.

TAPROOT The principal swollen, downward-growing root of a plant.

TERMINAL At the tip of a stem or branch, usually applied to a bud, rosette, or flower.

TOP-DRESSING An inert material, usually decorative, that is applied to the potting mix surface around a plant, to aid drainage, decrease erosion, or prevent moisture loss.

TUBER A swollen, usually underground storage organ, derived from a stem or root, that stores water and food during *dormancy*.

TUBERCLE A small wartlike swelling on cactus stems, formed by the horizontal division of a *rib*.

VARIETY A distinct variant, occurring in the wild, of a species.

WHORL Ring of three or more leaves or stems arising from the same point, usually on the stem of a plant.

WINDOW A layer of semitransparent cells, containing calcium oxalate, at the tip of a *succulent* leaf. The window protects the *chlorophyll* in the plant body from being destroyed by very strong sunlight by diffusing the light before it reaches the *chlorophyll*, thus enabling *photosynthesis* to take place.

ZYGOMORPHIC Bilaterally symmetrical, applied to a flower that has one or more unequal parts.

USEFUL ADDRESSES

CANADA

Societies and Journals

Burnaby Cactus and Succulent Club
Victor Wright
4261 Gatenby Avenue
Burnaby, BC V5G 3M8
(604) 298-5421

Cacti and Other Succulents
8591 Lochside Drive
Sidney, BC V8L 1M5

Toronto Cactus and Succulent Club
P.O. Box 334
Brampton, ON L6V 2L3
(416) 877-6013
Cactus Factus

Nurseries and Suppliers

Vandusen Gardens
5251 Oak Street
Vancouver, BC V6M 4H1
(604) 525-5315

UNITED STATES

Societies and Journals

Cactus and Succulent Society of America Inc.
Membership Committee
P.O. Box 35034
Des Moines, IA 50315
Cactus and Succulent Journal

Los Angeles Cactus and Succulent Society
5149 Jeffdale Avenue
Woodland Hills, CA 91364
Cactus Chronicle

New York Cactus and Succulent Society
312 West 49th Street
New York, NY 10019

The Desert and Botanical Garden Society
1201 North Galvin Parkway
Phoenix, AZ 85008
(602) 941-1217
Agave

Nurseries and Suppliers

Abbey Gardens
4620 Carpenteria Avenue
Carpenteria, CA 90313
(805) 684-5112

Arid Land Greenhouses
3560 West Bilby Road
Tucson, AZ 85746
(602) 883-9404

Cactus by Dodie
934 E. Mettler Road
Lodi, CA 95242
(209) 368-3692

Cactus by Mueller
10411 Rosedale Highway
Bakersfield, CA 93312
(805) 589-2674

Cactus Gem Nursery
5485 White Drive
Batesville, AR 75201

The Cactus Patch
RR 2, Box 159
Radium, KS 67550-9111
(316) 982-4670

Succulenta
P.O. Box 480325
Los Angeles, CA 90048
(213) 933-8676

Sunnyvale Cactus Nursery
679 Pearl Street
Reading, MA 01867
(617) 944-5959

Seeds

Cactus and Succulent Society of America Seed Depot
27821 S.E. Sun Ray Drive
Boring, OR 97009

Living Stones Nursery
2936 North Stone Avenue
Tucson, AZ 85705
(602) 628-8773

Mesa Gardens
P.O. Box 72
Belen, NM 87002
(505) 864-3131

Miles' to Go
P.O. Box 6
Cortario, AZ 85652
(602) 682-7272

New Mexico Cactus Research
P.O. Box 787
1132 East River Road
Belen, NM 87002
(505) 864-4027

INDEX

Page numbers in **bold** refer to entries in the Plant Catalog; *italic* page numbers refer to illustrations in other sections. Synonyms, or old plant names, of plants featured in the Plant Catalog are cross-referenced to current names. Old names of genera that have been amalgamated into genera in the Plant Catalog are also listed.

ACKNOWLEDGMENTS

ADDITIONAL CONTRIBUTORS
Claire Calman (pp. 38–45)
Keith Grantham (pp. 20–25)

AUTHOR'S ACKNOWLEDGMENTS
I would like to take this opportunity to thank all those people who, over the years, have shared their enthusiasm for these plants with me. Their generosity, help, guidance, and useful pieces of information have all helped to increase my enjoyment from this hobby. I would also like to thank my family for their forbearance – jobs in the greenhouse always seem more necessary than those in the home or garden. Finally, I would like to thank Dorling Kindersley for the opportunity to present a broad selection of these interesting and colorful plants. Their photography, editorial, and design teams have produced a magnificent book.

DORLING KINDERSLEY would like to thank Claire Calman, Joanna Chisholm, Serena Dilnot, Shona Grimbly, Elisabeth Haldane, and Jackie Matthews for their editorial help; Jill Hamilton, Laaren Brown Hort, Ray Rogers, and Julee Binder for their help with the North American edition; Isobel Maclean for the index; Tracey Clarke and Kate Sarluis for design assistance; Diana Morris and Christine Rista for picture research; Chris Anderson, Helga Lien Evans, Helen Gatward, Tanya Hines, Teresa Pritlove, and Thomas Read for general help; Emma Hutton, Joanna Figg-Latham, Karen Mackley, and Debbie Rhodes for DTP; Miles Anderson, Trevor Cole, C.W.E. and S.N. Harland, David Hunt, Peter T. Mitchell, and Gordon Rowley for horticultural advice; for loaning plants: Miles Anderson at Bach's Cactus Nursery in Tucson, The Chelsea Gardener, Chuck Hansen at Arid Lands in Tucson, Jane Evans and Gene Joseph at Plants for the Southwest in Tucson and World's End Nurseries; for loaning props: Brats, The Chelsea Gardener, Classic Pot Emporium, Clifton Nurseries, Covent Garden General Store, Fulham Palace Garden Centre, Grahame and Green, The Hungry Cowboy, London Graphics, Macondo South American Crafts, Marston & Langinger Showroom, Robert Dyas Hardware, Santa Fe Trading Post, Fiona Barkham at Suttons Seeds, and World's End Nurseries; Maria D'Orsi and Diana Mitchell for prop research; Juliet Payne, Chris Pietrzak and Merelina Dynoe White for transporting plants and props.

PICTURE CREDITS

KEY TO PICTURES
t = top; c = center; b = bottom; l =left; r = right (Figures refer to page numbers.)

All photography by Peter Anderson except for: Arcaid, Richard Bryant 42–3; Prof. W. Barthlott 14tc; The Bodleian Library, Oxford 22tr; Bridgeman Art Library, London / Collection Georg Schafer, Schweinfurt 23tr; Bruce Coleman Limited, John Cancalosi 17tr, Eric Crichton 23bl, Hans Reinhard 16–17; Elizabeth Whiting & Associates / Tim Street-Porter 44–5; ET Archive Museum of Mankind 25cr; Roger Ferryman 20bl; The Garden Picture Library, Linda Burgess 40bc, Ron Sutherland 42bl; Steve Gorton (DK Studio) 12tr, 24tl, 46–7, 75tr, 78–9, 81bl, 93bl, 95tl, 95bc, 117tr, 119tc, 146–7, 148–9, 150–51, 152–3, 156bl, 156br, 159br; Keith Grantham 12c, 18cl, 20cc, 21tc, 21cc, 25tc; Jerry Harpur 44bl; Harry Smith Horticultural Collection 97bc, 97tr, 97br, 120bc, 128br, 135tr, 139bl, 161cl; Terry Hewitt 72bl, 97bl, 98tr; *Houses and Interiors* 40tr; Hunt Institute for Botanical Documentation 21tc; Dave King 4br, 5, 28–9, 30–31, 32–3, 38–9, 48–9, 50–51; The Mansell Collection 20tl, 22bl; Susie Moore 16cl; Terence Moore 14b, 25bl; Nature Photographers / Paul Sterry 14–15; Clive Nichols 42tc; Jerry Pavia 44tc; Photos Horticultural / Michael Warren 97bc; Planet Earth Pictures / J. Provenza 18–19; Robert Harding Picture Library, James Merrell, IPC Magazines 1992 41.

ILLUSTRATORS David Ashby and Amy Lewis for Plant Catalog profile artworks; Karen Cochrane for the map on pp. 20–21 and the diagram on p. 150.